MEMORY
OFFENDED

———

The Carmelite convent at Auschwitz. (*Courtesy of Marcel Saba/Filip Horvat.*)

MEMORY OFFENDED

The Auschwitz Convent Controversy

EDITED BY CAROL RITTNER
AND JOHN K. ROTH

PRAEGER

New York
Westport, Connecticut
London

Library of Congress Cataloging-in-Publication Data

Memory offended : the Auschwitz convent controversy / edited by Carol
  Rittner and John K. Roth.
    p. cm.
  Includes bibliographical references and index.
    ISBN 0–275–93606–6 (alk. paper).—ISBN 0–275–93848–4 (pbk. :
alk. paper)
    1. Judaism—Relations—Catholic Church. 2. Catholic Church—
Relations—Judaism. 3. Auschwitz (Poland : Concentration camp)
4. Holocaust memorials—Poland—Oświęcim—Public opinion.
5. Convents—Poland—Oświęcim—Location. 6. Carmelite nuns.
7. Oświęcim (Poland)—Religious and ecclesiastical institutions.
I. Rittner, Carol Ann, 1943–   . II. Roth, John K.
BM535.M44   1991
261.2′6—dc20   90–47333

British Library Cataloguing in Publication Data is available.

Library of Congress Catalog Card Number: 90–47333
ISBN: 0–275–93606–6
     0–275–93848–4 (pbk.)

First published in 1991

Praeger Publishers, One Madison Avenue, New York, NY   10010
An imprint of Greenwood Publishing Group, Inc.

Printed in the United States of America

The paper used in this book complies with the
Permanent Paper Standard issued by the National
Information Standards Organization (Z39.48–1984).

10 9 8 7 6 5 4 3 2 1

TO ELIE

The memory of the righteous is a blessing.
                                —Proverbs 10:7

Contents

Illustrations

Preface

One chapter in this book is an interview with Elie Wiesel, a Jewish survivor of Auschwitz and the 1986 Nobel laureate for peace, conducted by Carol Rittner, R.S.M., on August 29, 1989. Her last question asked him, "Given all the problems facing humankind, where on the list of priorities do you place the controversy over the Auschwitz Carmelite convent?" That question, a good one then, also makes a good beginning for this book now.

The fall of the Berlin wall and the reunification of Germany, the apparent end of the Cold War, the Gulf Crisis precipitated by the Iraqi invasion of Kuwait—all of those surprises in 1989 and 1990 were yet to come as Rittner interviewed Wiesel and then began work on this book with John K. Roth. If those attention-riveting events—and others that may follow after this writing—overshadow a dilemma concerning nuns at prayer in a building that was formerly part of the Nazi death camp at Auschwitz, Wiesel's answer to Rittner's question helps to keep things in perspective. "What is so agonizing," Wiesel replied, "is that we live in a time when there is more than one *number one* priority. We cannot ignore any of them."

Wiesel might have added that we cannot ignore any of them because the world's crucial problems are related—not just in the present but also because of the past. Sea changes in Europe and turmoil in the Middle East—what happened at Auschwitz *then* affects what happens *now*. Likewise, what does and should continue to happen at Auschwitz *now* has important things to say about the world's prospects for the future, particularly insofar as that future involves relationships between Jews and Christians. Motivated by that conviction, Carol Rittner and John K. Roth found others who shared it.

We are immensely indebted to all of the writers who contributed to this book. Their caring efforts brought it to life. The book we envisioned was not one that anybody could write alone. A chorus of voices, not a solo, was necessary to comprehend and interpret the score. The eloquence of the contributors shows that each one makes a distinctive contribution. We hope and believe that their work can also create a harmony larger than the sum of their parts.

Writers depend on editors, and ours were superb. At the Greenwood Publishing Group, Dr. James T. Sabin had faith in the project. His steady and patient encouragement kept us moving. Production editor Arlene Belzer and copyeditor David Baker transformed a complex manuscript into a finished book. Our thanks go to them.

During critical moments important help came from many other persons, too. At the National Archives in Washington, D.C., Robert Wolfe found the maps we wanted. Mr. Wolfe also provided photographs, as did Richard L. Rubenstein, who took his camera to Auschwitz while he wrote his essay for us. Elan Steinberg of the World Jewish Congress in New York assisted us in documenting the chronology of events surrounding the Auschwitz convent controversy. Eugene Fisher of the National Conference of Catholic Bishops, Washington, D.C., did the same. Leads for the bibliography came from sources too numerous to mention here, but Gena A. Morgan organized them into usable form. And the Sisters of Sion, in France, Canada, and elsewhere helped us check some facts. To these people—each and all—we are deeply grateful.

Christians and Jews worked together on this book. The hope it contains is that they will find more and even better ways to do so in the future. Given all the problems facing humankind, that priority must not be ignored. By attending to it well, we may show, as Elie Wiesel's closing words to Carol Rittner said, that "humanity's fate is not sealed, that everything is still possible."

This is the place . . .
people
lived
and vanished
overnight
in this place.
—Elie Wiesel, at Auschwitz, August 1, 1979

MEMORY OFFENDED

Introduction: Memory Offended

Carol Rittner and John K. Roth

> If we stop remembering, we stop being.
> —Elie Wiesel

Heated controversy in late twentieth-century Jewish-Christian relations has swirled about two religious words—*convent* and *covenant*. In the Christian tradition, a convent is a community of nuns who aim to serve God and humankind by living, working, and praying together in a cloistered place. Convents exist because Christians typically consider themselves related to God in a covenant. The essence of that covenant is summed up in the biblical phrase: "I will be their God, and they shall be my people."

Arguably no idea has changed human history more than the belief that one's community or tradition has a special favored relationship with God. Christians did not invent it. Inheriting the conviction from their elder Jewish brothers and sisters, who understood themselves to be God's "chosen" people, Christians did go on fatefully to assert that theirs was a "new and everlasting covenant between God and humanity" and that "Jesus sealed this new covenant with his own blood."

Pope John Paul II used those words in a homily given during a general audience at the Vatican on August 2, 1989. Long accustomed to such formulas, most Christians found his views on that occasion to be unremarkable. Jewish reaction was different. It sensed ancient poison in the formula and dissented from it. That poison involves allegations about the Jewish people's "infidelity to God"—also the pope's words.[1]

Jewish religion is profoundly sensitive about "infidelity to God." This sensitivity rightly alerts it to a Christian tendency as destructive as it is old. That propensity is to accept what Jews find unacceptable: namely, that a "new" covenant, established through Jesus, took the place of the "old," abrogated the Jews' status as a chosen people, and, by implication, damned them.

In recent decades, relationships between the Vatican and the Jewish people had been better than during John Paul II's rocky reign. Understandably Jewish leaders felt it important to question his August 1989 pronouncements about Jewish "infidelity to God." They expressed relief when the Vatican's "clarification" no longer used those words. Yet the clarification did not put to rest the deep-seated problem that brought to a head this episode in Jewish-Christian controversy during the summer of 1989. To see why, turn from covenant to convent.

That turn leads to Oswiecim. Located in the pope's native Poland, this ill-fated community came to be better known by a German name—Auschwitz. Situated on its outskirts was the infamous Nazi concentration and death camp. About 1.5 million men, women, and children—90 percent of them Jews— perished in this place.[2]

Auschwitz took Polish and Christian lives by the thousands. It wasted Jewish life much, much more. Elie Wiesel, an Auschwitz survivor, says, "Do not trust your eyes. There is no sun here." He calls Auschwitz "the place of eternal night."[3] Its darkness covers not only the 900-year-old town of Oswiecim but also the world as a whole. Today Auschwitz is nearly synonymous with the Holocaust or *Shoah*, as it is often called, the Nazis' unprecedented, systematic, and unique attempt to destroy European Jewry. Tempting though it might be to put this catastrophic past behind us, humankind can ill afford to do so. For Wiesel's judgment is correct: "If we stop remembering, we stop being."[4]

Remembering, however, is easier said than done, because the need to remember raises hard questions. What, for example, most deserves to be remembered, and how is remembering best done?[5] Those issues help to reveal what is at stake in two observations. First, one can visit Auschwitz without seeing, or even knowing, that Polish Carmelite nuns have been meditating in the *Theatergebäude* or Old Theater at the site of the original Auschwitz camp. This structure, which predates World War I, has been put to various uses. During the Holocaust, for example, it served as a storehouse not only for loot taken from those who were gassed but also for the Zyklon B that dispatched Auschwitz's primarily Jewish victims. Second, and for reasons directly related to the location and nature of the *Theatergebäude*, the convent cloistered within its walls got headlines—too many of them. Its existence made memory offended.[6]

The Auschwitz convent controversy escalated when a February 1989 deadline for relocating the nuns came and went without their departure. It got uglier that July, when Jewish demonstrators took their protest to the convent grounds and Polish workers responded violently. Stormy debate followed. All of the disputes involved conflicting views about history, about proper and improper ways of remembering, and about religious sensitivities that involve rival claims about covenants.

Auschwitz is a tragically fitting place to trace results of that latter rivalry in particular. What happened there from 1940 to 1945, and thus in 1989 and beyond as well, is inconceivable without beliefs about God held first by Jews and then by Christians. Specifically, the claim that Christianity's "new" covenant superseded Judaism's "old" one helped to make the Holocaust happen by inciting anti-Jewish contempt in which Nazism would later flourish. That flourishing implicates Christianity in a twisted road that led to Auschwitz, which, in turn, made the Carmelite convent problematic and controversial.[7]

On April 27, 1940, less than a year after Germany began World War II by invading Poland, Heinrich Himmler, head of the Nazi SS, ordered the construction of a concentration camp at Oswiecim, about forty miles west of Cracow and in Upper Silesia, a southwestern Polish province that had been annexed to the Third Reich.[8] Near this bleak town, which is located close by the confluence of the Sola and Vistula rivers and along major railroad lines, stood a former military barracks. This configuration of some twenty dark and dreary red brick buildings served as the nucleus for what was to become both the most notorious installation in a vast network of Nazi concentration, forced-labor, and death camps and the largest place where Jews were dispatched by poison gas.

Auschwitz became several camps in one. The original camp was the *Stammlager* (main camp), Auschwitz I, once Himmler ordered the establishment of a second section on March 1, 1941. Located about two miles from Auschwitz I, this area—Auschwitz II or Birkenau—eventually became the major killing center in the Auschwitz complex. At the peak of its operations, Birkenau included four large, permanent, gas chamber–crematoria installations, each with the capacity to destroy 6,000 persons daily. A third section, Auschwitz III, was also known as Buna-Monowitz, taking its name from the Buna synthetic rubber factory at Monowitz, which the prisoners at Auschwitz III and its many forced-labor subcamps were forced to construct.

"This is the place," Elie Wiesel's poetry reminds us, "people lived and vanished overnight in this place."[9] In all of its dimensions, Auschwitz spelled death. Human beings were worked until they perished. Others died of starvation and disease, or were murdered in gas chambers. Deportees came from every European quarter and included, for example, German "undesirables," Soviet prisoners of war, Gypsies, Polish priests and nuns, members of the French Resistance, and Jews—especially, first and foremost, Jews. Auschwitz and the other killing centers (Chelmno, Sobibor, Belzec, Treblinka, and Majdanek—all on Polish soil) were the creation of a German nation highly endowed with learning and culture. The 1930s and 1940s brought home the fact that the heart of darkness does not lie in the upper reaches of some far-off, primitive place, but much closer to home. The Holocaust was more than just another brutal chapter in the history of humankind. It looms as a central event of the twentieth century—indeed perhaps of any century—because the institutionally organized, state-sponsored murder of the Jews, and the persecution of so many other victims of the Nazis (Gypsies, homosexuals, Jehovah's Witnesses, Poles, Communists, the mentally and physically disabled, Slavs, Russians, Ukrainians, political opponents, and others) took place within a regime that existed and functioned with the cooperation of thousands of "ordinary people" who trafficked in extraordinary evil.

The Holocaust stands as the definitive refutation of a grand illusion that guarantees human beings will automatically become better as they become more formally educated. It is a constant reminder of the terrible truth that large numbers of seemingly decent people found it possible to dehumanize and slaughter their fellow human beings—methodically, systematically—not for anything they had done but for who they were racially defined to be.

In late February 1990, ground was broken for a new interfaith center close by but clearly removed from the grounds of the Auschwitz camp site.[10] Eventually it is supposed to provide a home for the Carmelite nuns whose presence provoked the Auschwitz convent controversy. This resolution, however, leaves much unresolved, for as the events of 1989–90 testify, Auschwitz and its legacy still scar the earth. Jews point to the silence of God and human beings as the Holocaust's enormity was being perpetrated. For most of them, silence—not formal religious sites, least of all Christian ones, which strike many Jews as evidence of "Christianizing" intentions that would "de-Judaize" the Holocaust itself— is the only appropriate response to Auschwitz, a place that defies meaning. Not everyone, however, agrees.

At issue is what constitutes a fitting Auschwitz memorial. In light of the magnitude of all that happened at Auschwitz, this issue seriously jeopardizes the dialogue and goodwill between Christians—particularly Catholics—and Jews. It is quite clear that the dialogue has not gone deep enough on either side.

"For a quarter of a century," Peter Steinfels observes, "Roman Catholic and Jewish representatives have examined their traditions and tried to root out sources of prejudice and misunderstanding." Yet, more than twenty-five years after Vatican II (the twenty-first Roman Catholic ecumenical council, convened by Pope John XXIII, which deliberated from 1962 to 1965 and substantially improved Catholic-Jewish understanding), and despite many good intentions from all parties involved, "relations between Catholic and Jewish leaders have fallen into exceptional disarray."[11]

Numerous events in the 1980s, and lasting memories about them, contribute to this situation: Pope John Paul II's meetings with Yasir Arafat and Kurt Waldheim; the Vatican's continued unwillingness to extend full diplomatic recognition to the State of Israel; the two sermons given by the pope in August 1989 that seemed to depreciate the value of Judaism by recognizing it only as a prelude to Christianity; and certainly not least of all, the tense dispute over the presence of the Polish Carmelite nuns in the Auschwitz convent.

Led by their superior, Sister Maria Teresa, a group of about a dozen nuns from the Order of Discalced Carmelites (O.C.D.)* moved into the *Theaterge-bäude* at the site of Auschwitz I on August 1, 1984.[12] Apparently, after repeated requests from Sister Maria Teresa, they obtained the approval of Polish author-ities, as well as Catholic church officials, but it is equally clear that they occupied the Old Theater without any dialogue with members of the Jewish community inside or outside of Poland.

The nuns in the Auschwitz convent have rarely spoken to outsiders, and there is not a great deal of public information about them individually.[13] Their order is cloistered—withdrawn from the outside world—and the nuns' days are spent quietly in work, contemplation, and prayer. Each convent has considerable au-tonomy, and the Auschwitz Carmelites seem to have a very conservative profile that led them to spurn the progressive steps taken in the mid–1980s by the majority of their order. In turn, they have received support from very traditional, even fundamentalist, movements in the church. It is thought that most of the nuns come from Poznan in central Poland. One of them, however, may have grown up near the Auschwitz camp and dedicated herself early on to atone for the sins committed there. The nuns intended to pray for all the victims of the Nazis. The convent in the *Theatergebäude*, however, became not simply a Catholic house of prayer next to or within the boundaries of the Nazi camp, but the pivot around which animosities and suspicions, charges and denunciations came to revolve.[14]

For Jews, the Carmelite convent and tall cross erected in its garden, however well intentioned the origins, have been wrong-minded, insensitive, and an in-trusive offense.[15] In Jewish eyes, that Christian presence compromises the unique and absolute significance of the place. One hesitates to say what was more problematic—the praying nuns or the cross. What seems clear is that the nuns did not grasp the fact that for Jews the symbol of the cross—complicated by the attitudes and opinions of the Auschwitz Carmelite superior as revealed in a widely published newspaper interview—is problematic, arousing deep anxiety in the Jewish psyche and bringing to the fore centuries of suspicion and hostility between Catholics and Jews, particularly those of Polish background.[16]

Jews found the convent compounding the losses suffered by their people because it seemed to rob the Holocaust of its Jewish particularity and uniqueness. Some Christians, especially Polish Catholics, have defended the convent on the ground that they, too, have a right and an obligation to memorialize their brothers and sisters who also perished in large numbers at Auschwitz.

Polish Catholic attitudes reflect the fact that many Poles view the German occupation of their country and the human material losses they suffered between 1939 and 1945 as a "national crucifixion." For many Poles, Auschwitz sym-

*Editors' note: Officially known as the "Discalced Carmelites," they are alternately referred to in this volume as "Carmelites," "Carmelite nuns," "Car-melite sisters," and "Sisters of Our Lady of Mount Carmel."

bolizes the martyrdom of Poland during World War II. Put rather simplistically, often the Polish attitude is that "Jews have no monopoly on the victims of Auschwitz." Because tens of thousands of non-Jewish victims of the Nazis also endured the horrors, also died there—many of them among the very earliest to perish—it is often difficult for Poles, Catholic or non-Catholic, to understand and accept the prevailing Jewish points of view on this matter.

Many Jews are convinced that what is at issue here is really a deep-seated antisemitism. Vulgar as it was, the statement attributed to Israel's Polish-born Prime Minister Yitzhak Shamir—"They [Poles] suck it [antisemitism] in with their mother's milk"—resonated with the secret or open opinion of many Jews about Poles.[17] On the other hand, Cardinal Jozef Glemp's sermon (August 26, 1989) in Czestochowa at Jasna Gora, the shrine of the Black Madonna and Poland's most important national site, not only exacerbated the situation but also resonated with the opinion of many Polish Catholics. Indeed it did so with many non-Jews, irrespective of whether they were Polish or Catholic.

The Polish primate asserted that Jewish criticism was coming from a people who consider themselves in a "position of people raised above all others." And echoing an ancient antisemitic canard, however inadvertently, Cardinal Glemp also claimed that Jewish "power lies in the mass media which are easily at your disposal in many countries."[18] Coming, as they did, from the highest ranking leader in the Polish church, such words were not to be taken lightly. A witch's brew resulted. The delicate questions of religious propriety and national sentiment were mixed with a difficult deposit of history: lingering antisemitism among Poles, a Polish need for national assertion, and some amount of Jewish anti-Christianity.

To most Christian minds, especially to those of Catholics, prayer and penance are required to make reparation to God for the sins of those who perpetrated, or cooperated in, the hideous cruelty carried out in the ash-filled place that was Auschwitz. To deny Christians this right seems, particularly to Polish Catholics, to deny them the fulfillment of a religious obligation: acknowledgment of their dependence on the mercy of God.

Who better than a group of cloistered Discalced Carmelite nuns, a Roman Catholic religious order founded in the fifteenth century, could live out this reparation for the sins of humankind? Their lives are dedicated deeply and profoundly to confronting the world and God at an intense spiritual level. In the best and most loving dimension of their tradition, they live an enclosed life of voluntary poverty, sacrifice, and prayer. Theirs is a way of spiritual atonement for "the sins of the world." Yet here is precisely where some of the most crucial issues are joined.

As Christians must constantly seek to understand Jews as Jews, so Jews must seek to understand Christians—perhaps Catholics especially—as Christians, also trying to appreciate, although they may not always comprehend, their beliefs. Difficult as it is for both sides, Jews must understand that it is possible to offend

Christians, just as Christians must come to terms with a legacy that has not only offended but also done immense harm to Jews.

The Carmelite sisters are human beings. Subject to the same ignorance, prejudice, and misunderstandings as the rest of us, they do not always live up to the ideals of their lifestyle or of their following of Jesus, whom Christians believe to be the Christ of God. Surely this fact is evident when one reads and reflects on the profoundly insensitive comments made by the Carmelite superior in the previously noted interview.[19]

Compounding her prejudices, even anti-Jewish attitudes, and her theological understanding—some would say "unnuanced" theological understanding—is the fact that within Poland itself, and at Auschwitz specifically, the Jewish aspect of the Holocaust has been underplayed, even neglected. Hopeful currents of change are appearing in this regard, but in a country denuded of its own Jewish population and cut off by more than forty years of state-imposed ignorance from prevailing currents of thought in the outside world, it is not easy for Poles to appreciate the uniqueness of the Jewish Holocaust or to empathize with the worldwide Jewish community. Poles see themselves as victims, not only of the Germans during World War II but also of the Soviets after the war, which perhaps—including now the reunification of Germany—has never really ended for the Poles.

Auschwitz is in Polish territory. It is, one might even say, intertwined with Oswiecim. All of this makes it difficult for many Polish Catholics to revise their understanding of Auschwitz. At the time of this writing, Auschwitz itself still stands as a monument to multinational losses—Soviet, Czech, and French, for example, as well as Polish. Official guides, as many visitors can attest, rarely mention, let alone emphasize, Jewish losses. Rather, the Jews are lumped together with the "victims" and "prisoners" of more than twenty different countries whose nationals were enslaved, suffered, and died in the huge Auschwitz network.

So, how does one confront the past? How should one remember and memorialize, recognizing that our identities and needs are both those of a shared humanity and of a varied particularity—cultural, ethnic, national, religious—without which humanity is lost? As each generation grows further and further from Auschwitz and what led to it, people find it more and more difficult to remember together, particularly when they already remember differently. Judd Levingston argues persuasively, "The issue of religious memory is as problematic as the issue of historical memory. Jews and Poles . . . may not be able to agree on the most fitting memorial to those who perished. Jews and Poles will remember a different set of experiences in the 1930's and 40's. Poles will remember invasion and war, Jews will remember hiding and being hidden, endless journeys in boxcars, and the chimneys of Auschwitz."[20]

Christians are enjoined to remember that their tradition's long history of antisemitism helped to pave the way to Auschwitz. That history gives Christians a special, repentant responsibility to ensure respect for the losses suffered by the Jewish people in the Holocaust and at Auschwitz in particular. The responsibility cannot be fulfilled when Christians fail, as some are doing, to understand carefully enough what Jews presently find fitting or offensive in attempts to remember and to memorialize Auschwitz.

All the more, there are good reasons why it is important that the new center for dialogue and information at Auschwitz be built and that it should include the relocated Carmelites. Without such moves—and the continuing effort of Christians and Jews to re-establish and deepen their dialogue—the rift between Christians and Jews, the actions and reactions within and between the communities as a result of the Auschwitz convent controversy, will only serve to harden positions, to increase the strain, and, for some, to rupture completely the relationship between Jews and Christians.

What is needed is careful and sensitive listening that leads to understanding. All of us, Jews and Christians, need to stretch our thinking and expand our hearts, perhaps to the breaking point, to include the suffering of "others" in our consciousness and thereby to break down the barriers that destructively divide communities into "us" and "them." And we must do these things even as we struggle to bear our own particular suffering. Otherwise, how shall we come to recognize that our moral claim to life is not only individual but also shared and social? In the moral community of human beings, each of us is related to the other, and we must expand our universe of moral concern and obligation to include not just those who are "our own" but also those who are "not our own" and yet are still one with us in our common humanity.

Serious people who wish to learn from history have much at stake in understanding the profound importance of what happened to the Jews during the Holocaust and to millions of other peoples who were swept into the Nazi net of death. Likewise, we have much to learn about and from the dialogue between Christians and Jews concerning what constitutes a fitting memorial at Auschwitz. For lurking within the controversy are deeper issues than what are the boundaries of Auschwitz, who suffered more in this place, and should the nuns and their convent ever have been there.

Consider, for example, that religions—at their best—are indispensable sources of encouragement and hope. At their worst, they give birth to twins—exclusivity and intolerance—that breed vilification and hatred. The remedy is not to eliminate religion but to resist the temptation for one religion to make its tradition "chosen" to the detriment of others.

The lesson that still needs learning—by analogy it applies to all faiths, not just to the Jewish and Christian traditions—can be grasped at Auschwitz. When a socially dominant faith exalts itself over others, the inference among believers is that they, as people, are exalted. The next twist of logic, that they are free to eliminate the others, is recorded in almost every chapter of human history.

For Jews and Christians, perhaps for all religious traditions, Auschwitz is the paradigm for our time. That a convent's location should be a matter of controversy indicates the need for a fundamental spiritual and political reappraisal of love and justice.

Some clues about how that reappraisal might work come from Rabbi Irving Greenberg, an influential author and the founding president of the National Jewish Center for Learning and Leadership. Speaking at a 1989 symposium on "The Anatomy of Hate," Greenberg stressed how the Jewish tradition makes a fundamental claim: Human beings are created in the image of God. They are comparable to God, and yet, the claim makes clear, human persons are not divine and should not usurp God's place. But as religious traditions have developed, at least in the West, such usurping—idolatry is a traditional word for it—is what so often happens. It happens whenever individuals and groups absolutize what is relative, when they equate their ways with God's. Such absolutizing breeds conflict and hate, because anyone who fails to "see the light" opposes what is "good" and "right." Branded "evil," such opponents are even demonized. They become targets of hate, if not of annihilation.

Perverse though it is, Greenberg contends, such logic lurks within the most fundamental religious claims, including those about covenants that we have noted before. If that logic cannot be excised completely, self-criticism promoted by those same fundamental claims can provide a remedy. "Recognition of guilt and failure," Greenberg affirms, "is a sign of health." In the specific case at hand, the point to remember is that human beings are comparable to God, and hence of infinite worth, and yet they are not God, and hence their ways are not absolute. The net result, Greenberg argues, should be a pluralism—not to be confused with an indifference-breeding relativism—that respects human life by checking and balancing power, internally and externally, and by guaranteeing basic rights, especially those of the weak.

Complementing Greenberg's suggestion that there is something insidious in religion's logic, Bishop Krister Stendahl, a leading Swedish Christian scholar from Harvard University who also spoke at the conference on "The Anatomy of Hate," notes that "there is in the ground metaphors of the Biblical perception, as in the case of so many religions, an endemic pattern of powerlessness. But when that book becomes the holy scriptures of those with power, danger is at hand." The notion that a group is somehow "chosen" by God or in a special covenant with God provides a case in point. Such belief can be formidable in encouraging downtrodden people to break the shackles of injustice, but when success follows and the powerless become the powerful, the logic of "chosenness" or "covenant" may bear the fruits of conflict and hate.

By their fruits you shall know them, Stendahl urges, is the practical test that Jesus encouraged. Christians profess that the proper fruits are those of love, but Stendahl confesses that he is "afraid of that word," which has covered a multitude of sins, not enough by redeeming life but too much by destroying it in the name of love. Religiously speaking and acting, love itself needs to be redeemed, and Stendahl's suggestion toward that end is that love needs to be understood and enacted as *esteem*. Love-as-esteem, suggests Stendahl, involves a "kind of curiosity and suspicion that it is the one who is different from me who has something to give and to add. When love becomes that, then it is the opposite to hatred."[21]

Can religion become less the source of conflict and more the source of understanding and human solidarity? And can it do so, in particular, in a world scarred by Auschwitz and destined to contain wide varieties of religious and nonreligious experience in relation to the Holocaust? The answer, we believe, can and should be "yes," but it will be "yes" only to the degree that religious life fosters a sense of its own fallibility, an emphasis on self-criticism, a willingness to show esteem to others, and a sensitivity that sees with feeling the particularity and uniqueness of each other's suffering. Those qualities, in turn, depend on listening and sharing in good faith, on striving for better appreciation of the positions that others hold as well as of one's own. Those qualities also depend on accepting responsibility, humbly and where appropriate in a spirit of repentance, for the things that one's own tradition has done to create and perpetuate conflict, sorrow, and loss. Such an outlook would not negate religious particularities. It would contextualize them to emphasize understanding of the fact that we all belong to the same human species and that there is a fatal interdependence wherever the actions of its members are concerned.

Memory Offended speaks to this situation. Indeed its contents and their authors stress the very thing most needed: mutual understanding. Using the Auschwitz convent controversy as a prism, the essays that follow—each one by a distinguished writer who speaks from the particularity of his or her experience and tradition—refracts light to illuminate both the facts surrounding it and, more importantly, to identify, analyze, and comment on the long-range issues, questions, and implications that still lie hidden within the controversy and its aftermath.

In their own ways, each contributor has responded to the editors' request to address three main questions. First, how does the Auschwitz convent controversy and its seeming resolution reflect and impact the most important issues in Jewish-Christian relationships? Second, in both the Jewish and Christian traditions, what assumptions most need to be re-examined, what obstacles most need to be overcome, what pitfalls most need to be avoided, and what strengths most need to be utilized to address the issues in ways that might improve those relationships? Third, are there lessons Jews and Christians can learn as a result of this controversy?

The essays that follow deserve to speak for themselves. We choose to let them do so without further editorial summary—except for a brief concluding observation. Organized into three main parts that explore, first, the history and politics of memory, then the psychology of memory, and finally the theology of memory, the authors' contributions do not always say the same things about the Auschwitz convent controversy. They do, however, share a conviction—"if we stop remembering, we stop being"—and a spirit that can move people beyond "memory offended." Both that conviction and that spirit are grounded in the recognition that, if Jews and especially Christians had disputed less whose covenant was "old" or "new," false or true, and nurtured more a mutual respect, as well as a shared concern for the civility, justice, and love that both traditions enjoin, the Holocaust and Auschwitz in particular could have been prevented. Then a convent in Oswiecim, Poland, would not be controversial.

Events went another way. They leave Jews and Christians to ponder pain-filled relationships that involve much more than the physical location of nuns at prayer. At stake, as all the contributors to this jointly crafted, interdependent book better understand for having worked together, is nothing less than a fundamental reassessment that might help to mend the world.

NOTES

1. The texts from which these quotations are taken can be found, along with other documents pertinent to the Auschwitz convent controversy, in this book's appendixes.

2. Scholars continue to study and correct statistics about Auschwitz. We use the statistics endorsed by eminent historians such as Yehuda Bauer. See his "Auschwitz: The Dangers of Distortion," *Jerusalem Post* (International Edition), 30 September 1989, which is reprinted in the appendix.

Bauer debunks the conventional claim that 4 million people died in Auschwitz, a figure that is usually broken down further to suggest that 2.5 million of these victims were Jews and 1.5 million of them were Poles. The effect of these erroneous figures, argues Bauer, is to make Auschwitz more a place of Polish victimization than it really was. By his reckoning, about 1.3 million Jews perished there—most by gassing. Some 215,000 Poles were imprisoned in Auschwitz. About 83,000 of them died there—less than 4,000 by gassing.

For additional trustworthy analysis of the statistics about Auschwitz, see Aharon Weiss, "Categories of Camps—Their Character and Role in the Execution of the Final Solution of the Jewish Question," *The Nazi Concentration Camps*, ed. Yisrael Gutman (Jerusalem: Yad Vashem, 1984), 115–32. Another important article, unpublished at the time of this writing but scheduled to appear in *Yad Vashem Studies* (Vol. 21, 1991), is Franciszek Piper's "The Number of Victims in Auschwitz-Birkenau." The work of Weiss and Piper basically supports Yehuda Bauer's analysis although Piper's very conservative figures—1.1 million total deaths at Auschwitz, including 960,000 Jews and 70–75,000 Poles—are lower.

3. Elie Wiesel, "Listen to the Wind," *Against Silence: The Voice and Vision of Elie Wiesel*, 3 vols., ed. Irving Abrahamson (New York: Holocaust Library, 1985), 1:166. The epigraph for *Memory Offended* is derived from this poetic statement, which was first made by Wiesel at Auschwitz on August 1, 1979.

4. Elie Wiesel, "Let Him Remember," *Against Silence*, 1:368. The line is from a text adapted from a lecture at Schara Tzedeck Synagogue, Vancouver, B.C., May 6, 1978.

5. The question "Who comes to Auschwitz to remember?" is also noteworthy. The Auschwitz-Birkenau site was opened as a museum by the Polish government in 1947. Visitor estimates from 1947 to 1988 suggest that more than 19 million people have come to that place, and about 4 million of those persons are non-Polish. Jews go there in increasing numbers, but the great majority of those who visit Auschwitz are Polish

Catholics. See Dan Fisher, "Auschwitz: Jews, Poles Differ on Its Primary Significance," *Los Angeles Times*, 18 September 1989.

6. The chronology that follows this introductory essay, as well as the documents provided in the appendix, provides considerable detail about many more facts that are pertinent to the Auschwitz convent controversy. Three other excellent information sources are: Norman Solomon, "The Carmelite Convent at Auschwitz," *Christian Jewish Relations* 19 (September 1986): 42–46; Alan Montague, "The Carmelite Convent at Auschwitz: A Documentary Survey," *IJA Research Reports* 8 (1987); and Karen Adler, "Controversy over the Carmelite Convent at Auschwitz 1988–89," *IJA Research Reports* 7 (1989).

7. While the Auschwitz convent drew the strongest reaction, it is significant that the Carmelite convent at Auschwitz is neither the only nor the first location where Christian places of prayer and meditation have been situated adjacent to or within Nazi death camps. Consider, for example, the Sobibor killing center, which was constructed in the spring of 1942 in the eastern part of the Lublin district in Poland.

Sobibor's specific purpose was to help implement what the Germans euphemistically called "the Final Solution of the Jewish question." There nearly 250,000 Jews lost their lives, including some 35,000 from the Netherlands. In 1987, Polish Carmelite monks finished building a chapel on the site where an earlier and smaller Catholic chapel had existed. Sobibor's administration turned that early wooden structure into part of the camp itself. Some reports indicate that the Nazis executed Jews in that place. There has been Jewish protest about the 1987 development, but as of this writing it has not matched the intensity of the Auschwitz convent controversy.

Another example exists at Birkenau, or Auschwitz II. This part of the Auschwitz complex, constructed in 1941, was the camp's main killing center. Just outside the barbed-wire perimeter of Auschwitz II, situated just across a narrow road, there is a former Nazi building that is clearly identified on Auschwitz-Birkenau maps as the "new commandant's office." This structure was converted into a Catholic parish church early in the 1980s. Little protest occurred at the time, nor has there been much since. For more detail, see John Thavis, "No Protests Over Birkenau Church," *National Catholic Reporter*, 22 September 1989 and also this book's Afterword.

Christian sites, including a Carmelite convent in existence since 1964, can also be found adjacent to or within the boundaries of the concentration camp at Dachau, which was located in Germany about ten miles northwest of Munich. Controversy about their presence has been minimal, and some of the reasons are worth noting. Dachau was not a killing center where Jews were dispatched by gassing on arrival. Opened in March 1933, this camp did imprison Jews, but its inmates also included large numbers of non-Jews who were considered threats to the Third Reich. Indeed once the "Final Solution" was under way, Jewish prisoners in Dachau were usually deported to the killing centers in Poland. The German system, in sum, had camps of different kinds, and there was a substantial difference between a concentration camp like Dachau and a killing center like Sobibor. If Auschwitz combined the functions of both, it nonetheless remains the largest of the killing centers that targeted Jews. The Christian presence at Dachau, therefore, is rightly far less problematic than its existence at Sobibor, Birkenau, or Auschwitz I. The controversy about the Carmelites at Auschwitz may yet touch the Christian presence at the other killing centers as well.

8. For a succinct history of the Auschwitz camp, see Jozef Buszko, "Auschwitz,"

Encyclopedia of the Holocaust, ed. Israel Gutman et al. (New York: Macmillan, 1990), 1:107–19.

9. Wiesel, "Listen to the Wind," *Against Silence*, 1:167.

10. One fortunate effect of the Auschwitz convent controversy is that it helped to generate additional deliberations to reconsider how the Auschwitz-Birkenau site itself can best be preserved to memorialize those who perished there, and utilized to teach the living about the tragedy that happened in that place. In the autumn of 1989, for example, the Polish government established a new commission to plan for the future of the State Museum of Auschwitz. Suggestions for changes in the State Museum have been sent to the commission by an international group of Jewish academics and intellectuals who produced the Yarnton Declaration at their May 6–8, 1990, meeting in Oxford, England. The commission held an international meeting later in 1990 to consider further how the State Museum should be changed and developed.

11. Peter Steinfels, "Catholics and Jews Exchange Hope and Misunderstanding," *New York Times*, 17 September 1989.

12. Action of a different kind occurred in 1972. In that year, the European Rabbinical Conference met in Geneva, Switzerland. It asked Polish authorities for permission to build a synagogue in Auschwitz. The request was denied.

For more detail on the nuns moving into the Old Theater at Auschwitz, see Stefano M. Paci, "The Convent Again under Fire," *30 Days*, March 1989, 30–31.

13. Much of the information that follows about the Auschwitz Carmelites is taken from Adler, "Controversy over the Carmelite Convent at Auschwitz 1988–89," 3. See also Colonel Francis A. Winiarz's report of his interview (September 29, 1989) with Sister Maria Teresa, the superior of the Carmelite convent at Auschwitz, " 'We're Not Moving a Single Inch.' " *Polish Daily News*, 1 November 1989. The article is reprinted in the appendix.

14. The precise location of the *Theatergebäude*—inside the boundaries of the camp or not—is more than a quibble in the Auschwitz convent controversy. Karen Adler's analysis is helpful. "The building housing the nuns," she writes, "lies beyond a wall, and it has therefore been said that the convent was not part of the concentration camp. But other buildings nearby, also outside the wall, include the commandant's headquarters, a railway siding where inmates were brought, and an execution site. Many Jews have therefore had difficulty with the idea that the building—a former storehouse for gas, the very symbol of Auschwitz, itself the predominant symbol of the Holocaust—had nothing to do with the Holocaust itself" ("Controversy over the Carmelite Convent at Auschwitz 1988–89," 3).

In addition, the registration documents submitted to the United Nations Education, Scientific and Cultural Organization (UNESCO) by the Polish government in 1978 to win inclusion for the Auschwitz-Birkenau camp site on UNESCO's World Heritage List include the *Theatergebäude* as part of Auschwitz I.

It is also worth noting that the *Theatergebäude* stands just on the other side of the camp wall from Auschwitz I's notorious Block 11 and the execution wall adjacent to that block. It was in the cellars of Block 11 that the first gassing experiments took place at Auschwitz. This part of Auschwitz is especially dear to Poles, for many of them— including Father Maximilian Kolbe, who was canonized by his fellow-Pole, Pope John Paul II, on October 10, 1982—lost their lives in Block 11 or at the "Wall of Death," as the execution site is still called.

15. In November 1987 a cross appeared atop the *Theatergebäude*. It eventually was

removed, but another one was erected in the convent's garden. This particular cross has an intriguing history. Its existence dates back to June 7, 1979, when Pope John Paul II went to Auschwitz and Birkenau on his first papal visit to his native Poland. The pope celebrated Mass on the grounds of Birkenau, and the cross that came to stand in the convent garden was originally used as part of that religious service. See Henri Tinco, "À Auschwitz, le carmel de la colère," *Le Monde*, 18 July 1989.

Pope John Paul II's visit to Auschwitz-Birkenau on June 7, 1979, remains important in the Auschwitz convent controversy. The pope spoke about the redemptive Auschwitz martyrdom of Father Maximilian Kolbe and, significantly, Edith Stein, a Jewish convert to Christianity who became a Carmelite sister. He also referred to Auschwitz as "the Golgotha of the modern world." In one way or another, the seeds for the Auschwitz convent were probably planted during the pope's 1979 visit to Auschwitz. If so, they had much more than sprouted by May 1985, when the pope visited the Benelux countries.

In honor of this visit, the pope's friend Father Werenfried van Straaten, head of a German charitable organization called Aid to the Church in Need, which has provided support for the Catholic church in the Soviet bloc, decided to take up a request received from the Auschwitz Carmelites and launch a fund-raising drive to establish fully the Auschwitz convent as a gift to the pope.

The fund-raising appeal—it appeared in a special bulletin of a journal published by Aid to the Church in Need, was timed to coincide with the pope's stay in Belgium, and generated about $150,000—called the convent "a spiritual fortress and guarantee of the conversion of strayed brothers from our countries as well as proof of our desire to erase outrages so often done to the Vicar of Christ."

Early Jewish protests targeted this fund-raising effort, its particular language about conversion, and the Catholic presence at Auschwitz, but these protests became much more widespread only after Michel Bailly published an article about the matter in a Brussels newspaper, *Le Soir*, on October 14, 1985. Bailly quoted part of the fund-raising appeal, and his article was a catalyst in bringing worldwide attention to the Auschwitz convent.

For more detail on the fund-raising drive for the Auschwitz convent, see Montague, "The Carmelite Convent at Auschwitz: A Documentary Survey," 3; and Paci, "The Convent Again under Fire," 30–31.

16. See the Winiarz/Sister Maria Teresa interview, " 'We're Not Moving a Single Inch.' "

17. See Dan Fisher, "Auschwitz: Jews, Poles Differ on Its Primary Significance," *Los Angeles Times*, 18 September 1989, and Mary Curtius, "Israel's Bittersweet Diplomacy," *Boston Globe*, 24 September 1989. Curtius indicates that the specific remark attributed to Shamir was provoked by a reporter for the *Jerusalem Post*, who, according to Curtius, asked the prime minister "why the affair of the Catholic convent at the Nazi death camp of Auschwitz had triggered antisemitic outbursts in Poland."

18. For a more complete text of Cardinal Glemp's sermon, see the appendix.

19. See the Winiarz/Sister Maria Teresa interview, " 'We're Not Moving a Single Inch.' "

20. Judd Levingston, "The Legacy of the Convent at Auschwitz," *Sh'ma*, 27 October 1989.

21. The statements quoted from Irving Greenberg and Krister Stendahl are from unpublished remarks they made at a session on "Religion and Hate," which was part of an international symposium on "The Anatomy of Hate." The Symposium, sponsored

by The Elie Wiesel Foundation for Humanity, convened at Boston University, March 19–21, 1989. Additional symposia on this theme were held at Haifa, Israel, June 3–5, 1990, and Oslo, Norway, August 26–29, 1990. Further information can be obtained from the foundation's office at 666 Fifth Avenue, 11th Floor, New York, NY 10103.

Chronology: Events Pertinent to the Auschwitz Convent Controversy, 1933–90

Carol Rittner and John K. Roth

January 30, 1933	Adolf Hitler becomes Chancellor of Germany. The German Jews soon feel the effects of the Nazis' anti-Jewish policies of segregation and forced emigration.
July 20, 1933	The Nazi government signs a concordat with the Vatican in which Germany guarantees the freedom of the Catholic religion and the right of the church "to regulate its own affairs," as long as they are purely religious. In return, the German Catholic church dissolves its political organizations, thus virtually abandoning political activity in the Third Reich. The agreement was signed on behalf of the Holy See by the papal secretary of state, Cardinal Eugenio Pacelli, later Pope Pius XII.
January 26, 1934	Germany and Poland sign a ten-year nonaggression pact.
March 21, 1937	Pope Pius XI issues an encyclical, *Mit brennender Sorge* ("With Burning Concern"), which denounces the Nazi racial myth and castigates the German government for violating its concordat with the Vatican. But the encyclical fails to oppose unequivocally the Third Reich's antisemitic policies.
March 2, 1939	After the death of Pope Pius XI, Cardinal Eugenio Pacelli (1876–1958) is elected pope. He takes the name Pius XII.
August 23, 1939	A Soviet-German nonaggression pact is signed in Moscow by Molotov and Ribbentrop. It includes a secret agreement to partition Poland.
September 1, 1939	World War II begins with Germany's invasion of Poland. The Germans occupy the western half of the country, including Warsaw, Poland's capital city.

September 17, 1939   Soviet troops invade Poland and occupy the eastern half of
                        the country. As a sovereign state, Poland disappears from
                        the map of Europe.

April 27, 1940   Heinrich Himmler, head of the Nazi SS, orders the estab-
                        lishment of a concentration camp at Oswiecim (Auschwitz),
                        Poland. Situated about forty miles west of Cracow, the camp
                        has major rail lines nearby, a key factor in Auschwitz's
                        eventually becoming the major death and concentration
                        camp in the Nazi system.

March 1, 1941   Himmler orders expansion of the Auschwitz camp and con-
                        struction of Birkenau (Auschwitz II) begins in October.

June 22, 1941   Germany attacks the Soviet Union. All of Poland now falls
                        under German occupation.

July 31, 1941   Nazi leader Hermann Göring appoints Reinhard Heydrich
                        to implement "the Final Solution of the Jewish question."

September 3, 1941   The first experimental gassings with Zyklon B occur at
                        Auschwitz. Most of the initial victims are Soviet prisoners
                        of war.

January 20, 1942   Under Heydrich's direction, the Wannsee Conference plans
                        how to annihilate European Jewry. Before the end of World
                        War II, between 5 and 6 million European Jews lose their
                        lives in the "Final Solution." About 1.3 million of them
                        perish at Auschwitz.

Summer 1942   Following an inspection of Auschwitz-Birkenau by Heinrich
                        Himmler, the decision is taken to update and expand the
                        camp's killing capacity. With much of the construction
                        being handled by the J. A. Topf und Söhne company of
                        Erfurt, Germany, there are four gas chamber-crematorium
                        units in operation by the early summer of 1943. They can
                        "process" thousands of human beings daily.

Late 1942   Himmler orders non-Jewish Poles to be sent from Auschwitz
                        to other camps, while Jews from other camps will be trans-
                        ferred to Auschwitz. The order is not completely carried
                        out, but from 1943 on, the entire Auschwitz complex be-
                        comes a predominantly Jewish camp. Of the 215,000 Poles
                        imprisoned in Auschwitz, a majority survived. Many of
                        those who died lost their lives not in Auschwitz but in other
                        camps. (For more detail on the latter points, see the article
                        by Yehuda Bauer in this book's appendix.)

January 27, 1945   Soviet troops liberate Auschwitz.

May 7, 1945   Nazi Germany surrenders unconditionally to the Allies. Be-
                        tween 1939 and 1945, more than 6 million Polish people
                        have lost their lives and much of Poland is devastated.
                        Included in the Polish losses are about 3.5 million Polish
                        Jews, some 90 percent of Poland's Jewish population. By

1948, a Communist government, which includes strong antireligion policies, is firmly established in Poland. Meanwhile postwar agreements have shifted Poland's borders westward, and millions of its people have been resettled. The Soviet Union maintains control of much of Poland's eastern regions. As compensation, Poland obtains former German lands east of the Oder and Neisse rivers.

1947 The Polish parliament makes the Auschwitz-Birkenau site a "Monument to the Suffering of the Polish Nation and Other Peoples." Estimates about the number of visitors to the Auschwitz-Birkenau site from 1947 to 1988 indicate that more than 19 million persons went there during that period. About 4 million of these were non-Polish, many of them Jewish, but apparently the great majority who come to Auschwitz-Birkenau are Polish Catholics.

1958 Pope Pius XII dies. He is succeeded by the Cardinal Archbishop of Milan, Italy, Angelo Giuseppe Roncalli, who takes the name John XXIII.

January 25, 1959 On the Feast of the Conversion of St. Paul, Pope John XXIII announces that he intends to convene an Ecumenical Council for the Universal Church. That council, which is known as Vatican II, literally revolutionizes the Roman Catholic church and its stance toward human history.

November 22, 1964 A Carmelite convent, named "Heilig Blut"("Carmel of the Precious Blood"), opens at Dachau, the former concentration camp located near the German city of Munich.

1965 A Jewish memorial synagogue is dedicated on the site of the camp at Dachau.

October 28, 1965 *Nostra Aetate* ("In Our Times"), the Catholic church's "Declaration on the Relationship of the Church with Non-Christian Religions," including Judaism, is promulgated by Vatican II.

April 30, 1967 The Protestant Church of Reconciliation is completed on the site of Dachau.

1972 The European Rabbinical Conference, meeting in Geneva, asks permission of Polish authorities to build a synagogue in Auschwitz. The authorities refuse permission.

1978 Cardinal Karol Wojtyla, the archbishop of Cracow since 1964, is elected pope of the Roman Catholic church. Taking the name of John Paul II, he is the first non-Italian pope since 1523, the first Polish pope in history, and the first pope from a Communist country.

1979 The United Nations Educational Scientific and Cultural Organization (UNESCO) announces that the 1978 proposal—supported and encouraged by the World Jewish Congress—

from the People's Republic of Poland to add the Auschwitz concentration camp site to UNESCO's World Heritage List has been approved. The 1972 UNESCO Convention for the Protection of World Cultural and National Heritage, ratified by Poland in 1976, makes clear that Poland will have the "duty of ensuring the . . . protection, conservation, presentation and transmission to future generations" of the site. The Polish application to make the Auschwitz site a protected place includes a list of buildings and a plan of the area. Both contain the *Theatergebäude* or Old Theater building, where the belongings of those who were gassed were kept. The building also served as a storehouse for the Zyklon B that was used in the gas chambers. It is this building that will become the Carmelite convent in 1984.

June 7, 1979

During his first papal visit to his native Poland, Pope John Paul II goes to Auschwitz I and Birkenau. In Birkenau he celebrates Mass and his sermon makes particular reference to the fate of Jews and Poles. Calling Auschwitz "the Golgotha of the modern world," the pope also makes special mention of Father Maximilian Kolbe and the converted Carmelite sister, Edith Stein, who both lost their lives at Auschwitz.

March 5, 1982

Pope John Paul II tells participants in Jewish-Catholic dialogue that relations between Jews and Christians have been "marked by misunderstandings, resentments" but that Christians are on the right path toward reconciliation.

September 15, 1982

Pope John Paul II receives Palestinian Liberation Organization leader Yasir Arafat in a private audience. He tells Arafat that terrorism is "unacceptable," but Jewish leaders protest that the meeting gives the PLO added status and dignity.

October 10, 1982

Father Maximilian Kolbe, a Polish Franciscan priest who voluntarily took the place of another prisoner, a married man with children, as he was being led to his death in Auschwitz, is canonized by Pope John Paul II. Because some of Kolbe's writings reflect an antisemitic bias, his canonization strains Catholic-Jewish relations.

1983

A former Nazi building, just outside Birkenau's barbed-wire perimeter and clearly identified on Auschwitz-Birkenau maps as the "new commandant's office," is turned into a Catholic church and opened as an extension of the main parish at Oswiecim. Few, if any, objections are voiced. Also during this year, Jozef Glemp becomes a cardinal in the Roman Catholic church.

August 1, 1984

A small group of nuns from the Order of Our Lady of Mount Carmel, with the approval of Polish authorities and

Catholic church officials, but apparently without any dialogue with members of the Jewish community either within or outside of Poland, moves into the *Theatergebäude* or Old Theater building at the site of Auschwitz I.

May 1985

On the occasion of Pope John Paul II's visit to the Benelux countries, and with a prior Carmelite request for support, Father Werenfried van Straaten, a Dutch Dominican priest and founder of the anti-Communist German charitable movement, Aid to the Church in Need, based in Konigsten, West Germany, launches an international appeal to Catholics, asking them "to give a convent at Auschwitz as a gift to the Pope." Jews in Belgium and France are particularly offended, exacerbating Catholic-Jewish tensions. As the year continues, prominent Catholics in Belgium, Holland, and France voice objections, too, although, in general, Catholic reaction focuses on the fund-raising appeal of Aid to the Church in Need and displays more ambivalence about the Auschwitz convent itself.

May 5, 1985

Despite widespread protests from World War II veterans' groups, members of Congress, and Christian and Jewish groups in the United States and abroad, President Ronald Reagan and Chancellor Helmut Kohl of West Germany visit Bitburg's Kolmeshohe military cemetery, where soldiers from the Second SS Panzer Division are buried, to honor soldiers killed during World War II.

December 11–13, 1985

Edgar Bronfman, president of the World Jewish Congress, visits Poland and discusses the Auschwitz Convent issue with Adam Lopatka, Polish religious affairs minister.

February 17–18, 1986

Belgian Jewish leaders meet with Cardinal Franciszek Macharski, the archbishop of Cracow, and Adam Lopatka. Markus Pardes, president of the Co-ordinating Committee of Jewish Organizations in Belgium, concludes that the Carmelite convent can be removed "only if great international pressure from all Jewish organizations and communities, as well as our Catholic friends, is exerted on Cardinal Macharski and the Vatican." Cardinal Macharski follows up with a document detailing support for the convent.

April 14, 1986

John Paul II becomes the first pope ever to visit a Jewish house of worship. He goes to Rome's main synagogue, embraces Chief Rabbi Elio Toaff, describes the Jewish people as Christianity's elder brothers, and emphasizes the Church's rejection of antisemitism.

April 15, 1986

In a letter signed by five prominent rabbis—Sir Immanuel Jakobovits (Britain), René-Samuel Sirat (France), Max Warchawski (Strasbourg), Mordechai Piron (Zurich), and Moses Rosen (Romania), the Presidium of European Rabbis urges Pope John Paul II to abandon the Auschwitz convent project.

July 22, 1986

Meeting in Geneva, Switzerland, Jewish and Catholic leaders affirm that "the lonely sites of Auschwitz and Birkenau are recognized today as symbols of the Final Solution, under which title the Nazis carried out the extermination (known as the *Shoah*) of 6 million Jews, one and a half million of whom were children, simply because they were Jews." Catholic participants include Cardinals Godfried Danneels (Brussels), Albert Decourtray (Lyon), Jean-Marie Lustiger (Paris), and Franciszek Macharski (Cracow), the latter having recently returned from a visit to Israel that included time at Yad Vashem, the memorial to Jewish Holocaust victims. The Jewish participants include Theo Klein, Rabbi René-Samuel Sirat, Markus Pardes, Professor Ady Steg, and Tullia Zevi.

1987

Polish Catholic monks finish construction of a chapel on the site of the Nazi death camp at Sobibor.

February 22, 1987

Jewish and Catholic leaders—including all of those who signed the July 22, 1986, document—reach agreement indicating that "within two years" the Auschwitz convent would become part of a new center of "information, education, meeting and prayer . . . outside the area of Auschwitz-Birkenau camps." This agreement further states, "There will, therefore, be no permanent Catholic place of worship on the site of the Auschwitz and Birkenau camps. Everyone will be able to pray there according to the dictates of his own heart, religion and faith."

May 1, 1987

Edith Stein (aka Sister Teresa Benedicta of the Cross), a Jewish philosopher who converted to Catholicism and then became a Carmelite nun, is beatified by Pope John Paul II during a mass in Cologne, West Germany. Her beatification intensifies the issue of whether her death in Auschwitz was that of a Christian martyr or of a Jewish victim of the Holocaust. While in Cologne, the pope addresses the city's Jewish Central Committee and underscores the need to "remain alert for all new forms of antisemitism, racism, and neo-pagan religious persecution."

June 15, 1987

Pope John Paul II receives Austrian president Kurt Waldheim in a private audience at the Vatican. Protesting that Waldheim was involved in Nazi activities, including knowledge of war crimes, Jewish leaders express outrage about this meeting.

November 1987

A large cross appears atop the Auschwitz convent building. Eventually it is removed, but another is placed in the convent garden.

June 23–24, 1988

During a pastoral visit to Austria, Pope John Paul II says the country suffered under the Nazis and calls attention to Catholics who were persecuted during World War II. Visiting Mauthausen, the site of a Nazi concentration camp, he speaks about the victims' agonies but does not specifically mention the Jews, prompting Vienna's chief rabbi, Paul Chaim Eisenberg, to deplore the omission. Some Jews charge that the pope has deliberately ignored Austria's history of antisemitism and Jewish suffering during the Holocaust. On June 24, in an address to leaders of the Jewish community in Vienna, John Paul II comments on "the *Shoah*, the murder of millions of Jews in the concentration camps."

February 22, 1989

The "within two years" deadline passes without the Carmelites moving from the Auschwitz convent. Polish church officials state that the move will still be made but that logistics prevented doing so on schedule. Protests escalate from Jews and concerned Christians, too.

July 14, 1989

Led by Rabbi Avraham Weiss, Jewish demonstrators from the United States protest at the Auschwitz convent. Polish workers eject the protestors after they climb over the convent fence. Two days later and without intervention, Rabbi Weiss holds another protest at the convent.

July 22, 1989

An extension period for the nuns' relocation—it had been requested by Cardinal Decourtray—passes without their leaving the convent site. Decourtray issues a communiqué in which he says, "We beg our Jewish dialogue partners to forgive this delay, which is due to real obstacles, the seriousness of which was not recognized by any of the signatories to the [1987 Geneva] agreement." Theo Klein, president of the European Jewish Congress, calls for a freeze in Jewish-Christian relations and requests that Jewish leaders not meet with the pope.

August 2 and 9, 1989

In homilies given during two general audiences at the Vatican, Pope John Paul II says the Old Testament "shows many instances of Israel's infidelity to God." He also refers to a new covenant "established in Christ's redemptive sacrifice." These statements intensify Jewish-Catholic tensions.

August 10, 1989

Cardinal Franciszek Macharski, archbishop of Cracow and a signatory to the July 1986 and February 1987 agreements, decries Jewish "bad faith" and announces that, in the atmosphere of mistrust, it is "impossible to continue construction of the Center" near Auschwitz.

August 26, 1989

At celebrations marking the Feast of the Blessed Virgin Mary in Czestochowa at Jasna Gora, the shrine of the Black Madonna, Poland's holiest icon, Polish primate Cardinal

Jozef Glemp addresses a religious gathering—including Poland's new prime minister, Tadeusz Mazowiecki—and states that Jewish "pronouncements against the [Carmelite] nuns [at Auschwitz] offend the feelings of all Poles." He further states that Jewish "power lies in the mass media" and that the media are easily at the disposal of Jews.

August 27, 1989   Pope John Paul II issues an encyclical on the fiftieth anniversary of the outbreak of World War II. In it he states "emphatically that hostility or hatred towards Judaism is in complete contradiction to the Christian view of the dignity of man."

August 29, 1989   U.S. Catholic leaders protest Cardinal Glemp's remarks. Glemp reiterates support for the Auschwitz convent, arguing that previous agreements need to be "renegotiated . . . by competent people."

August 31, 1989   Solidarity leader Lech Walesa calls Cardinal Glemp's comments of August 26 "a shame and a disgrace." He also advocates an international commission to resolve the convent controversy.

September 3, 1989   Three French and Belgian cardinals—Decourtray, Lustiger, and Danneels—all signers of the 1987 agreement, dispute Glemp. "If four cardinals, including the archbishop of Cracow, are not qualified to represent the Catholic side," they protest, "then who possibly could be?"

September 9, 1989   The official Polish press agency announces that Cardinal Jozef Glemp has canceled a scheduled visit to several cities in the United States. The announcement does not refer explicitly to the Auschwitz convent controversy but mentions "circumstances unfavorable for pastoral purposes" as a reason for the cancellation.

September 11, 1989   With delegates from seventeen countries in attendance, the European Jewish Congress urges prompt relocation of the convent "outside the camp" and expresses hope that Jewish-Catholic dialogue "will not suffer lasting damage."

September 16, 1989   The international edition of the *Jerusalem Post* quotes Israel's Polish-born Prime Minister Yitzhak Shamir as saying that Cardinal Glemp's remarks reflect a national antisemitism in Poland and that Poles "suck it in with their mother's milk." Within days, the *Los Angeles Times*, the *Boston Globe*, and other newspapers in the United States carry the story. Sharp reaction to the Shamir quotation follows from Poland and from some Jewish sources.

September 19, 1989   Cardinal Johannes Willebrands, president of the Commission of the Holy See for Religious Relations with Judaism, issues a statement affirming support for the measures stipulated in the Geneva declaration of February 1987.

September 20, 1989	Cardinal Jozef Glemp writes to Sir Sigmund Sternberg, chairman of the International Council of Christians and Jews, stating that he agrees to abide by the 1987 agreement to relocate the Auschwitz convent.
September 23, 1989	A statement issued at Discalced Carmelite World Head-quarters in Rome affirms that "all along the position of the general of the order, Fr. Philip Sainz de Baranda, O.C.D., has been that agreements [regarding the Auschwitz Carmel] must be honored." (The Carmelite nuns, although women, are under the authority of the male superior general of the Discalced Carmelite Order in Rome.)
September 27, 1989	Vandals damage the remains of a thirteenth-century Carmelite monastery in northern Israel, apparently in protest against the Auschwitz convent.
September 29, 1989	In a widely cited interview article by Colonel Francis A. Winiarz, Sister Maria Teresa, the superior of the Auschwitz convent, is reported as stating that the Carmelites "are not moving a single inch."
October 7, 1989	News accounts report on a recent trip to Poland by Kalman Sultanik, vice-president of the World Jewish Congress. They state that Sultanik has learned that eight of the fifteen nuns at the Auschwitz convent have been moved. The accounts state further that Polish government officials told him that it was possible the nuns would soon be completely relocated at their own request.
November 1, 1989	The *Polish Daily News* publishes an interview article by Colonel Francis A. Winiarz and Sister Maria Teresa, the superior of the Carmelite convent at Auschwitz. Winiarz indicates that the interview occurred on September 29, 1989. He quotes Sister Maria Teresa as saying, "You can tell the Americans that we are not moving a single inch. And like the Pauline Monks who bravely withstood the Swedish siege of their monastery at Czestochowa in 1655, we are here to stay!"
December 1–2, 1989	Krystyna Marszalek-Mlynczyk, under-secretary of state at the Ministry of Culture and Art, chairs a meeting of the Polish commission established in the autumn of 1989 by the Polish prime minister, Tadeusz Mazowiecki, to consider the future of the State Museum of Auschwitz. The commission's proposals include "broadening of the exhibitions to include elements illustrating the place of the Jews in Auschwitz and the uniqueness of the Shoah."
February 19, 1990	Ground is broken for the new interfaith center that will replace the convent at Auschwitz, as specified by the February 1987 agreement.

February 27, 1990	Poland establishes formal diplomatic relations with the State of Israel.
May 8, 1990	Responding to indications from Poland's recently established official commission to consider substantial changes for the museum and monuments at Auschwitz-Birkenau, a group of Jewish academics and intellectuals from nine countries meets at Yarnton Manor, Oxford, England, on May 6–8. The resulting Yarnton Declaration observes that "disquiet has been expressed in many quarters at the instrumentalization of the Auschwitz site and the increasing introduction of religious and other symbols. Accordingly, no further unilateral changes should be introduced in the physical organization of the Museum without consultation, and innovations not authorized by the authorities responsible for the administration of the Museum should be stopped."
September 3–6, 1990	In their first formal meeting in five years, the Vatican's Commission on Religious Relations with the Jews and the International Jewish Committee on Inter-Religious Consulations hold talks in Prague, Czechoslovakia. Noting that Catholics have not reacted vigilantly enough against antisemitism, their joint statement calls for a deepening spirit of cooperation between Jews and Catholics.
November 30, 1990	The Polish Episcopate issues a pastoral letter to mark the "25th Anniversary of the Conciliar Document, *Nostra Aetate*," Vatican II's "Declaration on the Relationship of the Church to Non-Christian Religions."
December 5–6, 1990	Marking the twenty-fifth anniversary of the Vacatian II document *Nostra Aetate*, Pope John Paul II and leaders of the Roman Catholic church confer at the Vatican with members of the International Jewish Committee on Inter-Religious Consultations. Echoing the September 1990 Prague meeting of the International Catholic-Jewish Liaison Committee, John Paul calls antisemitism "a sin against God and humanity." While continuing to urge the Vatican's recognition of the State of Israel, Seymour Reich, the Jewish committee's chairman hails the Vatican's meeting as "the beginning of a new chapter" in Catholic-Jewish relations.
December 9, 1990	Lech Walesa, one of the founders of Solidarity, is elected president of Poland. Some critics accuse him of making comments during his campaign that were antisemitic in spirit if not in fact.
January 20, 1991	The pastoral letter issued on November 30, 1990 is read in every Catholic church in Poland. Decrying the evil of antisemitism, the pastoral letter expresses "sorrow for all the injustices and harm done to Jews" in Poland.

1. This aerial photograph of Auschwitz I was taken by a reconnaissance mission of the Mediterranean Allied Air Forces on April 4, 1944, the first Allied flight over Auschwitz. The picture was taken during Sortie 288 flown by the 60th South African Photo Reconnaissance Squadron based in Bari, Italy. (*Courtesy of the National Archives, Washington, D.C.*)

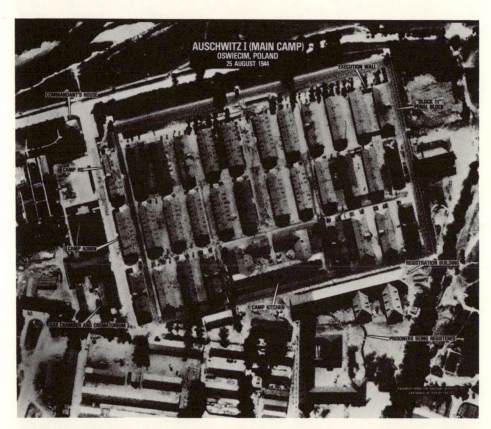

Within the image: AUSCHWITZ I (MAIN CAMP) OSWIECIM, POLAND 25 AUGUST 1944

COMMANDANT'S HOUSE
EXECUTION WALL
"BLOCK 11" PENAL BLOCK
CAMP HQ
CAMP ADMIN
REGISTRATION BUILDING
GAS CHAMBER AND CREMATORIUM I
CAMP KITCHEN
PRISONERS BEING REGISTERED
ENLARGED FROM THE ORIGINAL NEGATIVE
CAPTIONED IN 1978 BY THE CIA

2. This photograph is an enlarged detail of the one taken by the 60th South African Photo Reconnaissance Squadron during Sortie 694 on August 25, 1944. The enlargement and the captioning were done by the CIA in 1978. The photo includes the *Theatergebäude* or Old Theater, which appears just below the caption "Block 11" Penal Block. Identified by survivors as a building for "loot storage" and/or the place where Zyklon B canisters were stored, it eventually became the site of the controversial Carmelite convent. (*Courtesy of the National Archives, Washington, D.C.*)

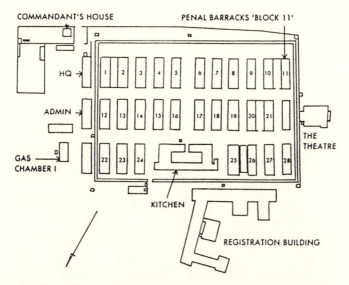

COMMANDANT'S HOUSE   PENAL BARRACKS 'BLOCK 11'

HQ →

ADMIN →

GAS ——
CHAMBER I

THE THEATRE

KITCHEN

REGISTRATION BUILDING

3. This map is a detail of the one submitted to UNESCO by the Polish government in support of its 1978 proposal to incorporate Auschwitz in the World Heritage List. The map clearly indicates as part of Auschwitz I the building that became the Carmelite convent. (*Courtesy of Christian-Jewish Relations.*)

4. Showing the Carmelite convent building from inside the barbed-wire boundary and wall of Auschwitz I in December 1989. Note the edge of the barracks and the guard tower, which can be located, along with the building itself, on the map above. (*Courtesy of Richard L. Rubenstein.*)

5. The cross pictured in this photograph stands in the convent garden. The cross was originally used in religious services led by Pope John Paul II on the grounds of Auschwitz II (Birkenau) on June 7, 1979. (*Courtesy of Richard L. Rubenstein.*)

6. This photograph, taken inside Auschwitz I, shows the cross in the convent garden visible above the barbed-wire boundary and wall of the camp. (*Courtesy of Richard L. Rubenstein.*)

Part One

The History and Politics of Memory

1

The Convent at Auschwitz and the Imperatives of Pluralism in the Global Electronic Village

Richard L. Rubenstein

The painful controversy over the location of the Carmelite convent within a few yards of Auschwitz has brought to the surface many of the persistent wounds of the still unmastered trauma of World War II. Some of the most difficult aspects of Jewish-Christian and Jewish-Polish relations were once again made manifest. Fortunately, communication did not break down and the dispute appears to be on its way to a resolution, albeit a less than perfect resolution.

To deepen my understanding of the controversy I visited the city of Cracow and the nearby sites of Auschwitz and Birkenau during the week of December 11, 1989. As I will explain, although I understand and share the feelings that compelled leaders of the Jewish community to request that the convent be re-located, the visit convinced me that it would have been better had there been no such request in the first place. However, after emotions had become inflamed and unduly harsh words uttered, honoring the February 22, 1987, agreement of Catholic and Jewish leaders to relocate the convent a short distance away from the main camp as well as to establish an interfaith center became the only way to calm down a situation that had gotten so badly out of hand as needlessly to jeopardize the very real progress made in Jewish-Catholic relations since Vatican II.

Jewish-Christian relations carry a special burden in the post-Holocaust era of the global electronic village. Both traditions make claims to exclusive knowledge of God's revealed will. Unfortunately, the claims are contradictory. Each tradition finds itself in the position of disconfirming that which the other takes to be decisive and nonnegotiable in the divine-human encounter. Moreover, because of Christianity's supersessionary claims concerning Judaism, far more is at stake in the differences between these traditions than between either tradition and Hinduism, Buddhism, or Shinto.[1] In the past, the Christian church has used whatever strategies were necessary to maintain its cognitive monopoly within the territories in which it was dominant. To the extent that Jews were permitted domicile, it was only under conditions in which the Christian cognitive monopoly was not seriously challenged. Very often negative images of the Jew, which were largely a consequence of church teaching and the relegation of Jews to occupations regarded as degraded in premodern societies, served to reinforce the cognitive monopoly.

Given the global proliferation of low-cost communications media, no institution, political or religious, can any longer maintain a cognitive monopoly, a lesson the Communist leaders of Eastern Europe have learned to their very great distress. Moreover, in religiously and ethnically plural societies such as the United States, the mainstream religious institutions, Protestant, Catholic, and Jewish, have come to accept a measure of ecumenical accommodation and cooperation. Nevertheless, the tension between exclusive religious claims and the imperatives of pluralism has yet to disappear. In times of stress and conflict, the forces making for dialogue can easily be overwhelmed. This possibility became manifest in the convent controversy.

At the height of the controversy, there was a marked difference between the positions taken and the words spoken by Cardinal Jozef Glemp, the primate of Poland, and such Western Catholic leaders as Cardinal John O'Connor of New York, Cardinal Bernard Law of Boston, and Cardinal Franz Koenig, the former archbishop of Vienna, and, finally even Pope John Paul II himself. Cardinal Glemp oversees the Catholic church in a country in which its religious monopoly is unchallenged and in which its principal ideological adversary, atheistic communism, has been thoroughly discredited in the eyes of most Poles. Apparently, Glemp saw far less reason, at least in this instance, than did his peers outside of Poland, to balance the church's exclusivistic and traditionally negative attitudes toward the Jews with the imperatives of ecumenical cooperation.

During my visit to Poland, I was questioned concerning my own views on the convent controversy. I also had the opportunity to discuss the dispute with a number of well-informed and well-intentioned Poles. Their basic view is that Poles in large numbers perished at Auschwitz. They therefore believe Auschwitz is an appropriate location for the convent. Given the historic link between Polish national identity and Roman Catholicism, none of my Polish informants could understand why anyone would object to the nuns devoting their lives to reconciliation and prayer for those murdered at Auschwitz. No Pole with whom I spoke regarded the convent as an attempt to appropriate Auschwitz as a Polish and Christian rather than a Jewish site. Moreover, even those who believed it best for the sake of interreligious concord to relocate the convent saw nothing wrong with its present location.

The fundamental difference between the attitude of most Poles and that of Jews and even many Western European and American Christian leaders was, I believe, epitomized by a question put to me on December 13 at the State Cultural Center in Cracow following a lecture on "Religion and Politics in the United

States'' in which I sought to offer an overview of the political attitudes of America's many religious groups.

''Do you think it is a good thing that America has so many religions?'' I was asked. Like most Poles the questioner was not used to religious pluralism. He was genuinely puzzled by America's ethnic and religious diversity and had difficulty in understanding how it could possibly work. He did not see how pluralism could be consistent with national identity. To be Polish meant to be Roman Catholic or, in the case of atheistic Communists, to be the offspring of Polish Roman Catholics. Moreover, in spite of forty-five years of Soviet-imposed Communist rule, Polish society was never secularized. In many ways it remains a sacralized society.

Although there was no hint of ill-will in the way the question was asked, its implications mirrored many crucial elements in the tragic history of Jewish-Polish relations. To the extent that the newly independent Poles were unable or unwilling to create a genuinely pluralistic state in 1918 after World War I, the presence of Europe's largest Jewish minority, 10 percent of Poland's population, was bound to be untenable. Lacking power to maintain themselves as a viable minority with its own distinctive religion, language, and culture, Poland's Jewish community was condemned to permanent pariah status at best and outright elimination at worst. In reality, the community was doomed to be eliminated. Only the method of implementation remained in doubt until World War II.

When after almost two centuries of foreign rule Poland regained its inde-pendence, one of the most important questions confronting the nation was whether it would be a pluralistic community consisting of a federation of East European peoples such as Belorussians, Ukrainians, Jews, ethnic Germans, and Lithuanians, albeit led by Poles, or a homogeneous religio-ethnic community. Marshall Josef Pilsudski's (1867–1935) vision was of a Polish-led multiethnic federation; the vision of an ethnically and religiously homogeneous Poland was fostered by Roman Dmowski (1864–1939), the most important leader of the ultra right-wing, antisemitic National Democratic Party, popularly known as the *Endecja*. To this day *Endecja* remains a powerful force in Polish life. According to Abraham Brumberg, a leading authority on contemporary Poland, Cardinal Jozef Glemp has professed sympathy for *Endecja*, a fact confirmed to me by responsible Polish observers on my recent trip.[2]

In the first decade of the twentieth century, Dmowski reflected on the reasons why Poland had not regained its independence and sovereignty. According to Dmowski, Poland's ethnic pluralism and its religious toleration together consti-tuted the nation's fundamental flaw. Poland contained too many unassimilable minorities, the Jews being the most unassimilable. Dmowski argued that the Poles would only regain their independence when they no longer needed any help from the minorities. He called upon the offspring of Poland's gentry to abandon agriculture and to train as professionals, managers, and technicians in order to provide the nation with the cadres necessary for a modern industrial society. He was especially insistent that they displace the Jews as Poland's commercial and professional class.[3] In 1914, Dmowski wrote that the whole tradition of European Christian society was alien to "the Jew." Hence he considered the Jew to be "the most dangerous enemy of Polish civilization, bent on destroying all vestiges of those institutions and ideals that a Pole would hold dear."[4]

Dmowski served as one of reborn Poland's delegates at the Paris Peace Conference of 1919. In the confusion following the Bolshevik revolution and the German collapse, Polish forces occupied territory on practically all of its borders containing large numbers of Germans, Jews, Belorussians, Ukrainians, and Lithuanians. Reports of pogroms and widespread terrorism against Jews in newly independent Poland aroused concern among the Allies. Stephen Bonsal, an American official, was assigned the task of sounding out Dmowski on the Jewish question. Dmowski told Bonsal that the Jews "constitute at least ten percent of our population, and in my judgment this is eight percent too much. . . . Unless restrictions are imposed upon them soon, all our lawyers, doctors and small merchants will be Jews."[5]

Dmowski's frankness did not help his cause. The Allies compelled Poland to sign a treaty guaranteeing equal rights for all of her minorities. Articles 10 and 11 of the Minorities Treaty specifically applied to Jewish religious and cultural autonomy. The treaty was signed on June 28, 1919, the very same day Poland signed the Treaty of Versailles guaranteeing her independence.[6]

From the start Jews and Poles had fundamentally different perceptions of the Minorities Treaty. The Jews assumed that the rights specified in the treaty had the force of international law. By contrast, the Poles saw the treaty as an affront to their national honor and dignity imposed upon them by foreigners. When the Jews criticized the Polish government for not living up to the provisions of the treaty, they were bitterly resented, a resentment which was intensified when influential American Jews supported their coreligionists.

Caste also played an important part in Polish–Jewish relations. This issue has been discussed insightfully by sociologist Celia S. Heller. According to Max Weber, "A caste is . . . a closed status group."[7] Heller adds that as a distinct caste in Poland, "the Jews were considered the outsiders, the strangers in their midst. They were also considered the epitome of inferiority."[8] Understandably, Jews were not prepared to identify with the Polish status hierarchy. I would add that the Poles rather than the Jews were able to enforce their definition of social reality because caste relations reflect power relations. No matter what constraints the Allies wrote into the Minorities Treaty, no consortium of foreign powers could compel the Poles to alter their status hierarchy. As Heller observes, violation of the Minorities Treaty was regarded as a defense of Polish honor rather than a breach of faith.[9]

Nevertheless, Marshall Pilsudski was strongly opposed to antisemitism. According to Richard M. Watt, Pilsudski apparently saw himself as the heir of Poland's kings in their role as protectors of the Jews. Although unofficial harassment of the Jews continued, the government of Prime Minister Kazimierz

Bartel, Pilsudski's choice, acted to repeal many of the old tsarist laws that had been enacted to harass Jews. For example, the government announced its opposition to the *numerus clausus* at Polish universities and the police and courts acted to protect Jews against physical assault.[10] Pilsudski was also strongly opposed to *Endecja*, and there was persistent hostility between him and Dmowski.

There are some Jewish authorities who argue that Pilsudski's opposition to antisemitism was more cosmetic than real.[11] For example, as long as Galicia had been a part of the Austro-Hungarian Empire, thousands of Jews worked in the state-owned railroads, post office, and other bureaus. After Poland gained independence, Pilsudski's position notwithstanding, Jews were barred from positions in all state bureaus and state-owned enterprises.[12] In any event, there was an immediate upsurge of anti-Jewish violence following Pilsudski's death in 1935. The government approved an economic boycott of Jewish merchants, and the police became permissive about anti-Jewish violence. Prime Minister Felicjan Slawoj-Skladkowski announced his approval of "an economic fight for survival between Jews and Poles."[13] According to Emil Lengyel, sixty-nine Jews were killed and 800 wounded in Polish anti-Jewish violence during 1936.[14] The difference between the government's Jewish policy and that advocated by *Endecja* began to narrow. In a famous speech before parliament Boguslaw Miedzinski, the regime's leading parliamentarian, declared, "Personally, I love Danes very much, but if we had three million of them in Poland, I would implore God to take them away as soon as possible."[15]

The theme of the Jews as a surplus population that Poland wanted to eliminate was taken up by government leaders. The theme was set forth in the *Theses on the Jewish Question* formulated by OZON, the progovernment "Camp of National Unity."[16] The theses were subsequently elaborated upon by Miedzinski. According to Edward D. Wynot, Jr., with Miedzinski's elaboration the theses "constituted the official program of the Polish authorities on the Jewish question."[17] Miedzinski advocated "the removal of this alien body" from Poland.[18] In July 1939, a little more than a month before the German invasion, the official government journal, *Gazeta Polska* declared: "The fact that our relations with the Reich are worsening does not in the least deactivate our program in the Jewish question—there is not and cannot be any common ground between our internal Jewish problem and Poland's relations with the Hitlerite Reich."[19]

The government's anti-Jewish policies were supported by the Roman Catholic church, which regarded the Jews as agents of secularization, liberalism, and Bolshevism. In 1936, Cardinal Augustus Hlond, the primate of Poland, openly supported the regime's anti-Jewish measures although opposing overt violence. In a pastoral letter read in most Polish churches, the cardinal declared: "A Jewish problem exists and will continue to exit as long as Jews remain Jews." The cardinal counseled the faithful: "One ought to fence oneself off against the harmful moral effects of Jewry, to separate oneself against its anti-Christian culture, and especially to boycott the Jewish press and the demoralizing Jewish publications.''[20] According to Celia Heller, Hlond was regarded as belonging to the moderate wing of the church. However, although we read Hlond's letter in the light of subsequent events, we must remember that he wrote as he did before Vatican II and from the perspective of a prelate for whom the church's cognitive monopoly in matters religious was nonnegotiable.

By the late 1930s, most Poles regarded the elimination of the Jews as an overwhelmingly important element of public policy. Nevertheless, Poland's leaders, both religious and secular, had no workable plan to implement the removal other than harassment and discrimination. Their basic objective was to encourage Jewish emigration. Unfortunately, emigration had ceased to be an option for all but a very tiny minority. The Jews of Poland were locked in a deathtrap from which there was to be no escape.

If the Poles did not know how to "solve" their Jewish problem, the Germans under Hitler did. In the late 1930s, the Jewish policy of both official Poland and National Socialist Germany shared a common objective, namely, the elimination of the Jews from their respective societies. They did, however, differ radically in the methods they were prepared to use. Whatever violence was inflicted on Jews by Poles, no more than a very tiny minority favored outright extermination. Although the church was a principal force in the negative definition of the Jews, it set limits on what the Poles could do to them. When the invading Germans exterminated the Jews, they achieved the objective of Poland's Jewish policy, but they did so by means the Poles themselves were unwilling to adopt. Moreover, there were selfless and heroic Poles who saved Jews at the risk of their own lives. Although many stories can be told, the story of Wladyslaw Bartoszewski, retired professor of history at the Catholic University of Lublin, is especially moving. After having been imprisoned at Auschwitz, Bartoszewski was released in 1941 at the age of nineteen. He then returned to Warsaw, where he found a nine-foot wall erected around the part of the city which had become the Warsaw ghetto. Bartoszewski became the liaison between the Polish underground and the Jewish leadership within the ghetto. At great personal risk he attempted to rescue some Jews and to make the world aware of what was taking place. When I met Bartoszewski in Poland in 1965, he showed me two documents, his Auschwitz identity photos and the testimonial certificate in his honor given to him by Jerusalem's Yad Vashem.[21] Nevertheless, the sober weight of historical scholarship compels one to ask whether the majority of the Poles regarded the Germans as having "solved" their Jewish problem for them.

Nor did the killing of Jews in Poland stop with the war's end. There were pogroms in Cracow, Chelm, Rzeszow, Kielce, and elsewhere.[22] In 1946 on the basis of a false rumor that Jews had kidnapped a Christian boy and killed him in a ritual murder, Poles murdered seventy Holocaust survivors in Kielce. The Jews of Kielce turned to Bishop Stefan Wyszynski of Lublin with the request that he condemn the massacre in order to stem the violence. Although the facts concerning the Holocaust were by that time well known, the bishop not only refused but added that he was not altogether convinced that Jews did not commit ritual murder! Shortly thereafter he became a cardinal and the primate of Poland. Moreover, Cardinal Josef Glemp was Wyszynski's hand-picked successor as primate. His homily dealing with Jewish-Christian relations delivered to pilgrims at Poland's national shrine of Our Lady of Czestochowa on August 26, 1989, proved to be the most controversial statement of any religious leader involved in the dispute.[23]

Government hostility to Jews, Judaism, and Zionism continued after the war. In the countries of Soviet-dominated Eastern Europe, Stalinist antisemitism sought the total obliteration of Jewish cultural life. After the death of Stalin in 1953 and the rehabilitation of Wladyslaw Gomulka, a modicum of Jewish cultural life was restored. This came to an end with the Six Day War of 1967. Minister of the Interior Mieczyslaw Moczar utilized antisemitism as a means of displacing Gomulka. Not to be outbid, Gomulka instituted his own antisemitic campaign in the press, radio, and television. Moreover, in recent years Cardinal Glemp has accused Solidarity of having been infiltrated by "Trotskyites," according to Abraham Brumberg, a code word for Jews.[24] At present there are fewer than 6,000 Jews in Poland, but Anna Husarska, an editor of *Gazeta Wyborcza*, Solidarity's daily newspaper, has recently written in the *Washington Post* of the "persistence of anti-Semitism in Poland." According to Husarska, "For the past 44 years Polish public opinion has been manipulated by the state-monopolied media. Until a few years ago, most of the rare appearances of the word 'Jew' in official print were more or less open insults." When Husarska wrote objectively about the demonstration by Rabbi Abraham Weiss and six companions at the site of the Auschwitz Carmelite convent and the physical and verbal violence inflicted upon the group by Polish construction workers, she received insulting responses from more than one hundred readers, many of which used unprintable language. She has written that any doubts she had about the persistence of antisemitism in Poland were dispelled by these communications.[25]

Given the history of the Jews in Poland both before and after the war, it is not difficult to understand why the placement of the convent at Auschwitz would elicit an emotional response, especially among Holocaust survivors. In spite of the help and rescue extended to Jews by some Christians during the Holocaust, it is impossible for Jews not to see in the pre–Vatican II definition of the Jews as deicides the legitimating ideology which cast the Jews wholly outside of any shared universe of moral obligation with Christians and thereby made genocide morally acceptable.

There was also a distinctively Jewish aspect of the issue of memory in the convent controversy. No curse is more terrible for Jews than, "*Y'mach sh'mo v'zichrono.*" ("May his name and memory be wholly blotted out.") That curse has been visited upon the millions of Jewish families who died and whose remains were incinerated without a trace at Auschwitz. Even for the surviving community of Israel as a whole, there is the fear of the appropriation and obliteration of memory. Such an attempt is being made by pro-Nazi Holocaust revisionists. Moreover, although Jews were killed simply because they were Jews, at Auschwitz, Treblinka, Sobibor, Majdanek, Babi Yar, and Mauthausen in Austria, they are memorialized as Poles, Austrians, Russians, Hungarians, and Germans. When alive they were regarded as despised aliens. Only in death were they permitted to augment the number of nationals that countries like Poland, the USSR, and Austria were willing to claim as their own war victims.

There is also fear of the theological appropriation of memory, an ancient issue between Judaism and Christianity. Christians regard the books of the Hebrew Scripture as witnesses to Christ as Lord. Paul of Tarsus explicitly denied that his Jewish contemporaries could understand their own Scriptures:

Since we have such a hope, we are very bold, not like Moses, who put a veil over his face so that the Israelites might not see the end of the fading splendor. But their minds were hardened; for to this day, when they read the old covenant, that same veil remains unlifted, because only through Christ is it taken away. Yes, to this day whenever Moses is read a veil lies over their minds; but when a man turns to the Lord the veil is removed (II Cor. 3:12–16).

After the fall of Jerusalem in 70 C.E. membership in the Jewish community was conditional upon acceptance of the rabbinic interpretation of Scripture as authoritative, at least in matters of Halakhah or Jewish religious law. Nevertheless, because of the overwhelming numerical and cultural predominance of Christianity as a world religion, the Christian reading of Scripture came to carry far greater weight and influence. Under the circumstances, it is understandable that many Jews were fearful that the presence of the convent and its tall cross at Auschwitz would initiate a process in which the distinctive Jewish content of the Holocaust would be lost to memory and ultimately assimilated to a Christian interpretation of the event.

Theological appropriation of the Holocaust can become a problem even when the intention is to heal and to reconcile. On June 24, 1988, Pope John Paul II visited the site of the Mauthausen concentration camp in Austria where tens of thousands of Jews were put to death. In his remarks at the camp site he referred to four camp victims but made no mention of Jewish victims. The pontiff's omission was criticized by Paul Grosz, the president of the Austrian Jewish community. The next day during a visit to Lorch, Austria, the pope told an audience of 80,000 during a prayer service, "Not far from here is Mauthausen, where Christians, Jews and others were persecuted for many reasons, including their religion. Their suffering was a gift to the world."[26]

The idea that the suffering of those who perished in the camps was a gift is consistent with the image of Christ offering himself as a sacrificial offering for the sins of the world. The pope understandably interpreted the sufferings of the camp victims in terms of the symbolism of his own tradition. It was, however, a symbolism altogether foreign to Jews, who cannot see the greatest catastrophe in their history as a gift of any sort whatsoever.

In his speech at Mauthausen the pope also stated, "It would be unjust and not truthful to charge Christianity with these unspeakable crimes.''[27] The pope is undoubtedly correct. Nevertheless, he failed to address the question whether the Christian identification of the Jews as deicides created a moral climate in which millions of Europeans could, at least during wartime, regard extermination of the Jews as a legitimate enterprise. Nor did the pope consider the fact that many of the major war criminals, such as Franz Stangl, the SS commandant at the Treblinka death camp, were assisted in their flight from justice by Vatican and other church officials.[28]

At some level the Jewish sensibilities were understood and appreciated by the Catholic leaders, including Cardinal Franciszek Macharski of Cracow, Cardinal Albert Decourtray of Lyon, Cardinal Godfried Danneels of Malines-Brussels, and Cardinal Jean-Marie Lustiger, who on February 22, 1987, signed the original agreement to relocate the convent. It was also understood by the Polish Bishops' Commission for Relations with Judaism. On September 6, 1989, the commission urged the construction of the proposed new interfaith center near the Auschwitz camp after Cardinal Franciszek Macharski of Cracow had suspended the project.

Nevertheless, as stated above, I believe it would have been better had there been no request to relocate in the first place. *The indispensable precondition of diaspora Jewish religious life has always been religious pluralism.* Roman Dmowski campaigned to eliminate Jews from Poland because he regarded religious and cultural pluralism as fundamental causes of the political, moral, and cultural debilitation of the Polish people. In his eyes, he was acting for the good of his own people. If pluralism is rejected, one can only criticize the *methods* by which governments achieve religious, cultural, or ethnic homogeneity but not the objective itself.

In spite of the bitter history of Polish-Jewish relations, acceptance of the imperatives of pluralism would have led the Jewish leaders to recognize the fact that Poles wanted to render homage to the memory of their fellow countrymen and coreligionists at the place where they perished. The presence of the convent at Auschwitz cannot in any way minimize the fact that Auschwitz was a place of utter extermination for Jews. Thousands of Poles perished in Auschwitz. Nevertheless, as the case of Wladyslaw Bartoszewski shows, it was also possible for Poles to be released. By contrast, extermination was the fate awaiting all Jews without exception. This should not mean that Poles and other Roman Catholics ought not to be able to pray for their dead at Auschwitz. *Pluralism entails recognition of the religious requirements of diverse religious communities.*

Unfortunately, too many things went wrong after the signing of the 1987 agreement. Having been a signatory to the original agreement, Cardinal Franciszek Macharski of Cracow had an obligation to see that it was carried out. When it became evident that the deadline would pass without implementation, the Jewish signatories should have been informed openly and frankly. Instead, there was no communication and the twenty-four-foot cross was placed in the yard adjacent to the convent. Absence of frank communication could hardly inspire trust and, in fact, had the effect of awakening Jewish apprehensions.

The situation grew worse on July 14, 1989, with the protest demonstration led by Rabbi Avraham Weiss at the site of the Auschwitz convent. The fact that the rabbi and his group were violently assaulted by Polish construction workers whose leader yelled "Heil Hitler" while a priest egged them on and the nuns stood by without protest further exacerbated the conflict.[29] Old memories of Polish anti-Jewish violence were inevitably reawakened.

The assault on the rabbi and his colleagues was inexcusable. Nevertheless, neither the rabbi nor anyone else had the right to enter the convent precinct without permission. When Rabbi Weiss first appeared at the door of the convent, he announced that he had come in peace and that undoubtedly was his intention. Nevertheless, if the Polish assault against the Jews triggered unpleasant Jewish memories, neither the rabbi nor the leaders of the world's major Jewish organizations took into account the primal associations the rabbi's actions triggered in Poles. Whatever positive associations prayer shawls, sacred books, and Hebrew chanting have for Jews, they have no such associations for Poles. In his description of the demonstration, the rabbi gives no indication that he had any understanding of the kind of fearful primal associations that could be triggered in the psyches of theologically unsophisticated Polish Catholics when uninvited males enter a domain reserved for women who have devoted their lives to chastity and prayer. At the most primitive level, the symbolism involved in the idea of male invasion of a precinct reserved for pious virgins carries with it the most unfortunate sexual associations. Let us remember that these people have no experience with American-style demonstrations. Clearly, there was a major communication problem.

Rabbi Weiss's demonstration and the Polish workers' violent response brought the controversy to a head. It was featured on page 1 of the *New York Times*. We cannot discuss in detail the many well-publicized statements and events that took place thereafter. A few, however, are crucial to our theme.

On August 10, 1989, Cardinal Macharski announced that he was abandoning plans to construct a center for Christian-Jewish dialogue adjacent to Auschwitz as per the 1987 agreement. The cardinal also declared that the timetable for removal of the convent was unrealistic. He accused "some Western Jewish centers" of staging a "violent campaign of accusations and slander, outrageous aggression." Referring to the demonstration at the convent, he said, "The nuns, their human and Christian dignity, were not respected. The peace to which they are entitled was disturbed. The Christian faith, as well as symbols and piety were not respected."[30] The cardinal's statement put the blame for breaking the convent agreement on the Jewish side. There was, however, suspicion that this was only a pretext and that the decision to break the agreement had been made before the February 1989 deadline for its implementation. Furthermore, at that point, save for Rabbi Weiss, none of the major Jewish groups had done anything more than seek its implementation, an altogether legitimate enterprise.

Rabbi Weiss's convent demonstration was another matter. The cardinal's statement stressed the fact that Rabbi Weiss had entered the convent grounds without authorization. The cardinal had no words of regret for the assault upon the rabbi. In his statement responding to the cardinal, Rabbi Weiss stressed the violence against the demonstrators and the cardinal's bad faith in breaking the agreement. The rabbi declared, "Cardinal Macharski's statement is repugnant. In seeking to break the Jewish-Catholic accord of 1987 which he personally signed . . . the Cardinal has, in almost classical anti-Semitic terms, chosen to portray Jewish victims as aggressors. It was not we who beat Polish Catholics. It was Catholic Polish workers of the convent who assaulted us, as the nuns and the priests looked on in silence."[31] Just as the cardinal expressed no concern for the construction workers' assault, the rabbi apparently had no understanding of and made no mention of the profound symbolic offense committed by the demonstrators in entering the convent grounds as they did. Insensitive to each other's symbols and memories, both sides succeeded only in angering each other.

The conflict was further exacerbated by the seemingly unrelated remarks made by Pope John Paul II at his weekly general audience of August 2, 1989. This was after the demonstration at the convent but before Cardinal Macharski issued his statement. In the homily the pope declared that the Old Testament showed many instances of the Jewish people's "infidelity to God." He further declared that the prophets were sent

to call the people to conversion, to warn them of their hardness of heart and to foretell a new covenant still to come.

The new covenant foretold by the prophets was established through Christ's redemptive sacrifice and through the power of the Holy Spirit. . . . This "perfect gift from above" descends to fill the hearts of all people and to gather them into the church constituting them the people of God of the new and everlasting covenant.[32]

The pope's remarks were an expression of the traditional Christian claim that the church had superseded Israel as the people of God in the new covenant established by Jesus Christ. In weighing the claims of religious exclusivism against those of ecumenical pluralism, in this instance the pope tilted the balance in favor of exclusivism. The pope's remarks were immediately protested by Jewish religious leaders, who reminded the pope of an occasion on which he had tilted the balance the other way. In 1980 when the pope spoke to Jewish leaders in Mainz, Germany, he referred to the Jewish people as "the people of God, of the Old Covenant never revoked by God." All doubt as to the pope's present position was put to rest the following week when on August 9 the pope told visiting pilgrims that God had created a new covenant with his people through Christ because of Israel's "infidelity to its God." Implicit in the pope's remarks was the view that simply by being devotedly loyal to the teachings of their rabbis Jews were unwittingly in rebellion against God and that only by accepting Christ as their Lord could Jews truly be reconciled to God. Although it was never said, one could draw the further implication that there was only one proper way to memorialize the dead at Auschwitz, that is, in and through Christ. No room for pluralism here. Because of the great moral authority of the pope, his remarks aroused all of the Jewish fears that their tragedy was being assimilated to Christian meanings.

The controversy threatened to become a major crisis in interreligious relations with Cardinal Jozef Glemp's homily at the Polish national shrine of Our Lady of Czestochowa on August 26 and his statements to the press on August 28. The Czestochowa homily attracted worldwide attention. As is their wont, the newspaper accounts emphasized the cardinal's most inflammatory statements, all of which appear in his concluding comments. The body of the homily was devoted to reflections on Polish-Jewish relations on the fiftieth anniversary of the start of World War II. Understandably, the cardinal was especially concerned with the question why the convent controversy has arisen ''40 years after the ovens of the crematoria were extinguished?'' While most Jews would take issue with the cardinal's analysis of the history of prewar Polish-Jewish relations, it can be characterized as the prelate's sincere attempt to give what he regarded as a balanced account.[33]

The same cannot be said of his concluding remarks beginning with the statement: ''We have committed our faults against the Jews, but one would like to say: 'Dear Jews, don't talk with us from the position of a nation above all others and don't lay down conditions that are impossible to fulfill.' ''[34] Referring to the Carmelite sisters, he continued: ''Do you not, respected Jews, see that in your actions against them you injure the feelings of all Poles, and our sovereignty obtained with such difficulty? Your power is the mass media, which are, in many countries, at your disposal. Do not let them act to kindle antipolonism.''

He then turned to the subject of Rabbi Weiss's demonstration at the convent: ''Not long ago a squad of seven Jews from New York committed an assault on the convent at Auschwitz. It's true that it didn't come to the murder of the sisters, nor to the destruction of the convent, because they were stopped, but don't call these assailants heroes. Let us maintain the standards of the civilization in which we live.'' The cardinal also argued that the convent was appropriately located at a part of the huge Auschwitz complex where mostly Poles died: ''Let us differentiate between Oswiecim-Auschwitz, where mostly Poles and other nations perished, and Brzezinka-Birkenau, the camp a few kilometers away, where mostly Jews perished.'' He concluded his remarks addressed to Jews with counsel on how antisemitism might be diminished in Poland: ''If there is no antipolonism, there will be no antisemitism in us.''

The cardinal added further heat to the controversy on September 2 when he termed the 1987 agreement on the convent ''offensive.'' He also said, ''I want this accord to be renegotiated. It has to be done by competent people and not just by any cardinal who doesn't understand these things.''[35] This was, of course, a direct rebuke to his fellow cardinals who had negotiated the original agreement.

Criticism of the cardinal came swiftly from many quarters. *Gazeta Wyborcza*, the Solidarity daily newspaper, featured a front-page editorial denouncing the cardinal's remarks, declaring that they ''caused real not artificial or paper pain.''[36] Cardinal John O'Connor of New York said that he was shocked by Cardinal Glemp's remarks. He said, ''Normal decent people could construe from such a statement that the blame be shifted to the Jews for demanding that a signed accord be carried out. I don't think that is right. I don't think that is charitable. And it certainly doesn't represent my opinion.''[37]

Cardinal Albert Decourtray of Lyons, Cardinal Jean-Marie Lustiger of Paris, and Cardinal Godfried Danneels of Brussels, three of the four cardinals who had signed the accord, issued a statement which said: ''Cardinal Glemp could only have been speaking for himself in talking of renegotiating the Geneva accords, particularly since until now he has always let it be known that Cardinal Macharski was solely responsible and that the Polish Conference of Bishops, on March 9, 1989, had committed itself in turn by giving its support to the realization of this accord.''[38]

In the United States, Catholic religious and lay leaders urged that the nuns be relocated. The religious leaders included Cardinal Bernard Law of Boston, Archbishop Roger Mahony of Los Angeles, Cardinal Edmund Szoka of Detroit, and Cardinal John Krol, retired archbishop of Philadelphia. The latter two are of Polish descent. Among the prominent Catholic laypersons who urged that the accord be kept were William F. Buckley and Michael Novak. Patrick J. Buchanan was prominent among those who defended Cardinal Glemp. He denounced the Jewish community's attitude and gave evidence of little interest in pluralism. Even in Poland there was support for relocation among Catholic religious leaders. On September 6, 1989, the Polish Bishops' Commission for Relations with Judaism indicated their support, but reminded Jews of the importance of supporting construction of the interfaith center which had also been part of the agreement.

I was queried about Cardinal Glemp's statement when I lectured in Cracow. By that time the cardinal had reversed his position, and I had no desire to stir up further controversy. I did, however, take issue with two of the cardinal's statements. As stated above, I believe that Rabbi Weiss's group was profoundly in error in having entered any part of the convent without permission. Nevertheless, the cardinal's statement that ''seven Jews from New York attacked the convent,'' and his accusation that the nuns were not killed because Rabbi Weiss's group ''was restrained'' were inflammatory in the extreme. Whatever may have been the prelate's intention, his words could only fan the flames of hatred. There is absolutely no evidence that Rabbi Weiss or any member of his group had any intention of harming the nuns in their ill-advised, insensitive, American-style demonstration. If the rabbi's behavior had unpleasant associations for Poles, the cardinal's wholly unfounded accusations could very easily have elicited associations with the age-old canard of ritual murder. Certainly, the primate of Poland had an obligation to measure carefully his words when he spoke at Poland's most sacred shrine.

It also seemed to me that the cardinal gratuitously raised yet another false and inflammatory issue when he warned Jews not to use their alleged power in the mass media "to inflame anti-Polish sentiment." Poland's struggle to liberate itself from communism and to put its economic house in order has received considerable support from almost all American newspapers. When President Bush proposed giving Poland a minimum of financial support, he was widely criticized for being niggardly and ungenerous. If Jews have the media power Cardinal Glemp alleges they have, they have used it in support of contemporary, Solidarity-led Poland, rather than to arouse hostility against Poland.

Apparently, Cardinal Glemp did not understand that responsible Jews have no interest in arousing anti-Polish sentiment. The history of the Jews in Poland will in all likelihood continue to be viewed differently by Jews and Poles. Nevertheless, Jews have absolutely no interest in hostility toward the present Solidarity-led government. On the contrary, both in Israel and the diaspora they have every reason to want it to succeed in liberating Poland from the moral, political, and economic legacy of communism. On the Polish side, Poland's real problems would appear to be overwhelming, but with fewer than 6,000 Jews remaining in Poland, there is no rational reason for continued Polish-Jewish hostility. Whatever antisemitism exists in Poland is an obsession that can only divert attention away from the country's real problems.

The controversy was brought to closure on September 19 when the Vatican's Commission for Religious Relations with the Jews issued a statement signed by Cardinal Johannes Willebrands to the effect that the Holy See is "prepared to make its own financial contribution" to the construction of an interfaith center at Auschwitz as called for in the 1987 agreement to relocate the Carmelite sisters.[39] On September 23 the Discalced Carmelites' generalate in Rome issued a statement to the effect that the position of the general of the order had been all along "that agreements must be honored." Finally, on September 20 Cardinal Glemp sent a letter to Sir Sigmund Sternberg, chairman of the executive committee of the International Council of Christians and Jews declaring, "It is my intention that the Geneva declaration of 1987 should be implemented." Of the well-known personalities who had spoken out on the issue, only Patrick Buchanan issued a dissent, and an angry one at that.[40]

Before Vatican II it would have been highly unlikely that Catholic leaders such as Cardinal O'Connor, Cardinal Law, and the signatories of the 1987 agreement would have publicly taken issue with Cardinal Glemp or even that the agreement would have been signed at all. What had changed was the way the church balanced the claims of pluralism with its own claims to exclusive truth. Put differently, those Catholic leaders who had taken issue with Cardinal Glemp had accepted the reality of pluralism to a far greater degree than did he. No Catholic leader could really see anything wrong in and of itself in the location of the convent or in the erection of the twenty-four-foot cross. Only when Jewish sensibilities were weighed in the balance were church leaders willing to consider relocating the convent. Given the church's cognitive monopoly in religious matters in Poland, its unique role in preserving Polish cultural autonomy in the face of Soviet-imposed communism, as well as Poland's tragic history since 1939, it is easy to understand why Cardinal Glemp was less concerned with the imperatives of pluralism than were his colleagues in the West and even in the Vatican.

Nevertheless, in the era of the global electronic village none of the major religious traditions any longer enjoys a cognitive monopoly even in countries like Poland where they continue to enjoy the loyalty of an overwhelming majority. When events like the end of the Berlin wall are instantaneously visible by hundreds of millions throughout the world and distance is no longer a factor in the encounter of the world religions, some degree of accommodation to pluralism is indispensable for all of the major religions. This does not mean that they can or necessarily should give up their exclusive claims. Intelligent men and women can find a viable way to balance these claims with the imperatives of pluralism. With the Jewish community in Europe largely destroyed, some church leaders there could have argued that the church could easily reject Jewish demands that the agreement be kept. Such a posture might have worked for a time in Poland and elsewhere on the continent. It could not have worked in the United States, where Jews and Christians have important reasons for maintaining dialogue and encouraging interfaith cooperation. Even in Europe, the Vatican recognized that moving the nuns was far better than a public breach, especially on an issue concerning how the dead at Auschwitz are to be remembered.

NOTES

1. For an elaboration of this problem from the perspective of the theory of cognitive dissonance, see Richard L. Rubenstein, *The Age of Triage* (Boston: Beacon Press, 1983), 132–35.

2. Abraham Brumberg, "Silence on Anti-Semitism," Letter to the Editor of the *New York Times Book Review*, 27 January 1985. See also Brumberg, "A Parting for Solidarity and the Church?" *New York Times*, 1 September 1989.

3. See Richard M. Watt, *Bitter Glory: Poland and Its Fate, 1918 to 1939* (New York: Simon and Schuster, 1982), 40–41.

4. Roman Dmowski, *Upadek mysli konserwatywnej w Polsce* (Warsaw: 1914). Cited by Edward D. Wynot, Jr., " 'A Necessary Cruelty': The Emergence of Official Anti-Semitism in Poland, 1936–49," *American Historical Review* 76 (October 1971): 1036.

5. Stephen Bonsal, *Suitors and Supplicants: The Little Nations at Versailles* (New York: Prentice-Hall, 1946), 124. Cited by Watt, *Bitter Glory*, 75.

6. See Celia S. Heller, *On the Edge of Destruction: Jews of Poland Between the Two World Wars* (New York: Columbia University Press, 1977), 53–57.

7. Max Weber, *The Religion of India: The Sociology of Hinduism and Buddhism*, trans. Hans. H. Gerth and Don Martindale (New York: The Free Press, 1958), 39.

8. Heller, *On the Edge of Destruction*, 58.

9. Ibid., 57.

10. Watt, *Bitter Glory*, 360.

11. See *Encyclopedia Judaica*, s.v. "Pilsudski, Josef."

12. *Encyclopedia Judaica*, s.v. "Poland."

13. *Gazeta Polska*, 5 June 1937. Cited by Wynot, " 'A Necessary Cruelty,' " 1038.

14. Emil Lengyel, "Europe's Anti-Semitic Twins: Poland," *Current History* 48 (1938): 45.

15. *Gazeta Polska*, 12 January 1937. Cited by Wynot, " 'A Necessary Cruelty,' " 1039.

16. OZON was established by leaders of the Government party on February 21, 1937.

17. Wynot, " 'A Necessary Cruelty,' " 1048. The theses and Miedzinski's commentaries were published in the official *Gazeta Polska*, 22, 25, 26, 27 May 1938 and 4, 9, 12 June 1938.

18. Wynot, " 'A Necessary Cruelty,' " 1050.

19. *Gazeta Polska*, 23 July 1939. Cited by Wynot, " 'A Necessary Cruelty,' " 1057.

20. Cardinal Augustus Hlond, *Listy Pasterskie* (Poznan: 1936), 192–93. The pastoral letter is dated February 29, 1936. Cited by Heller, *On the Edge of Destruction*, 113.

21. For an account of Bartoszewski's experiences see Wladyslaw Bartoszewski, *The Warsaw Ghetto: A Christian's Testimony* (Boston: Beacon Press, 1987).

22. Heller, *On the Edge of Destruction*, 295. See also *Encyclopedia Judaica*, s.v. "Poland."

23. The full text of Cardinal Glemp's homily is to be found in *Origins* 19 (5 October 1989): 291–94. See also the appendix to this book.

24. Brumberg, "Silence on Anti-Semitism" and "A Parting for Solidarity and the Church?"

25. Anna Husarska, "Malice or Misunderstanding Over Auschwitz?" *Washington Post*, 17 August 1989.

26. "John Paul Cites Suffering of Jews," *New York Times*, 26 June 1988.

27. See the response to the pope by Alfred Lipson and Samuel Lipson, "A Reply to the Pope's Request," *New York Times*, 16 July 1988. The Lipsons are Holocaust survivors.

28. This subject is discussed by Gitta Sereny, *Into That Darkness: From Mercy Killing to Mass Murder* (London: André Deutsch, 1974), 289–333. Sereny is a Roman Catholic.

29. See Avraham Weiss, "We Did Not Go to Auschwitz to Be Beaten," Letter to the Editor, *New York Times*, 12 September 1989.

30. John Tagliabue, "Polish Prelate Assails Protests by Jews at Auschwitz Convent," *New York Times*, 11 August 1989.

31. Religious News Service, 11 August 1989.

32. Alan Riding, "Jewish Group Protests Remarks Made by Pope," *New York Times*, 13 August 1989.

33. The full text of Cardinal Glemp's homily is to be found in the appendix to this book.

34. There is a difference between the translations offered here and in the *New York Times* (29 August 1989). The *New York Times* uses "do not dictate" where this translation says "don't lay down conditions."

35. John Tagliabue, "Polish Cardinal Terms Agreement on Auschwitz 'Offensive,' " *New York Times*, 3 September 1989.

36. John Tagliabue, "Polish Primate Criticizes Jews in Dispute on Auschwitz Convent," *New York Times*, 29 August 1989.

37. Ari L. Goldman, "O'Connor Assails Remarks by Glemp," *New York Times*, 30 August 1989.

38. Youssef M. Ibrahim, "3 Cardinals Defend Convent Pact Against Attack by Polish Primate," *New York Times*, 4 September 1989.

39. *Origins* 19 (5 October 1989): 291.

40. Patrick J. Buchanan, "Hardball Is a Game That Two Can Play," *Washington Times*, 25 September 1989.

2

Jews and Poles: Remembering at a Cemetery

Ronald Modras

At the end of the seventeenth century, as many as three-quarters of the world's Jews made the Polish-Lithuanian Commonwealth their home.[1] It had become *Polin*, the Yiddish word for Poland and the Hebrew for haven, a place of rest. Often fleeing persecution or expelled, Jews came from Germany, Bohemia, and Hungary, as well as, though in lesser numbers, from Turkey, Italy, Portugal, and Spain. In time Poland supplanted the Rhineland and Spain as the leading center of Jewish creativity and culture in Europe. As late as 1939 the Jewish community in Poland numbered 3.3 million, second in size only to the one in the United States which was largely derived from it.

Today barely 6,000 Jews still live in Poland. The Holocaust rendered it virtually *Judenrein*. To all appearances and former appraisal, to quote Rafael Scharf, "The paths of 'two of the saddest nations on this earth' have parted forever." I say appearances and former appraisal because the Auschwitz convent controversy belied the conventional wisdom that was generated solely by numbers. So long as there is memory, the paths of these two nations will never part. Ashes unite them. As people often do, they will meet in cemeteries. Not surprisingly, their meetings thus far have not been altogether free of misunderstanding.

STRUGGLE OVER A SYMBOL

The avalanche of commentary engendered by the Auschwitz convent controversy brought to light not only considerable feeling but varying degrees of misinformation. American church historian Martin Marty was wide of the mark when he wrote that Auschwitz for Jews is a place so "profane" that no Catholic house of prayer can consecrate it.[2] Auschwitz is anything but profane. Though some Jews have called it defiled, Auschwitz functions as a sacred symbol. It has become a *holy* place, not in the popular sense of ennobling or uplifting but in the biblical sense of the word *kadosh*, beyond the ordinary, fearsome, capable of evoking shuddering and awe. Auschwitz has become hallowed ground, a *sanctum*. Not unlike Jerusalem's Western Wall for Jews or Mecca for Muslims, it has become a rallying point for collective experience. Not unlike the Church of the Holy Sepulchre for Christians, it has become a place of competing interests. Nothing is so unbecoming a sacred place as a turf war, but that is what the convent controversy became. Auschwitz was a place of common martyrdom amid uncommon horror, and for Jews and Poles both, albeit differently, it is holy.

Marty misstated the matter again when he wrote that "Hitler's people built Auschwitz while most of Catholic Poland was silent." Auschwitz was built by Austria as an army camp before World War I, when Poland was still partitioned by her neighbors. Between the wars it was a Polish army camp, until the invasion by Germany and the Soviet Union in 1939 partitioned Poland once more. Oswiecim, its Polish name, became Auschwitz when, like the rest of western Poland, it was directly annexed to the Reich. Auschwitz became a German city, its Polish inhabitants forced to move some distance away from the complex that was first transformed into a labor camp and then expanded into a death factory.

The first victims at Auschwitz were ethnic Poles, part of the Nazi plan to destroy Polish leadership and culture. The Jews came some twenty-one months after and in such overwhelming numbers that Auschwitz became the pre-eminent symbol of that horrific event we have come to call the Holocaust, the systematic attempt by Nazi Germany to destroy all of European Jewry. It points beyond itself to the murders perpetrated at labor camps like Dachau, Buchenwald, and Mauthausen, and death camps like Chelmno, Majdanek, Sobibor, and Treblinka. It symbolizes the murders of civilians not only in gas chambers but by shooting, hanging, overwork, and starvation. Auschwitz symbolizes the murders of 6 million Jews, 3 million ethnic Poles, and 2 million other victims: Gypsies, gays, lesbians, Soviet prisoners of war, and other Slavic peoples.

It was not Catholic Poland that was silent. Diplomat Jan Karski and the Polish government in exile brought detailed information about the ghettos and death camps to the West and pleaded for intervention on behalf of Jews. In effect it was the West that remained silent—Churchill's government in Great Britain, the Roosevelt administration, the *New York Times*, and, yes, Pope Pius XII and the leadership of the American Jewish community.

Auschwitz is a monument to more than inhumanity. It testifies to what political expediency, institutional self-interest, personal indifference, or fear can allow. It points to the guilt not only of the German perpetrators but also to the complicity of any and all who could have made a difference and did not. Wladyslaw Bartoszewski, who helped organize a Polish underground effort specifically to rescue Jews, did make a difference. But he exaggerates, I believe, when he writes that from a moral point of view only those did not fail in their humanity who died giving aid to Jews.[3] He and those like him do not bear the same moral burden as those who, safe in the West at no risk to their lives, still did nothing. Anywhere under German occupation, giving aid to Jews was dangerous, but only in occupied Poland did it automatically mean death not only for oneself but for one's family.

It appears to me, therefore, particularly inappropriate for Martin Marty to moralize to Poles about Auschwitz, when he writes: "Whatever else this place is, Catholic Poland, it is not yours to preempt." Marty, I presume, lost no family or loved ones at Auschwitz or any other death camp. He is an outsider. Catholic Poland is hardly pre-empting Auschwitz. It is already theirs, built by German engineering on occupied Polish soil, a warning to humanity entrusted to Polish keeping. It is not for us outsiders to dictate how it will be kept. We can ask and advise, but we have no more right to dictate terms to Poland than we have to dictate terms to Israel. Poles, like Israelis, are wary of outsiders making determinations for them. After outsiders allowed them to be partitioned in the eighteenth century and bequeathed them in 1945 at Yalta to the Soviet bloc, they have reason to be wary.

CARDINAL MACHARSKI

He did not have to do it. Cracow's Cardinal Franciszek Macharski did not have to agree to moving the Carmelite convent from the edge of the grounds of Auschwitz. I am glad and deeply grateful that he did so in 1987 at Geneva. And once he signed that declaration, he was, of course, bound to keep his word. But he was not bound by any norm of justice to sign the declaration in the first place. Cardinal Macharski is known to be a sensitive man with a profound respect for what Auschwitz means to Jews. It was out of that sensitivity and respect— charity, he said, not justice—that he made the agreement.

Macharski was unrealistic in accepting a two-year completion date. Neither did he act quickly, perhaps because not all his colleagues in the Polish hierarchy were in accord with the Geneva declaration. The archbishop of Warsaw, Cardinal Glemp, believed that Macharski had gone beyond his authority in signing it. Although Auschwitz lies within the boundaries of Macharski's archdiocese of Cracow, Glemp as primate could claim jurisdiction over all monasteries and convents in Poland, including this one. Despite ecclesiastical infighting behind the scenes, Macharski was in the process of keeping the agreement when a group of American Jews took matters into their own hands.

The cardinal had just days before completed a year-long process of bureaucratic red tape to purchase a new site for the convent. Progress was being made, although at a slower pace than had been anticipated at Geneva and with little assistance from Western sources to the economically strapped Polish church and nation. But the pace was not enough for a Bronx, New York, rabbi and his followers, who around noon on July 14, 1989, scaled the six-foot fence and occupied the yard in front of the convent. According to an on-site report, they made insulting remarks about the sisters, Poles, and the church, attached posters to the convent walls, and declared their intentions to remain until the Vatican intervened to move the cloister. The group refused requests to leave and after five hours were forcibly removed. They proceeded to confer with members of the press conveniently at hand. On July 16 they trespassed once again and occupied the convent grounds from 10:30 A.M. until 6:00 that evening.[4]

Jewish commentators are now willing to use words like "ill-considered," "boorish," and "crude" to describe the actions of the American demonstrators. Immediately after the incident, however, media attention was given to how, after five hours, they were forcibly removed. I have no doubt that the protesters were roughed up by the workers who removed them. Catholic intruders would have been treated no differently. These were not trained police but ordinary laborers unaccustomed to dealing with demonstrators of any kind, let alone experienced professionals like this particular group, whose actions had made them problematic to the American Jewish leadership long before this episode. (It is worth noting that the demonstrators excused the Polish workers as probably not knowing any better, preferring to blame instead the clergy who allegedly looked on.)[5]

This deliberate and successful attempt to create an international incident does not bear repeating except to reflect on the reaction of the press. Media attention was focused not on the trespass of the cloister's privacy but on the manner in which the trespassers were removed. Although leaders of American Jewish agencies are now willing to admit privately that they should have distanced themselves from the offensive protest, they did not. Instead press releases were sent out decrying "typical" or "traditional" Polish antisemitism.

In Poland Jewish leaders criticized the actions of the New York Jews as being contrary to the ethical principles of Judaism. From the West, however, came what Macharski described as "a violent campaign of accusations and defamation."[6] Macharski apparently did not know that the protesters in no way represented the mainstream Jewish community. From a widespread Polish perspective, understanding and respect were being required of only one side. Incensed at the provocation by the demonstrators and media abuse, Catholic Poles on all levels protested their rights to have their dead remembered at Auschwitz. A harried Macharski, much in the middle, issued a statement deploring the "atmosphere of aggression and disquiet" and called for peace. He announced a moratorium on any further action on moving the convent. Ambiguous as to whether it was temporary or indefinite, the announcement was conducive to anything but peace. But it was enough for Elie Wiesel to accuse Cardinal Macharski of bad faith and insulting Jewish honor.[7]

CARDINAL GLEMP

Insensitivity to others' feelings and ignorance abounded on all sides and at all levels in this episode surrounding the Auschwitz convent. But no one had to pay more dearly for it than Poland's Cardinal Jozef Glemp. His August 26,

1989, sermon at Czestochowa was, he claimed later, "a grand proposal for an open and complete dialogue" with Jewish leadership.[8] He apparently attempted to present what he believed to be a fair and balanced picture of the situation, making references to Jews enriching, loving, and giving their lives for Poland. But he also made references to crude stereotypes that come right out of the 1930s, identifying Jews with innkeepers, Communists, and influence over the mass media. It was these references that were singled out and reported at length in the Western press. The cardinal should have known better. Whether or not his ignorance was culpable, only God can judge. But his remarks immediately earned him an unprecedented rebuke on the front page of Poland's Solidarity daily and the invidious description of being an antisemite.

Antisemitism is a word that points to a very real and widespread phenomenon but is notoriously difficult to define. Permit me to illustrate. Speaking once at a temple to a class of teenagers, I asked if they had ever personally experienced antisemitism. I was told, "Yes, they think our fathers are all rich and that we've all had nose jobs." Not to discount the dangers of stereotyping nor the hurt these young people experienced, surely a word that includes adolescent stereotypes such as these with the Jew-hatred of Adolf Hitler seriously begs for some sort of further qualification.

Cardinal Glemp would deny, I presume, that he is antisemitic, that he bears hostility toward Jews. But in the 1930s his remarks about Jewish Communists and power over the press were the stock-in-trade of antisemites throughout Europe, including Poland, and the United States (one thinks of Father Charles Coughlin). Those remarks touched a raw nerve in most Jews and raised Jewish memories of an era in Polish history as controversial as it is complex.

INTERWAR POLAND, JEWS, AND THE CHURCH

Two extremes have arisen in the historiography of Polish-Jewish relations. One school of thought, espoused by nationalist Poles like Glemp, emphasizes Poland's long history of tolerance and hospitality, when Jews were welcomed and offered refuge. This camp focuses almost exclusively on Poland's remote past, like the Statute of Kalisz (1264) that along with obligations recognized Jewish rights and privileges. It points to the Council of the Four Lands, a unique institution that in the sixteenth century allowed Poland's Jews to govern themselves through a kind of parliament, affording them a political autonomy unprecedented in the rest of Europe. This school of historical thought emphasizes the heroism of the thousands of Poles who risked their lives and those of their families to help Jews under the German occupation. While it does not deny there were blackmailers and informers in Poland, it correctly points out that at the Yad Vashem Holocaust Memorial in Jerusalem, in the grove of trees honoring the righteous non-Jews who gave help to save Jews, more Poles and Dutch are honored than any other national group. In other words, this camp looks only at the positive aspects of Polish-Jewish history and tends to ignore the more painful.

The other extreme of historiography focuses almost exclusively on this century, particularly on the period between the two world wars in which Polish Jews are described as living on the "edge of destruction" (Celia S. Heller). The interwar period in Poland is regarded as a rehearsal for the Holocaust: first the Poles pushed Jews to the brink, then the Germans pushed them over. Fixed on this era, this camp tends to view Poles and Polish culture as inveterately antisemitic. Illustrating this line of thought is Israel's Prime Minister Yitzhak Shamir, who in an interview expressed the opinion that Poles imbibe antisemitism with their mother's milk.[9] In this camp, to quote Hebrew University's Professor Ezra Mendelsohn, one can detect "the long-established Jewish point of view that most, if not all, gentile states (and gentiles in general) are anti-semitic, particularly East European states and East European gentiles."[10]

Distancing themselves from these extremes are scholars working in Poland, Israel, the United States, and England, particularly in connection with *Polin*, the journal of the Institute of Polish-Jewish Studies at Oxford. Emerging from this group of scholars is a recognition of the comparatively positive history of Polish-Jewish relations up to the end of the last century and the complexity of those relations and of the situation in which Jews and Poles found themselves subsequently. Yet Poland for many Jews more than any other country, even Germany, is identified with antisemitism. It is not only (though it is partially) because more Jews came from Poland.

More than any other country in this century, Poland represents the longstanding antisemitism of the Roman Catholic church. The toleration and autonomy which Poland's kings and aristocracy granted to Jews was deeply resented and decried by the church's hierarchy. In the eighteenth century Pope Benedict XIV wrote an entire encyclical criticizing Poland for allowing Jews to live in the same towns as Christians and to acquire political influence and economic power, all of which the pope called a "stain of shame."[11] When Poland was partitioned off the face of Europe, Catholicism as much as any other cultural force kept Poles from being assimilated into a Germany that was Lutheran and a Russia that was Eastern Orthodox. In successfully identifying the concepts Polish and Catholic, the church's leaders helped Poland to survive the partitions. The identification, however, meant Jews, no matter how long they had lived in Poland, were at best guests in Poland, at worst aliens.

There were many factors that led to animosity between Poles and Jews between the wars. Certainly a major one was poverty. Most American Jews are aware of the economic hardship suffered by Polish Jewry during the interwar period. Recent Jewish scholarship, however, has demonstrated that the poverty of the Polish peasantry was even worse.[12] Poles and Jews found themselves competing for jobs in a country that was economically underdeveloped and, given its resources, overpopulated. But economic hardship alone does not account for anti-Jewish feeling any more than prosperity guarantees its absence.

Poland's social and economic problems could have been met, I believe, if the Catholic church, the greatest moral force in Poland before the war, had been open to pluralism, dialogue, cooperation, all that we identify today with Vatican II and Pope John XXIII. The pre–World War II, pre–Vatican II church waged a war in behalf of Christendom. Although it welcomed the benefits that separation between church and state afforded it in a country like the United States, where Catholics were a minority, the church's leadership found a similar situation intolerable in traditionally Catholic countries like France, Italy, or Spain. In Poland bishops, clergy, and the Catholic press mounted a virtual crusade against a liberalism that would make the Catholic church equal to other religious bodies. Those who espoused such liberal ideas were regarded as enemies of the church and of Poland's traditional Catholic culture. Foremost among them, of course, were the Jews, who were encouraged by both churchmen and politicians to emigrate.

In great part because of the Catholic church and its struggle on behalf of a Polish Catholic culture, interwar Poland was an antisemitic country, both in its policies and in the attitudes of large sectors of its population. Poles are reluctant to admit that fact, possibly because they are accustomed to define themselves as victims, and victims are reluctant to admit that they have victimized others. The phenomenon, however, is not infrequent. Again to quote Professor Mendelsohn, who, like others, has drawn comparisons between interwar Poland and present-day Israel: "Israelis are in a good position to understand that any state which defines itself as a mono-ethnic entity, but which in fact includes within its borders members of other ethnic groups that cannot be absorbed, must act in a way which is deleterious to the interests of other ethnic groups."[13]

AN ECUMENICAL CENTER

An ecumenical center is being planned to house the Carmelite sisters a quarter of a mile from Auschwitz, a place for prayer, study, and meeting. It is to be a place where anyone who comes to Auschwitz will be able to learn the facts and reflect on their meaning. Here Poles will have an opportunity to acquire greater understanding of the Jewish perspective on the Holocaust. Until now, Poland's government has been compelled to follow the Soviet policy toward the Nazi victims, to make no distinctions and treat them all equally as martyrs of fascism. Here is a factor, often ignored, that contributed immensely to the convent controversy. The particularity of the Jewish martyrdom has either been understated or altogether ignored in Poland, not only in the schools but at Auschwitz itself.

That the overwhelming number of victims at Auschwitz were Jews killed simply because they were Jews is not immediately apparent upon visiting the camp, now a state museum. It is an omission that needs to be rectified. The Jews were singled out by the Nazis in a way that no other group was, and that singularity should be noted. The museum authorities under a new Polish government could make a difference in this regard.

The policy in Polish schools to ignore distinctions among the Nazi victims has led to a commonplace assumption in Poland of a certain parity: 3 million

Polish Jews were killed and 3 million ethnic Poles. But the significance of the tragedy for the two groups is strikingly asymmetrical. For ethic Poles it was 10 percent of the population but it was 90 percent of the Polish Jews. The 6 million constituted nearly one-third of world Jewry, destroyed by a state-sponsored, systematically planned program that targeted every Jewish man, woman, and child as an object for extermination. There is a uniqueness here, often acknowledged by Pope John Paul II. It is a singularity that requires recognition by more than Poles. An ecumenical center could contribute to that recognition.

Jews are rightly concerned about how the Holocaust will be remembered fifty years from now. The generation of survivors is now passing. In a decade or more their firsthand testimony will be gone. But Poles, Gypsies, and other groups are concerned not about a future possibility but a present reality, the fact that, for many people if not most, the martyrdom of the non-Jewish victims of the Nazis is either unknown or dismissed. Five million non-Jewish victims were also deemed expendable, as less than fully human. And there were millions more who were targeted right after Jews. The supplies of Zyklon B gas found in storage at the end of the war point to the fact that the Nazis had millions more victims in mind for their program of extermination than the relatively few Jews left in Europe. The Nazis planned to make Poland and the Ukraine colonies for German settlement and cultivation. The native populations required decimation.

An ecumenical center at Auschwitz could also serve as a natural meeting ground for theologians and religious leaders to search out the relationship between the crematoria and the cross. The Nazis were neopagans who despised Christianity as an offshoot of Judaism. But they were also apostate Christians, who perpetrated the Holocaust in the heart of historical Western Christendom. Was this purely accidental, or did the history of Christian antisemitism contribute to making the Holocaust possible? There is a clear distinction between the previously traditional theological antisemitism of the Christian churches and the racial antisemitism of the Nazis. But would the latter have been possible without the former? If not a direct cause, the tradition of antisemitism in the Christian churches can certainly be described as a *conditio sine qua non*. Would there have been so much indifference to the plight of the Jews if Christianity had not decreed them as marked with the sign of Cain? These are questions which Christian thinkers have yet to reflect on in serious numbers. An international ecumenical center at Auschwitz could draw the scholars and church leaders to grapple with the questions and draw the necessary conclusions.

Surveying the facts of the convent controversy, the Anti-Defamation League pointed to one "that the Jewish community might not want to face. As Christians are asked as partners in dialogue to acknowledge patterns of contempt in teaching and preaching, there should be a Jewish acknowledgement of prejudices against Christians and the need to overcome them."[14] There are Poles and Jews who point at each other's prejudice to excuse their own. Besides anti-Polish sentiment among Jews and anti-Jewish feelings among Poles, the ADL statement acknowledged the "Polish Catholic solidarity to the Jewish people expressed by clergy and lay leadership in their support of the Auschwitz agreement." Though visitors come to Auschwitz from all over the world, the greatest numbers, as one would expect, are Poles and Jews. An ecumenical center would provide a place for them to share perspectives and confront their mutual stereotypes and prejudices.

So long as there is memory, Jews and Poles will be meeting at Auschwitz as at a cemetery. But as people of goodwill on both sides of the controversy made clear, they need not meet as strangers.

NOTES

1. Chimen Abramsky, Maciej Jachimczyk, and Antony Polonsky, eds., *The Jews in Poland* (Oxford, Eng.: Blackwell, 1986), 1.

2. *Chicago Sun-Times*, 21 September 1989.

3. Wladyslaw Bartoszewski, "Some Reflections on Polish-Jewish Relations," *Polin*, 1: 286.

4. *Tygodnik Powszechny*, 30 July 1989.

5. Coalition of Concern, Bronx, N.Y., 3 August 1989.

6. Radio Vaticana, 10 August 1989.

7. *Jewish Herald*, 22 September 1989.

8. *Origins*, 5 October 1989, 294.

9. *Jerusalem Post* (International Edition), 16 September 1989.

10. Ezra Mendelsohn, "Interwar Poland: Good for the Jews or Bad for the Jews?" *The Jews in Poland* (Oxford, Eng.: Blackwell, 1986), 131.

11. Claudia Carlen, *The Papal Encyclicals* (Wilmington, N.C.: McGrath, 1981), 1:41–44.

12. Mendelsohn, "Interwar Poland," 131.

13. Ibid., 137.

14. Leon Klenicki, "The Carmelite Convent at Auschwitz, Past and Future," *Anti-Defamation League of B'nai B'rith*, October 1989.

3

The Auschwitz Convent Controversy: Mutual Misperceptions

John T. Pawlikowski

There is little doubt that the Auschwitz convent controversy produced the most serious threat to date to the general development of the Catholic-Jewish dialogue in the last twenty-five years. Yet, whatever fallout has resulted for the overall climate of Christianity's relationship to the Jewish people, the impact on Polish-Jewish relations in particular has been even more intense. And Polish-Jewish tensions over the matter have not completely subsided despite the new assurances from the Vatican and the Polish hierarchy that the convent will be moved. Many of these tensions in fact are not apt to disappear anytime soon because, as will be explained subsequently, they are deeply rooted both in twentieth-century Polish history as well as current discussions in Poland regarding the shape of the emerging post-Communist society.

The crisis of late summer 1989 has revealed both the depth and the limited outreach of a quarter-century of Christian-Jewish dialogue. Clearly the controversy over the convent has shown that many people remain totally unaffected by the contemporary encounter. The old antisemitic stereotypes remain painfully evident in the church, even at the highest ecclesiastical levels. Cardinal Jozef Glemp's remarks during the height of the crisis, which seemed to many to suggest classical antisemitic stereotypes of Jews as exercising excessive control over the media and posing a threat to Polish national sovereignty, are a case in point. And Jewish circles, both popular and leadership, were replete with unnuanced accusations of Polish antisemitism. The most outrageous example of this surely was Israeli prime minister Yitzhak Shamir's remark about Poles acquiring antisemitism through their mother's milk. While Shamir's words may well reflect unresolved anger over the death of a brother at the hands of Poles after the end of World War II, they were nevertheless unbecoming a head of state and, more importantly, misrepresented to the world the complex Polish-Jewish relationship.

If we are to understand the making of the 1989 Auschwitz convent crisis and
its ultimate resolution, which involves far more than the mere relocation of the
Carmelite convent outside the camp grounds, we need to probe more deeply the
historical and contemporary factors that generated such profound mutual mistrust
and misperceptions on all sides. In the following pages we shall attempt to
summarize some of these factors that remain ongoing realities and hence continuing sources of potential tensions between Polish Christians in particular and
the Jewish community.

JEWISH FEARS

Jewish fears concerning the Auschwitz convent in the end boiled down to one
reality—desecration of the *memory* of the millions for whom the site constitutes,
in the words of Elie Wiesel, "an invisible cemetery." Over and over again Jews
expressed profound concern, some even discerned a deliberate plot on the part
of the church, with respect to the veiling of the camp site in Christian garb. This
would in effect kill the victims a second time, as they would grow even more
invisible. In the minds of some Jews, what was happening at Auschwitz reflected
a general trend in the church, especially in Polish Catholicism, to "Christianize"
the Holocaust. This would quickly lead to the equation of Jews with all other
victims of the Nazis, eliminating all sensitivity to the immensity of the "Final
Solution" of the Jewish question. It would also cover over considerable Christian
complicity with the Nazis in this endeavor. It was not sufficient to kill Jews.
Now memory of their death would also be obliterated through universalization.
This for most Jews, especially survivors of the *Shoah*, was the ultimate frustra-
tion. Jews overwhelmingly would applaud the sentiments expressed by Catholic
theologian Michael Novak who, in urging that the convent be moved, wrote:
"Let Auschwitz-Birkenau remind us of the desolation proper to a place where
God was hidden. His absence (and that of human civilization) so grievously felt
amid immeasurable human suffering. Such desolation will not really make it far
from Him. On the contrary."[1]

There was yet another fear alive in the Jewish community during the height
of the crisis, at least in its European sector. Leadership on the Auschwitz convent
issue had been largely assumed by the European Jewish community, whose
representatives were the sole Jewish signatories to the original Geneva accord
of 1987 whose nonimplementation precipitated the 1989 crisis. In recent years
the Jewish community of Western Europe, reborn from the ashes of the *Shoah*,
has increasingly been seeing itself as a new "third force" in world Jewry. This
new European Jewish leadership has frequently adopted a far more aggressive
posture toward non-Jews, including the Christian community, with which it has
experienced little in the way of sustained dialogue. The Auschwitz convent
marked its first real test. And so pursuit of the goal of moving the convent
became relentless and aggressive, perhaps covering some fear of failure, particularly within the Belgian and Italian sectors of European Jewry. This factor in

no way invalidated the primary Jewish goal of preserving the memory of the Jewish victims, but it contributed an intensity to the debate on the Jewish side which frequently made it difficult for the Jewish leaders to appreciate Polish identification with Auschwitz.

POLISH FEARS

The basic fear of the Polish community likewise centered on *memory* of its victims, but in a somewhat more complex way. Repeatedly the Polish accusation, warranted or not, was that Jews were trying to take sole possession of the Auschwitz site, forgetting that it served as the premier camp for the extermination of the Polish leadership elite (academics, politicians, artists, clergy) in the Nazi effort to reduce Poland to a permanent state of servitude to the Third Reich. Poles often expressed great dismay at the seeming lack of information on the basic origins of Auschwitz as initially a camp for political prisoners (a short period) and then the primary center for the liquidation of Polish leaders. Only toward the end of 1942 did Auschwitz become predominantly Jewish, well after the Nazis had totally conquered Poland. This subsequent Jewish majority at Auschwitz must be clearly acknowledged by all.

The memory of this camp's human destruction has been permanently implanted in Jewish consciousness with the name *Auschwitz* at times being used as a synonym for the entire Final Solution. But this fact does not excuse, even in the eyes of those Poles who are quite prepared to acknowledge the ultimate significance of Auschwitz for the *Shoah*, the narrowness of remarks made by Ady Steg, president of the Alliance Israélite Universelle, at the first Geneva meeting on the convent situation held during July 1986, which was attended by Roman Catholic leaders from France, Poland, and Belgium and Jewish rabbinic and communal leaders from France, Belgium, and Italy. Professor Steg proclaimed to those assembled in Geneva that the Jewish people had acquired, through the martyrdom of its children, "inalienable rights to Auschwitz." He further declared that the memory of the hundreds of thousands of non-Jews who were murdered there should be preserved. But, he noted, "their murder was perpetrated as an 'extra measure' . . . a matter of subjecting the non-Jews to facilities which were installed for the working out of the Final Solution. In truth, Auschwitz, with its gas chambers and its crematoria, was conceived, constructed and put to use solely for the extermination of the Jews."[2] Apart from total insensitivity to the pivotal role played by Auschwitz in the Nazi onslaught against the Polish nation that constituted a integral part of the overall Nazi plan for "human purification" whose centerpiece was Jewish annihilation, Steg simply has his basic facts wrong. Poles were the majority of inmates at Auschwitz until 1942, when Jews took over that dubious role. The first killings by poison gas at Auschwitz, according to historian Richard C. Lukas, involved 300 Poles and 700 Soviet prisoners.[3]

A second Polish fear, rooted both in historical experiences and contemporary reality, is in some ways a corollary to the European Jewish fear of appearing too weak, spoken of above. The Polish psyche, both in Poland and in the foreign communities of Polonia, has been profoundly conditioned by examples of oppression and prejudice, particularly in this century. First it was the Nazis, then the Communists. Just when new possibilities for a measure of democracy and national self-respect were appearing on the horizon, into the picture come the Jews over the Auschwitz camp, which, as we shall explain subsequently, is as much a national political shrine for many Poles as a religious one. While some of the Polish reaction on this score was clearly interwoven with traditional Catholic and Polish antisemitic attitudes toward the Jews, it is necessary to understand that this other dynamic was also at work. Was the supposed power of the international Jewish community (in itself a definite antisemitic image) going to discredit the fledgling new experiment in democratic government and thereby undercut, perhaps gravely, its chances for survival? The fear was real even if some of its motivation was highly questionable.

MUTUAL MISUNDERSTANDINGS

Authentic communication between the respective leaderships during the crisis was negligible at best. Clearly here was an instance of the proverbial two ships passing each other in the night. On most major issues neither community really understood the basis for the other's stance. And by and large there was little effort from either side to find out.

Without doubt one critical issue that persisted throughout the crisis was the "rights" questions with respect to the camp. We have already encountered Ady Steg's claim of Jewish "inalienable rights to Auschwitz" based on the immensity of Jewish suffering there. But Polish claims in the main tended to be just as unbending. Auschwitz was on Polish national soil. So it was the right of Poles to determine what should happen at the site. And most Poles assumed that Jews had precipitated the crisis by failing to acknowledge legitimate Polish sovereignty over the camp and making counterright claims instead.

Looking at this "rights" dispute from a distance, we can say that from any analysis of the numerous statements issued on the Jewish side, the Jewish community must be faulted for not clearly acknowledging the central role of the Auschwitz camp for the Polish nation even though most did not go as far in positing Jewish claims as Professor Steg.

The failure on the Polish side has to be judged even more severe. Some Polish spokespersons such as Father Stanislaw Musial, S.J., secretary of the Polish Episcopate's Commission for Relations with the Jews; Jerzy Turowicz, internationally acclaimed editor of *Tygodnik Powszechny*; and Lech Walesa affirmed Jewish primacy at Auschwitz while at the same time insisting that Jews must understand "what place is occupied by Auschwitz in the collective consciousness of our nation."[4] Walesa, in comments made during his November 1989 visit to New York, acknowledged that "the biggest right at the place belongs to the

Jews.'' He recognized that "the Jewish community is the nation that has paid the highest price in the history of the world."[5] But he went on to add that the Polish nation has paid the second highest price, and therefore there is no question of anyone's having exclusive rights to Auschwitz. He urged the two victim peoples to refrain from fighting among themselves and to pursue a path of compromise instead.

On the whole, however, the statements of Musial, Turowicz, and Walesa were far from typical of the general Polish response to the crisis. Most Poles who responded to the situation with statements, articles, or letters-to-the-editor attacked Jews for supposedly denying any Polish rights to Auschwitz. Even within the circle of the Solidarity union whose daily newspaper *Gazeta Wyborcza* ran a strong editorial against Cardinal Glemp's infamous Czestochowa address, the general Polish response seemed to prevail, if we are to believe the analysis provided by Solidarity member Konstanty Gebert, who, writing under the pen name of Dawid Warszawski, reports on the outraged mail received by the newspaper as a result of its editorial.[6] While in some cases the charges may be justified, they all miss the point that the problem with the convent did not begin with the Jews. Rather it dates back to its very creation, which took place without any consultation whatsoever on the part of Polish church leaders with the international Jewish community, who alone could adequately speak for the Jewish victims buried there. So, in fact, what the convent crisis is about in large part is rectification of the original Polish Catholic mistake of totally excluding Jews from any voice about memorialization of victims at the camp site. This "priority of error" must be underscored because Poles overwhelmingly have accused Jews of trying to pre-empt their rights to the Auschwitz camp site. The truth of the matter is the reversal of that. Polish Catholics initially failed to acknowledge the distinctive bonding to Auschwitz existing within world Jewry.

A second major misunderstanding shared by the two communities during the course of the crisis is connected with the "rights" question. The distinctive rights of both groups need to be recognized with respect to Auschwitz, in part because of the differing approaches to the memorialization of the dead prevailing in each. For classical Catholicism it is considered honorable, even commendable, to erect monuments and chapels in cemeteries, which in the past at least were often located adjacent to a church. To pray for the dead or arrange for the celebration of Mass in their behalf traditionally has been strongly encouraged by the church. No doubt this is directly related to a strong belief in purgatory, where those who still are required to make amends for past sins must go prior to passage into heaven. Prayer for the dead is viewed as of direct benefit to the dead whose souls may still remain mired in purgatory, in terms of quickening their departure for heaven. In this sense it remains the most "productive" activity members of a community can undertake for their immediate and extended families who are deceased.

In the Jewish community the attitude toward memorializing victims is virtually the exact opposite of the Catholic position. Traditional Jewry has always been opposed to the erection of worship sites in cemeteries. And, unlike the situation in Catholicism, cemeteries have never been developed adjacent to a synagogue. Jews do pray in cemeteries, both on the day of burial and on the anniversaries of the death of loved ones. But the prayer texts for those occasions do not refer directly to death. In fact, they have been imported from other situations having no connection with the passage from life. Instead they focus first and foremost on the sanctification of God. Again, it is likely that theological understandings of the afterlife play a critical role. As descendants of the Pharisaic/rabbinic tradition of the Second Temple period, classical Jewry today accepts the notion of resurrection of the faithful individual. But this point of belief is emphasized far less than it is in Catholic theology. And one does not find in Judaism any sense of temporary purgation akin to the church's view of purgatory. Hence there exists no sense of responsibility on the part of the living community of faith to assist those who have gone before them in finally attaining heaven. Resurrection in Judaism is something that will occur once at the end of human history when all just Jews will enter the new kingdom inaugurated by the coming of the Messiah. Resurrection is entirely the activity of God. Humans can have little, if any, direct effect on its speed. The state of the dead in the interim period is of little concern to Jewish theology, in contrast to classical Catholic thought. Rather, praying in cemeteries is intended to remember the deceased person, but first and foremost to honor the Creator God, Lord of both the living and the dead, whose power continues to energize the people Israel as they move on through history toward the final Messianic era.

These fundamentally different, in some ways even opposed, perspectives on memorializing the dead will of necessity make the task of achieving harmony between Jews and Catholics an extremely delicate one that will require both understanding and sensitivity. Both qualities were in rather short supply among Poles and Jews in the midst of the convent controversy.

The dispute over the Auschwitz camp site also brought to the surface another continuing Polish-Jewish misperception—the issue of Polish antisemitism. The relationship between the two communities was only beginning to experience some healing of the scars caused by the film *Shoah* on this score when the convent controversy reached the boiling point. The tensions of summer 1989 were often intensified by linkages made between the convent situation and historical (and enduring) antisemitism among Poles. This was especially characteristic of the Jewish media. Typical was an editorial appearing in the *Jerusalem Post* that read as follows: ''Nor can the recent violent attack by Polish workers on a visiting group of protestors at the site be disconnected from the gruesome historical background of centuries-old Polish anti-Semitism.''[7] Such blanket accusations of Polish antisemitism further hardened the attitude of many Poles against Jewish claims to Auschwitz.

Clearly the question of Polish antisemitism, past and present, must be a part of any reconciliation effort in connection with the convent dispute. We may never achieve a total meeting of the minds on this question between the two communities. But each must be prepared to probe the issue far more extensively than has been the case until now if the syndrome of wholesale indictment/stubborn denial is to be overcome.

Polish society will have to come to grips, far better than it has thus far, with its legacy of antisemitism, rooted both in classic Christian stereotypes of the Jews and in social conditions particular to that nation. Some attempts have been made by the church as well as academic centers such as the Jagiellonian University and the Club of Catholic Intellectuals. The summer of 1989 found more than twenty professors from theological faculties in Poland participating for eight weeks in a program for Judaism, Jewish-Christian relations, and American religious pluralism, held at Spertus College in Chicago under the auspices of the Archdiocese of Chicago and the Polish Episcopal Conference (with the personal endorsement of Cardinals Glemp and Macharski). This program also involved extensive exposure to the varied life of the Chicago Jewish community. Upon their return to Poland in the midst of the convent controversy, a number of the participants wrote substantive articles urging reconciliation between Jews and Catholics with regard to the convent, based on the church's faithfulness to the original 1987 Geneva accord. And a national debate on Polish antisemitism was generated by an article published in the influential Catholic newspaper *Tygodnik Powszechny* in January 1987 by Professor Jan Blonski.[8]

Yet the widespread opposition to the Blonski article as well as the reaction to the Solidarity editorial on the convent issue reported by Warszawski gives us ample evidence of a continuing problem. Surely it needs to be stated, and *restated*, that Polish antisemitism is in the final analysis no more virulent than that embedded in other European societies, that Poland, unlike France and several other countries, parented no Nazi support group during World War II, and that Poland has the second highest number of "righteous" officially honored by the Yad Vashem national Holocaust memorial in Israel. But the reality of Polish-Jewish relations in the twentieth century in Poland, especially in the interwar and war years which has done so much to shape the contemporary Jewish consciousness of that land, is quite grim in many respects, according to the recent research undertaken by Father Ronald Modras[9] and others. Antisemitism was clearly in the ascendency in this period. It was affecting Polish political, academic, and economic life. A feeling was growing in some quarters, particularly with the rise of Polish religio-nationalism, that national life would be far more wholesome without the presence of Jews despite their longstanding involvement in so many dimensions of Polish society.[10]

Twentieth-century Polish religio-nationalism in particular remains relevant for the continuing dialogue between Poles and Jews about Auschwitz. This outlook placed the church at the very apex of Polish society, the guardian of its public morals and culture. Jews were seen as direct threats to this hegemony over Polish society by the church, being viewed as "internationalists," "secularists," and "unbelievers." As the struggle now begins in the post-Communist era to fashion a new social fabric in Poland, the question of church-state relations will move center stage. And for most of this century the internal "church-state" issue in Poland has directly involved Jews, who have been considered by influential Polish religio-nationalists as an alien force threatening the well-being of the society. What scared so many about Cardinal Glemp's claim that Jewish opposition to the convent was threatening Polish national sovereignty was its clear relationship to a religio-nationalistic argument that was especially vehement during the notorious period between the two world wars when Polish-Jewish relations sank to a low ebb. This viewpoint has shown some new ascendancy in Poland of late, and there are reasons to suspect Cardinal Glemp may be personally sympathetic to its basic argument. Not long ago he wrote a preface to a new volume by an author associated with this movement. And in the 1989 elections he supported certain candidates for the Sejm (Polish parliament) running in opposition to so-called "secularists" (in some cases Jews by birth).

This religio-nationalism is generally not supported by the Solidarity movement, which favors a role for the church more akin to that it exercises in the Western democracies and one more in line with Vatican II's Statement on Religious Liberty. Hence the considerable ongoing tension between Solidarity and Cardinal Glemp, which surfaced again in the midst of the convent controversy. This Solidarity viewpoint, which is probably shared by Cardinal Macharski and members of the Polish Bishops' Commission for Relations with Judaism, is far more willing to recognize the primacy of Jewish rights at Auschwitz (not to the exclusion, of course, of Polish rights) than the religio-nationalistic movement, for which Auschwitz stands as both a historical symbol and a sacred Polish Catholic religious site. The persistence of this religio-nationalistic outlook in Poland has the potential for creating ongoing problems between Christians and Jews over the Auschwitz site even if the Geneva accord is quickly implemented.

Without implying symmetry with Polish antisemitism, it is also necessary to recognize that current tensions between Poles and over the convent will not subside unless Jews are willing to confront the widespread stereotyping of Poles still current in world Jewry. Some of this is simply due to lack of knowledge, both of the complex history of Jewish life in Poland as well as Polish sufferings during the Nazi onslaught. This is not to say that many Jews today do not remember vividly antisemitic attacks against them or their immediate families in Poland. But these are often generalized and not placed in the total sociopolitical framework, particularly of the interwar years.

Dr. Stanislaw Krajewski, a Polish Jew working at the Institute of Mathematics in Warsaw and a contributor to this volume, has written of the problem of mutual misunderstanding. He admits that "most Poles do not recognize the exceptional character of the project to wipe out the Jewish people and either poorly understand or altogether ignore the Jewish significance of Auschwitz." But he likewise insists that people in the West, including Jews, simply do not appreciate the depth of Polish suffering at Auschwitz: "The historical fact is that the Nazis tried to crush the Polish nation; they not only introduced bloody terror but began to murder Polish elites and destroy Polish culture. The Auschwitz camp was used also for this purpose, and during its first two years of existence, *this* was its main function.''[11] I might add at this point that even Western Christians with extensive experience in Christian-Jewish dialogue frequently revealed insufficient awareness of the profound (and enduring) impact of the Nazi era on Polish national life. This generated a certain measure of hostility on the part of Poles to Western Catholic efforts at reconciliation over the convent controversy.

Beyond the question of Polish suffering at Auschwitz, Jews will also have to develop a heightened understanding of the constructive periods in Polish-Jewish history, for Jews went to Poland at times when many other European nations excluded them. A more sophisticated analysis of the multifaceted role of the large Jewish community in pre–World War II Poland is also required if we are to find our way through the current morass. Jews played significant roles in the fields of commerce, industry, law, and medicine even though they may have been somewhat more restricted in other social freedoms in comparison with the West.

Twentieth-century Poland saw the rise of a small group of Polish enthusiasts within the Jewish community together with a far larger group who supported Jewish nationalism in Israel (i.e., Zionism) and therefore were regarded by most Polish nationalists of the period as a hostile force. Also in existence at the time were a large block of Hassidic Jews who disdained both Polish and Jewish politics as well as a small, but influential, group of Jewish socialists and Marxists who were loathed by the Polish nationalists even more than the Zionists. In short, the Jewish community of interwar Poland was far different sociologically from that of Germany or France. The Jewish socialists and Marxists eventually took, for example, some important roles in the postwar Communist government, a fact that further intensified Polish-Jewish tensions.[12] Most Jews in Western Europe and North America are simply unaware of this complicated history of the Jewish community of Poland and its relationships to the broader Polish population.

WHAT NEEDS TO BE DONE

The first demand flowing from the crisis of 1989 is the need for rapid implementation of the 1987 Geneva accord. Perhaps some greater Polish input is necessary, but only within the framework of what was agreed upon by the original signatories. At this point, reports by the American Jewish Congress and the Oxford-based Institute for Polish-Jewish Studies indicate that Prime Minister Tadeusz Mazowiecki; the Polish minister of culture, Izabela Cywinska; and the leading Polish Bishops are not only firmly committed to rapid and complete implementation of the original agreement but also to the revamping of the camp memorial site itself in a way that will clearly show the uniqueness of Hitler's attack on the Jewish people within the context of his general onslaught against the Polish nation. The international community of Jews, Poles, and non-Polish Christians surely needs to support Polish leaders as far as they can. But they must be careful of public statements or actions that might harm the process. Both the American Jewish Congress and the Oxford Institute statements, for example, highlight the devastating impact of the Avraham Weiss incident on the constructive resolution of the crisis in Poland.

The convent crisis also illustrates the need to search for better ways to speak of the connection between Jewish victimhood and that of other target groups, especially the Poles and Gypsies. The present formulations offered by people such as Elie Wiesel, while they safeguard the uniqueness of the Jewish tragedy, do not adequately capture the reasons behind the attacks on the Gypsies and on the Polish nation. Many in both these groups simply died *because they were part of these groups* (not for what they did or said).

Finally, we must be careful about "numbers inflation" in speaking about Auschwitz itself and about the situation in Poland in general. Poles who try to place Polish suffering during the Nazi era on a par with that of the Jews by equating death by starvation and disease with the deliberate extermination of Jews in the camps are misguided. And Poles and Jews, as historian Yehuda Bauer rightly insists,[13] who deliberately exaggerate the number of victims at Auschwitz itself are in the final analysis only playing into the hands of the neo-Nazi revisionists.

There remains a good possibility that the intense controversy of 1989 over the Auschwitz convent may result in significant new advances in Polish-Jewish understanding and in an enhanced appreciation of Christian-Jewish dialogue generally. But this will happen only if we remain firmly bound to the original Geneva framework and if leadership asserts itself in all the involved communities which recognizes what ultimately is at stake—preventing the "killing of victims for yet a second time," as Elie Wiesel has put it, and crushing the seeds of political and religious fascism once and for all. If we fail, Hitler and his allies will be the only victors.

NOTES

1. Michael Novak, "To Honor Auschwitz's Catholic Dead—Move the Nuns," *Wall Street Journal*, 12 September 1989.

2. As quoted in the *American Jewish Committee Journal* (Spring 1987): 6.

3. Richard C. Lukas, *The Forgotten Holocaust: The Poles under German Occupation 1939–1944* (Lexington: The University Press of Kentucky, 1986), 38.

4. Jerzy Turowicz, Editorial, *Tygodnik Powszechny*, 22 June 1986. Quoted in *Christian Social Union Information Bulletin* 6 (June 1989): 30.

5. As quoted in Neil A. Lewis, "Walesa's View of Glemp Irks Jewish Leaders," *New York Times*, 18 November 1989.

6. Dawid Warszawski, "The Convent and Solidarity," *Tikkun* 4 (November/December 1989): 29.

7. Editorial, *Jerusalem Post* (International Edition), 7 July 1989.

8. *Tygodnik Powszechny*, 11 January 1987. For an English translation of this essay, with reactions, see Jan Blonski, "The Poor Poles Look at the Ghetto" and "Polish-

Jewish Relations During the Second World War: A Discussion,'' *Polin* 2 (1987): 321–58.

9. Ronald Modras, ''The Catholic Church in Poland and Antisemitism 1935–39: Responses to Violence in the Universities and the Streets,'' *Remembering for the Future: Jews and Christians During and After the Holocaust*, papers presented to an International Scholars' Conference, Oxford, England, 10–13 July 1988 (Oxford, Eng.: Pergamon Press, 1988), 183–96.

10. For some examples, see Shmuel Krakowski, ''The Polish Catholic Church and the Holocaust,'' *Judaism and Christianity under the Impact of National Socialism*, ed. Otto Dov Kulka and Paul R. Mendes-Flohr (Jerusalem: The Historical Society of Israel and the Zalman Shazar Center for Jewish History, 1987), 395–99.

11. Stanislaw Krajewski, ''Carmel at Auschwitz: On the Recent Polish Church Document and Its Background,'' *SIDIC* 22 (1989): 16.

12. Cf. Stefan Korbonski, *The Jews and the Poles in World War II* (New York: Hippocrene Books, 1989), 39–86.

13. Yehuda Bauer, ''Auschwitz: The Dangers of Distortion,'' *Jerusalem Post* (International Edition), 30 September 1989, and ''Higher Auschwitz Count Doesn't Aid Jews,'' *New York Times*, 23 December 1989.

4

Backward and Forward

Gabriel Moran

The year 1989 was not a good one for Catholic-Jewish relations. In particular, it was scarred by the controversy over the Carmelite convent at Auschwitz. A July protest at the convent escalated into an international incident. For weeks, newspapers around the world headlined stories about where fourteen Polish nuns should live.

For the past quarter-century, Catholic-Jewish relations have had their ups and downs, their movements forward and backward. But even that statement acknowledges progress over most previous centuries, when movement was either hostile or nonexistent. Still, it is depressing and confusing to be in the midst of attempts at understanding that seem constantly to go awry. Especially after this step backward at Auschwitz in 1989, we need to examine the case to see what there is to be learned. The convent controversy reveals deep problems about the basis of Catholic-Jewish and Christian-Jewish relations.

Many of the other contributors to this volume are more knowledgeable than I am about the history preceding the Auschwitz convent controversy, but I approach it as a classroom teacher who regularly has Jewish and Christian students in the same religion courses. There is still a large gap in each group's understanding of the other. I am much concerned that Jews and Christians often do not understand where the other's starting point is and how the two communities differ in the way they argue. So I wish to offer here an interpretive principle about the Roman Catholic church. I also wish to offer a personal footnote about the person who led the protest at the convent in July 1989.

A TWO-SIDED PRINCIPLE

The principle I will enunciate is two-sided. It is formulated from the Catholic Christian side and offered to Jews for their consideration. That is, it is a principle about possible Jewish misunderstanding of the Catholic church, and it can be put as follows: Neither underestimate the religious significance of the church's structure nor overestimate that structure's bureaucratic power.

In my experience, Jews generally understand Catholics better than Catholics understand Jews. However, what was central in the Auschwitz convent dispute was the Catholic church's structure. I am interested in Jews' understanding of that structure, not only because it would help Jews but also because Jews could help those Christians who wish to see certain important changes in the church.

Peter Steinfels, the religion editor of the *New York Times*, had one formulation of my two-sided principle. In an essay summarizing the controversy over the Carmelite convent, Steinfels wrote: "Catholics have also complained of Jewish tendencies to underestimate the papacy's religious significance and overestimate its bureaucratic power."[1] I would add that a religious or sacramental significance for Catholics includes not only the pope but many other people and places. A church building or a convent has a sacred character; nuns are considered consecrated, too. Some of these religious feelings may be mere nostalgia, soon to disappear. And the feelings are stronger among some ethnic or cultural groups. But the sensitivity for sacralized space and consecrated persons still runs deep, even among left-wing Catholics.

The spark for the 1989 collision at Auschwitz was a protest at the convent by Rabbi Avraham Weiss from Riverdale, New York, and a group of his students. The protesters undoubtedly came with peaceful protest in mind. That was not apparent, however, to workmen at the site, and they met the outsiders with some degree of force. Whatever else this exchange accomplished, it did get immediate international publicity and thus focused attention on the long-simmering dispute.

There followed statements fired from all directions. Not all Jews agreed with Rabbi Weiss, who had acted on his own without the advance support of any Jewish organization. But from the standpoint of most Jews and most U.S. Christians who spoke on the matter, the burden of the problem and the responsibility for a solution lay with the church.

The ensuing controversy included disagreement—so acrimonious and public as to be almost unprecedented—among some of the church's leading cardinals. It contained some disgraceful remarks by Poland's Cardinal Jozef Glemp in a sermon that echoed a centuries-old antisemitism. New York's Cardinal John O'Connor called Glemp's remarks "distressing" and "extremely harmful." Finally, the Vatican brought its influence into the controversy and pressured the Polish church to stand by the agreement it had previously made. The convent is again scheduled to be moved, although its relation to a planned center for Jewish-Christian conversation remains unclear.

The story of the Carmelite convent at the death camp goes back to 1984, when the convent was opened. At that time, there was little or no protest. Who would object to praying nuns? This is still the question that many bewildered Catholics ask, especially within Poland but also in other countries. Several other points about the story, however, tended to get lost along the way.

What upset Jews was a fund-raising campaign run by a Belgian foundation on behalf of the nuns. A letter suggested that the nuns were there to pray for the conversion of the Jews (conversion, of course, to Christianity). Some ambiguous language about the "enemies of Christ" worsened the situation. What puzzled me was why a group of contemplative nuns needed millions of dollars to carry on a life of prayer. Part of an answer to that question is that in this fund-raising and in subsequent discussions the convent was joined to a center for interreligious dialogue. Joining those two ideas may have seemed to be creative thinking, but this linking just caused further complications in discussing "the problem" and its solution.

Another key to the story, perhaps the most significant, was the erection of a large cross on the convent grounds. Jews have to understand the sacredness of this symbol and the good intentions behind the nuns' use of it. On the other hand, most Christians still do not understand what the symbol of the cross means to Jews. In particular, Christians need to grasp the inappropriateness of that symbol at Auschwitz.

In the middle of the Auschwitz flare-up, and for months afterward, there were many letters-to-the-editor asserting that Polish Catholics in great numbers, as well as Jews, died at Auschwitz. There is a truth here that Polish Catholics do not feel is acknowledged in the Jewish assertion of the Holocaust's "uniqueness."[2] In this Polish reaction, however, there has been an understatement of the particularity of Jewish suffering during the Holocaust. Each side needs to reformulate statements relative to the suffering of the other. That point takes me to one side of my two-sided principle: Care must be taken not to underestimate the particular significance of a place, including especially its potent religious dimensions, and to find appropriate ways to mark it with symbols. There is no inherent reason why there cannot be memorials that join rather than divide. However, an enormous cross cannot serve as a symbol to unite the two communities in their memory of tragedy.

In this context, it also bears remembering that Rabbi Weiss and his students violated the religious sensibilities of Polish Catholics. An essay by John Pawlikowski in *Commonweal*, while drawing the wrath of many Polish Catholics for his siding with the Jews, gently remonstrated against the Jewish failure to understand the sacramental character of the convent. For many Polish Catholics, that failure led to "violating sacred space."[3] Jews may not understand the emotional reaction of the Poles (some Christians do not understand it either), but Jews have to respect those feelings if there is to be progress.

THE BUREAUCRATIC SIDE

The second side of my two-sided principle—do not overestimate the church's bureaucratic power—probably poses greater problems than the first. My experience bears out Peter Steinfels' statement that Jews overemphasize the power of the church's bureaucracy, especially Vatican power. Many people who are not Catholics have a picture of the Catholic church as a unified whole with diocesan bureaucracy efficiently linked into the Vatican empire. This view can lead one mistakenly to conclude that a solution to a problem can easily be found if only the pope as supreme bureaucrat would issue an order. Once there was a saying: "Rome has spoken, the case is ended." Except in narrowly defined areas, the saying was probably never true. It certainly is not true today.

I am constantly amazed that many Jews are more interested than are Catholics in what the pope says. For example, in his weekly general audience of August 2, 1989, Peope John Paul II—significantly, he is himself Polish—made some typical unreformed statements on the topic of covenant: "We consider the coming of the Holy Spirit at Pentecost as the fulfillment of the new and everlasting covenant between God and humanity . . . sealed in the blood of Jesus Christ."[4] On other occasions, John Paul II has affirmed the continuing validity of God's covenant with the Jews. Which position does he really hold? I would guess that he believes—like the rest of us—many things that are not entirely consistent with one another. As a result, Pope John Paul II says things on various occasions that can sound as if he has changed his mind. Christians do indeed need to change their language, imagery, and thinking on the subject of covenant. That work is in the hands of thousands of scholars and teachers around the world. The transformation of Christian language in this area will take at least a generation or two. In August 1989, as on similar occasions, the Jewish reaction to the pope's remarks was as if he had issued a Supreme Court ruling which henceforth would bind every Roman Catholic. I cannot imagine that this particular papal remark had any influence on any Catholic scholar.

My perspective is that of a loyal Roman Catholic who reveres the symbol of the papacy and the religious sensibility that the pope can evoke. In the era of international television and jet travel, the significance of the pope has increased rather than decreased. Nonetheless, for tens of millions of Roman Catholics much of what the pope says does not interest us and some of what he (John Paul II or others) says we are likely to dispute. On a few issues of internal discipline, the pope could perhaps nudge things in one direction rather than another. But as Pope Paul VI found after issuing an encyclical on birth control, people do not change deep moral convictions because they are told to do so.

I would hope that Jews would understand this position of disagreeing with a leader's statements while remaining loyal to a tradition and hopeful of a better future for it. One learns to put up with things said by one's appointed leaders. When Pope John Paul II received Kurt Waldheim, I thought the timing was terrible but I could understand what the pope was doing as a head of state. However, the pope's particular words on that occasion—calling Waldheim a man of peace—seemed to me unnecessary and indefensible. The millions of us who felt that way did so not in disparagement of the papacy but, on the contrary, because we believed that such words weaken its religious significance. No institution these days, including the papacy, has credibility to spare.

The overestimation of the papacy and the Vatican was brought home to me a few years ago. A prominent Jewish scholar published an op-ed essay in the *New York Times* questioning the value of Jews' trying to talk with the Catholic church. The Vatican had just issued a statement that was terribly disappointing to Jews. Every time Jews think there has been progress, Pope John Paul II seems to say or do something that throws the conversation into disarray. The writer concluded: Why should Jews allow themselves to be set up this way? Why not just accept the fact that Jews cannot have a dialogue with the Catholic church at this time in history?

I wrote a letter to the *Times* expressing my sympathy with the author of the essay. I said that many Catholics also do not understand the Vatican's theology. But I expressed the fear that unwittingly the Catholic church was being equated with the pope and the Vatican. I offered the opinion that Catholics and Jews have plenty to talk about in places such as the United States. Being optimistic, I thought that eventually the pope and the Vatican would discover a new theology from such talks.

From previous experience with this kind of letter writing, I braced myself for the reaction. I expected a stream of abuse from right-wing Catholics for saying that the Vatican is less important than they think it is. I was totally unprepared for the reaction I did get. Nearly all the responses were from Jews, and the letters ranged from puzzled disagreement to furious outrage. What I had regarded as a simple reminder of a self-evident truth seemed to these letter writers to be fraud and deceit.

I am still puzzled by that reaction. Usually, if one gets such a response, it is possible to discover a sentence or a phrase that conveys an impression one did not intend. In this case, however, the target seemed to be the straightforward distinction I had made. To some writers I was deliberately confusing the issue and trying to excuse church failure on numerous issues. Other writers asked in genuine puzzlement what I could possibly mean by distinguishing between the terms "Catholic church" and "Vatican." That was a "distinction without a difference," said one writer.

What this small incident reveals, I think, is not merely that Jews and Catholics do not understand each other. More important is the fact that we lack a context of trust in which to offer explanations. Endless words flow back and forth, but it is not clear that we have settings in which real disagreements can be discussed and misunderstandings can be eliminated. There has been progress during recent decades, but mostly the contexts of understanding remain at the level of trust based on personal friendships. In the public arenas of discourse, there is not a funded experience of trust to fall back upon when the motives or wordings of a speaker are not immediately clear to the listener.

One of the results of hostility and tension is a crediting of one's opponents with a clearer plan and more power than they usually have. In regard to various bureaucracies of the Catholic church, I think that most Jews attribute more ability to church organization than it deserves. Bureaucratic secrecy can sometimes be a cover for frightening power and devious strategy. For the most part, however, bureaucracy hides ineptitude, laziness, and confusion. I suspect this problem is getting worse all over the world. Although television often exposes the confusion and incompetence, that exposure is not enough to make bureaucratic governments effective.

In particular, the Jewish emphasis on Vatican bureaucracy leads Jewish groups to go where they think all the power is located. Elias Mallon, a Catholic veteran of these discussions, pointed out that, if you go to the pope and cardinals first, where do you go if nothing happens? He noted that if you wish to move a convent, perhaps you start by dealing with the Carmelite superior of the convent.[5] Jews understandably know little of prioresses, superiors general, and conferences of major superiors. Perhaps the decisions about the Auschwitz convent still would have involved the ''top'' as they did, but the place to start was at the convent.

After the dispute settled down near the end of 1989, the prioress of the convent said that no one had yet consulted her. Cardinal Bernard Law of Boston had made one plea to the nuns that they simply move themselves, but the request was a public statement when the two sides were already frozen in their positions. A quiet approach to the nuns at a much earlier time might have been fruitful. Even if such direct consultation would have been unsuccessful in this instance, the basis for future deliberations might have been improved by showing respect for the local community's potential for action.

When trying to change an authoritarian system, it always seems most realistic to go right to the top. The drawback is that even if the decision is the desired one, the procedure has reinforced the power arrangement of the institution. My comments are not condescending instruction to Jews on how to interact with the Catholic church. Rather, I am making a plea to Jews that they help to change the church in its fundamental power structure. I know that this is asking a lot. We all have plenty to keep us busy in our own institutions. But I am presuming that Jews do not wish to spend their energies on new convent controversies every two years.

I am aware that throughout most of church history the papacy was often the defender of Jewish rights against local Catholic bigotry. That is a large part of the reason why Jews were so disappointed in the actions of Pope Pius XII and why Jews still look to the papacy whenever conflicts with the church arise.[6] I grant that it is still the pope's job to condemn Catholic bigotry; modern means of communication give him quick access and effective forums to do that job. Vatican bureaucracy, however, is a different story. Neither the pope nor any body of cardinals, archbishops, or bishops is very effective in organizational matters.

I do not expect any great improvement in efficiency and effectiveness in coming years, but I do not think that this is bad news for most Catholics and Jews. The Catholic church is rebalancing itself, filling in the institutional structure it lacks on local, regional, and national levels. There is no automatic guarantee that such a church will be easy for Jews to live with. Nonetheless, that form of Christian life would offer more ordinary means for creating a fund of trusted experience in which disputes would be handled with ordinary civility, quiet understanding, and intelligent compromise.

A PERSONAL FOOTNOTE

My personal footnote about the protest incident at the Auschwitz convent concerns Rabbi Avraham Weiss. I feel compelled to offer a word of defense to balance the harsh criticism he received. My defense is not of the particular tactic he used but of his personal motivation. I have known Rabbi Weiss—"Avi" to all his friends—for more than ten years. He was my student in half a dozen graduate courses. He has also taught for me on several occasions. I used to say that after a class session with Avi in the room I felt like I had been in a wrestling match. That was said with affection, not complaint. Our wrestling with ideas was never hostile or uncivil. I never took it as anything other than a passion for truth.

I also got to know Avi outside the classroom setting. I marveled at the energy he brought to work in his congregation. A new synagogue was built, and the size of the congregation rapidly expanded. Avi was keen on issues of justice (for example, those pertaining to feminism) that took both courage and political skill. I have attended services in his synagogue and celebrated Passover at his dinner table.

The press tended to play the July 1989 incident at Auschwitz as a case of religious defenders and secular attackers. It is true that Christians usually enter into discussions with Jews for "theological" reasons; Christians need Jewish religious ideas to make sense of Christianity. In contrast, Jews have usually had political interests in talking to Christians; the chief end in view is survival in an alien world. This theological-political contrast, however, can be overplayed. *Newsday*, for example, said mistakenly that the problem of the nuns' praying at Auschwitz was that Christians believe in a life hereafter and Jews do not—as though only Christians pray in memory of their dead.

I simply wish to state that Rabbi Weiss is one of the more spiritual people I know. Whether Christian, Jewish, or from other religions, students are struck by his profound religious sense when he explains his Orthodox Jewish belief and practice. He combines a life of prayer and social activism. He went to Bitburg, Germany, in 1985 to confront President Ronald Reagan, but, with a small group, he spent the night before praying in that German military cemetery where members of the Waffen-SS are buried. He disrupted traffic one week on the east side of Manhattan, but he did so by the ascetic practice of fasting in front of the Soviet embassy. He has been chained to the gate of the White House and has been a thorn in the side of pompous politicians on both the right and the left.

The Auschwitz incident, in other words, was not a one-time stunt. It was consistent with a spirituality that flows naturally into courageous activity. And there is no reason for not bringing in the news media to help one's cause. Rabbi

Weiss's activities have included ecumenical cooperation with Roman Catholics. Some of his harsh remarks about church officials, as well as his pending suit against Cardinal Glemp, are not born of an anti-Catholicism.

Several Jewish organizations condemned Rabbi Weiss's action because it was an individual venture without organizational backing. I am not trying to intervene in that disagreement. My word of defense is for the person I know and what I am sure was good faith in the attempt to move in a positive direction. As the event played out, it was easy to find grounds for criticism. Rabbi Weiss and his students miscalculated; then their attackers overreacted. I have tried to suggest above some of the reasons why such misunderstandings from both sides continue to occur.

I would guess that Rabbi Weiss thinks the project was successful. Undeniably, there was suddenly movement where there had long been stasis. To my way of thinking, the price in added bitterness was too high to pay for the resulting action. But I also think that well-intentioned people can genuinely disagree on the wisdom of such tactics. What I am certain of is that we need to develop better means of exchange. Otherwise incidents of conflict are likely to generate even more heat than Rabbi Weiss's aggressive but nonetheless restrained action.

NOTES

1. *New York Times*, 10 October 1989.
2. See Gabriel Moran, "Is the Holocaust Unique?" *Journal of Ecumenical Studies* 26 (Winter 1989): 211–16.
3. John Pawlikowski, "A Sign of Contradiction," *Commonweal*, 22 September 1989, 485–88.
4. *New York Times*, 13 August 1989.
5. Elias Mallon and Leon Klenicki, "Close Enough to Step on Toes." *Commonweal*, 6 October 1989, 521–26.
6. Yosef Yerushalmi, "Response to Rosemary Ruether," in *Auschwitz: Beginning of a New Era?*, ed. Eva Fleischner (New York: KTAV, 1977), 97–107.

The Struggle for Civility: The Auschwitz Controversy and the Forces Behind It

Michael Berenbaum

In the end civility and interfaith understanding triumphed—but only in the end. The recent controversy surrounding the convent at Auschwitz demonstrated how thin is the veneer of civility that masks fermenting religious differences, yet how deeply invested we are in preserving that facade because we recognize that we cannot deal with what lies underneath.

John Cuddihy has written persuasively about the role of American religion and the requirements of a pluralistic culture. In his work *No Offense*, Cuddihy argues that the rules of interreligious life are that we may not say in public what we believe in private lest we offend other faiths.[1] Thus Protestants cannot insist, "there is no way to the Father save through the Son." (When the Reverend Bailey Smith made such a statement a few years ago, he was immediately sent on an Anti-Defamation League sponsored trip to Israel and came back repentant, that is, well tutored in the decorum of mainstream religious life.) Catholics may not utter in public what was so commonly shared in the past: "there is no salvation outside the Church." Nonorthodox Jews outside of the State of Israel confine their affirmations of chosenness to synagogue ritual and to those secular mutterings that preserve status without insulting or demeaning others.[2]

Even religious teachings have been changed in order to reflect the culture of civility. *Nostra Aetate*, the earth-shaking pronouncement of Vatican II, clearly reflected the triumph of civility. A generation earlier, John Courtney Murray for the Catholics and Mordecai Kaplan for the Jews became the apostles of civility, radically reconstructing their own religious traditions in order to conform to the requirements of modern, pluralistic culture. Elsewhere, Cuddihy reminds us that civility can be an ordeal; much must be masked, much must be pasted over, even more must be left unsaid.[3]

The culture of civility has triumphed institutionally. The various bureaucracies of church and synagogue are meticulous in observing its requirements. In large forums and textual pronouncements, in published pieces and public broadcasts, no offense is given. But if such a culture has triumphed among the church and synagogue elite, its roots in folk religion—among the populace—are not deep, especially not among the most devout.

The events surrounding the Auschwitz controversy are well known; they need not be repeated here, at least not in detail. An agreement was worked out between European Jewish leaders and four cardinals of the church (Cardinal Godfried Danneels of Brussels, Cardinal Albert Decourtray of Lyons, Cardinal Jean-Marie Lustiger of Paris, Cardinal Franciszek Macharski of Cracow)—in fact, eighteen parties signed the original agreement—calling for the moving of the Carmelite convent outside the gates of Auschwitz to an interreligious center a kilometer or so down the road. The agreement was signed but not implemented.

ENTER THE RADICALS

As is well known Rabbi Avraham Weiss, the Riverdale, New York, Orthodox rabbi and veteran protester, who is well to the fringes of the Jewish establishment, led a demonstration at the Auschwitz convent. His words were words of peace, his deeds were deeds of confrontation. Once Weiss moved the conflict from the board rooms to the streets, events got out of hand. Weiss and his fellow demonstrators were beaten up by workers at the convent. Their presence on the sacred grounds of the convent was misunderstood by those who had *not* been trained in the culture of civility, and the mythic process began. Even in the era of television, when the protest was public and available, stories were told misrepresenting and distorting what had happened. They soon took on a life of their own, gaining widespread credibility. The state-sponsored Polish Press Agency described the protesters as "aggressive . . . invaders destroying the flowers that the nuns had planted." Only after a local paper published an accurate report of the peaceful protest was the initial press dispatch amended.[4] "We come in love and peace, said Rabbi Weiss" was the headline. Nevertheless, Weiss was viewed as attacking the convent, as threatening the nuns, as coming to murder them— echoes of earlier antisemitic myths deep within the traditions of the early church fathers, even if not widely preached today.[5]

Buffeted by myth and misinformation, the radicals silenced the moderates and suddenly the conflict threatened to undo twenty-five years of important ecumenical progress. What had been left unsaid was all of a sudden introduced into public discourse, and everyone became uncomfortable. Cardinal Macharski, the archbishop of Cracow, announced that he was abandoning plans to construct an interfaith center in protest at Weiss's protest. "Such attitudes and actions make it impossible for me to continue to construct the center."[6] Left unsaid by the cardinal of Cracow was why the initial agreement was not honored before the protest. The radicals came to dominate the monologues, and the facade of civility was ruptured.

Latent tensions surfaced. For example, the Jewish community has been deeply concerned about preserving the uniqueness of the Holocaust and the centrality of the Jewish experience under Nazism. In the United States, this issue had once threatened to break apart the President's Commission on the Holocaust. It had been a public controversy among two distinguished survivors, Elie Wiesel and Simon Wiesenthal. It is also part of the rivalry between New York's Museum of the Jewish Heritage and the United States Holocaust Memorial Museum; the former museum advertises itself as the lone repository of Jewish memories outside of Yad Vashem (as if the U.S. memorial is not a place where the Jewish tragedy will be remembered). The Jewish community has also been deeply suspicious of Roman Catholic efforts to discover—some would say invent—a tradition of Roman Catholic martyrdom in the Holocaust. Periodically there would be some controversy in the papers over one issue or another: over the beatification of Edith Stein (did she perish as a Catholic martyr or as the daughter of Jewish grandparents?); Pope John Paul II's holding a mass at Auschwitz in 1979 and not once mentioning the Jews; or the mural at the Sobibor church, which depicts the Holocaust as a crucifixion of Christ without any mention of Jews. Sobibor was a death camp where Jews constituted more than 95 percent of the murdered.

Once the controversy of the convent at Auschwitz erupted, all of these suspicions and angers were brought to the surface and the rage of the Jewish community could not be contained. Lurking behind all of these suspicions was lingering rage at the Vatican for its well-documented inaction during the Holocaust.

Even then, the culture of civility was still preserved. Euphemisms were used and the central issue could not be addressed. It was argued that "Auschwitz is holy to all people, no single faith could predominate," or that "Auschwitz was a place devoid of God's presence and should deliberately remain so." No one dared to confront the central issue of why the cross at Auschwitz was so offensive a symbol to Jews; no one dared to, because the controversy ensuing might destroy twenty-five years of interfaith cooperation. Yet clearly this was at the core of Jewish objections. Jews intuitively felt that the perpetrators of the Holocaust were Christians—Christians who may have defied the teaching of their tradition or who may have understood and been willing to act upon the undercurrent of Christian antisemitism that has been so central a part of Christian teachings. Clearly, as Franklin H. Littell, A. Roy Eckardt, Rosemary Ruether, and so many others have argued, the Holocaust could not have happened without Christianity and without the culture of the cross and its imperialistic designs on heathen cultures. This sensibility was deeply felt but could not be articulated in public, so it festered in private.

Furthermore, the very symbol of the cross towering over Auschwitz—representing the murder of an innocent Jew, which has transcendent meaning to more than half a billion people—was perceived as provocative to Jews, who experience an antitranscendent meaning in the murder of 6 million innocent Jews by the very same culture that reveres that one crucified Jew. Helen Fein has convincingly demonstrated that we must take seriously the role of Christian culture in the murder of Jews. There is a direct correlation between the religious piety of the country and the percentage of Jews killed in that country during Nazi occupation. The more devout the religious practice, the greater the percentage of Jews that were killed.[7]

With civility breached, the wolves could come out of the closet. Patrick J. Buchanan, the syndicated conservative columnist, used the controversy surrounding Auschwitz to free himself of inhibitions that constrained his complaints against the Jews, against Israel, against Yitzhak Shamir, whom he recalled was a Stern Gang terrorist. Buchanan lamented Catholic taxes going to pay for aid to Israel. Naturally, he went for the jugular. He also defended the behavior of Pope Pius XII, asserting as facts claims convincingly rejected by contemporary scholars. But the real targets of his animus were the contemporary church leaders who had toned down the faith in order to speak to the broader society. Buchanan clearly wanted to turn the clock back to pre–Vatican II Catholicism and to abandon the culture of civility. He deftly changed the topic. "Catholics Under Siege," he wrote. The target of his anger was clearly the culture of civility.

To Orthodox Catholics, the demand we be more sensitive to the Jewish concerns is become a joke . . . If U.S. Jewry takes the clucking appeasement of the Catholic cardinals as indicative of our submission, it is mistaken . . . Be not afraid, your eminence; just step aside, there are bishops and priests ready to assume the role of defender of the faith.[8]

Radicals drove the moderates from the news; they always do. Every journalist knows that "Dog bites man" is not news. "Man bites dog" is news. Hundreds of statements of interreligious understanding and mutual respect, dialogues and discussion cannot command the attention of the press, but one juicy incident, one attack, one instance of incivility commands massive attention.

Roman Catholic leaders were later to complain that they did not know that Rabbi Weiss was a fringe leader and not a mainstream figure. Indeed, at the height of the controversy the failure of the organized Jewish community to deal with the demonstration gave the impression to Jews and non-Jews alike that Rabbi Weiss was acting on behalf of the American Jewish community. Jewish organizations could not disown the demonstration after the protesters were attacked and after the antisemitic malice that was hurled against the demonstrators in the Polish press.

Yet, at several points during the controversy, responsible leaders of mainstream organizations offered to mediate the dispute, to call all sides together, and to seek an equitable solution. Their calls not only went unheeded, but unreported. For example, Miles Lerman, chairman of the United States Holocaust Memorial Council's International Relations Committee, spoke at Auschwitz on August 20, 1989, at the height of the controversy. In his audience were two Polish cabinet ministers and four members of the U.S. Senate Foreign Relations Committee, a former U.S. ambassador to the United Nations, and a former secretary of labor. He offered American backing for a resolution of the conflict. Lerman proposed "a meeting of the highest caliber with the representatives of the Vatican, the Polish prelates, France and the United States—to meet with the most respected spiritual and political leaders of the world Jewish community . . . to break the impasse . . . and to arrive at a logical and just resolution."[9] His effort went unreported. His words were of mediation and mutual understanding. That's not news. Similarly Kazimierz Smolen, the director of Auschwitz Memorial and himself a survivor of the concentration camp, appealed for the church to carry out the original agreement to relocate the convent. His words, too, were unheeded.

Sometimes radicals force a solution, for they reveal the full implications of what will happen if no solution is imposed. I am certain that such was the case when Cardinal Jozef Glemp, the Polish primate, made his antisemitic statements. Cardinal Glemp's words indelibly reinforced all the stereotypes of the Polish antisemitism that both church leaders and Polish officials have been working hard to combat. The motifs were all too familiar: an international cabal of Jewish influentials controlling the media and business, dominating the United States, and subverting the church from its real mission. Harsh as they were, Cardinal Glemp's statements proved singularly helpful in forcing a solution. He demonstrated the full consequences of letting the crisis linger. It would have undone the work of the post-Holocaust generation in achieving interreligious tolerance and understanding—the very hallmarks of civility.

ALL POLITICS IS LOCAL

Thomas P. "Tip" O'Neill, the former speaker of the U.S. House of Representatives said, "All politics is local." The controversy surrounding the convent was not only religious but also political, and the politics was not only global but also significantly local.

For example, the reason the initial agreement between the European Jewish leaders and the four Roman Catholic cardinals was not carried out was that the archbishop of Cracow, in whose diocese the convent was located, seemingly violated Polish national feeling by not consulting with his Polish colleagues and the primate of Poland before coming to the agreement. He was perceived as "kowtowing" to foreign cardinals and influential Jews and not paying sufficient attention to Polish national interests. Cardinal Glemp inserted himself into the dispute as the Polish primate, a first among equals, against his more regional rival. Local politics were to play a dominant role.

So too, on the morning after Cardinal Glemp's statement he was attacked by the Solidarity paper, which unequivocally condemned his remarks. Informed Polish sources indicated that the vehemence of the attack against Cardinal Glemp had nothing to do with the substance of his statements. Solidarity officials were still angry over the support he had offered to the Polish Communist regime when martial law was imposed in 1981. They did not get mad; they got even, by abandoning the primate in his moment of crisis and thus signaling to the world press that the cardinal was a reactionary figure who could be swept aside during turbulent times.

Cardinal John O'Connor of New York and Cardinal Bernard Law of Boston, Catholic leaders in cities with influential Jewish communities, were also quick to respond to the sensibilities of their local communities. They pushed toward a solution. Their influence was limited because they suffered from a case of "clientitus," that is, being overly responsive to local pressures.

Cardinal Glemp's statements set off a series of local crises. Months before the controversy, Cardinal Glemp had been invited to visit Chicago in September 1989 by Cardinal Joseph Bernadin of Chicago. More Poles live in that city than any place other than Warsaw. Had Cardinal Glemp come to Chicago, demonstrations would have ensued and the cardinal would have had to appear before hostile American media where other "equally unfortunate" statements would surely be made. At best, the Polish primate would require extensive coaching. At worst, his visit would prove a disaster. Cardinal Bernadin, a gentle man well schooled in the ways of American religion, could not be pleased by the dilemma he faced, nor were the cardinals of the other cities that the Polish primate was scheduled to visit—Detroit, Chicago, Milwaukee, and Washington, D.C.

The Jewish community of Chicago faced an equally painful problem. Living in the most ethnic of American cities, it had become very skilled at negotiating the labyrinth of interethnic politics. Left to its own devices, it could express its displeasure at Cardinal Glemp and the Auschwitz controversy without alienating the Polish community it had so tirelessly cultivated. But Chicago's Jews would not have been left to their own devices. Rabbi Avraham Weiss, who had been personally and falsely attacked by Cardinal Glemp, said that he would come to Chicago for a demonstration and a confrontation. In the confrontation between the Polish cardinal and the American rabbi, Weiss would enjoy the nearly unanimous support of the American Jewish community. He had achieved a measure of celebrity that was bound to attract the attention of the crowd. There was no way to control the situation.

In the end, Cardinal Glemp did not come to the United States. The timing of his visit was inopportune. After his remarks, the Vatican intervened and the rest is history. I suspect that when historians examine the records, they will discover that Cardinal Glemp's statements—and not the crisis that was looming—provoked Vatican reaction. Things had gone too far. Vital church interests in the ecumenical movement, in Vatican II, in the culture of civility, were at stake. It was time to cut one's losses and to bring the crisis to an end.

BUREAUCRATS AND THEIR BOARD ROOMS

At the height of the crisis over the Auschwitz convent, American Jewish leaders were deeply divided over the politics of organizational life. At stake was a Jewish organization few Jews had ever heard of, *IJCIC*, the International

Jewish Committee for Interreligious Consultations. Its membership includes the World Jewish Congress, B'nai B'rith, the American Jewish Committee, the Israel Interfaith Association, and the Synagogue Council of America, the latter an umbrella body of six organizations from the Orthodox, Conservative, and Reform rabbinic and synagogue groups. A quarrel had broken out among institutional bureaucrats in the various Jewish agencies over whether the World Jewish Congress (WJC) was playing too central a role in the interreligious dialogue and whether the other organizations were getting enough institutional mileage from their affiliation. Was the WJC not usurping the role traditionally played by the American Jewish Committee, a pioneer in interreligious activities? The Anti-Defamation League of B'nai B'rith and the American Jewish Congress clearly wanted to be part of the action. B'nai B'rith was not anxious to have its rival scion, ADL, usurp its honored place, and the Synagogue Council was wondering how all of these secular organizations could come to dominate interreligious dialogue.

Crisis or not, the war of the Jews continued unabated. A new organization was founded. Its launching was heralded by the usual public relations fanfare. It then went the way of many other organizations and disappeared from the scene. Nevertheless, the Jewish community was needlessly weakened by institutional rivalry.

The scandal of Jewish disunity could be dismissed as humorous or self-indulgent if it did not reveal a dramatic shift in power and responsibility in the Jewish community. A generation ago when the historic negotiations with the Vatican over *Nostra Aetate* were being conducted, the Jewish community was represented by Professor Abraham Joshua Heschel of the Jewish Theological Seminary. Behind the scenes, Heschel consulted with the spiritual leader of modern Orthodoxy, Rabbi Joseph Dov Baer Soloveitchik. Together they were quite a formidable team. Both had a charisma of person and the authority of learning that far transcended their institutional roles. They bestowed dignity on the offices they held, rather than deriving their stature from their titles. Both rabbis were well rooted in Jewish tradition and teaching. Both were concerned not only with immediate Jewish interests but with the long-term spiritual, cultural, and political well-being of their people. Neither was pushing a parochial institutional agenda. Neither was a fund-raiser. Heschel entered the portals of the Vatican without being overwhelmed by its power or history or overawed by the pope. He was the spiritual equal of everyone he encountered, and he represented a religious tradition that did not have to take second place to the great Roman Catholic church. Contrast this feeling with the butterflies in Golda Meir's stomach as she met with the pope for the first time. Meir described herself as astonished that a young Jewish girl from Milwaukee should be meeting with the Vicar of Christ. Certainly such astonishment "loaded" the meeting. So too, the various heads of Jewish organizations play inner institutional politics as they head for a papal meeting. They derive organizational status and support from their contacts with the Vatican, and thus they cannot make adequate representation on behalf of the Jewish people. Certainly, no personal criticism is intended as to the honesty, integrity, forcefulness, or motives of any individual representative. My point is structural—those who require these meetings for institutional purposes, those who derive their principal status from their office or rather than their person, are significantly less effective in their representative roles than the giants of a generation ago.[10] Woe to us, when bureaucrats replace authentic spiritual figures who can command respect for who they are and what they represent. The Jewish community is diminished by having all power pass to the institutional bureaucrats and their powerful financial backers.

INFORMATION AND TRUTH

Throughout the Auschwitz controversy, everyone was playing the numbers game. Truth was an orphan. Each party to the controversy rooted itself in the numbers of victims who were killed at Auschwitz. Four million was the figure most often repeated in the press. Four million soon became a sacred figure, yet the remainder of the sentence was all-important: Four million victims, more than half of them Jewish; 4 million victims, a preponderance of whom were Jews; or 4 million victims, many of them Jews. The figure of 4 million became a self-verifying figure; that is, journalists who saw the number in an earlier article, considered it a matter of fact and did not bother to inquire as to its origins.

Yehuda Bauer, the distinguished Holocaust historian of the Hebrew University, gave an interview to the *New York Times*, published on November 12, 1989, which challenged these figures. His interview was unoriginal. He had written a similar piece for the *Jerusalem Post* early in the controversy. For several years, Bauer has been speaking of 1.6 to 1.8 million victims of Auschwitz—1.35 million Jews, 83,000 Poles, 20,000 Gypsies, and 12,000 Soviet POWs. Bauer's interview was rooted in serious scholarship done by the French Jewish historian Georges Wellers, published a half-dozen years ago. Yet, so sacred had the 4 million number become by repetition in the press that Bauer's articles aroused immediate controversy. Survivors were upset that he was seeming to join the revisionists in diminishing the number of victims. Communal activists were appealing to the United States Holocaust Memorial Council, the Anti-Defamation League, and the World Jewish Congress, and local rabbis to intervene in the debate. Poles were outraged. So too, were Gypsies. The number 4 million was widely accepted without being rooted in fact or verified by history. It had gained credibility—not facticity—merely by repetition. We will hear the numbers invoked again and again in the future. Each time, truth will be orphaned.

Are we wiser now than in the heat of the 1989 Auschwitz convent controversy? I doubt it. However, those of us who work in the field of interreligious relations are more chastened. We know how much has been done to achieve interreligious understanding in the forty-five years since the Holocaust. We now know all too well how easily it can be undone. The roots of such interreligious understanding are shallow. Therefore, the task ahead is ever more urgent.

NOTES

1. John Murray Cuddihy, *No Offense: Civil Religion and Protestant Taste* (New York: Seabury Press, 1978).

2. Thus Charles Silberman refers to the American Jews as "a certain people," and John Cuddihy considers the debate over the uniqueness of the Holocaust as an attempt by Jews to confer status on Jewish identity in the absence of a religious legitimation for chosenness. See Michael Berenbaum, "The Uniqueness and Universality of the Holocaust," *A Mosaic of Victims*, ed. Michael Berenbaum (New York: New York University Press, 1990).

3. John Murray Cuddihy, *The Ordeal of Civility: Freud, Marx, Levi-Straus, and the Jewish Struggle with Modernity* (New York: Basic Books, 1974).

4. See Anna Husarska, "Malice or Misunderstanding Over Auschwitz?" *Washington Post*, 17 August 1989.

5. At the time of this writing, a libel suit against Cardinal Jozef Glemp, who accused Rabbi Weiss of wanting to murder the nuns, is still pending in the American courts.

6. John Tagliabue, "Polish Prelate Assails Protests by Jews at Auschwitz Convent," *New York Times*, 11 August 1989.

7. Helen Fein, *Accounting for Genocide: National Responses and Jewish Victimization During the Holocaust* (New York: The Free Press, 1979).

8. Patrick J. Buchanan, "Catholics Under Siege," *New York Post*, 24 September 1989. His syndicated column appeared in hundreds of papers under a variety of titles.

9. Report from the Jewish Telegraphic Agency, 22 August 1989.

10. One may speculate why Elie Wiesel did not lead the Jewish community on this issue. It could be that he was reluctant to get involved. It could be that personal charisma devoid of an institutional role can no longer propel one into a leadership position. Wiesel was the chairman of the United States Holocaust Memorial Council when he confronted President Ronald Reagan on Bitburg. It could also be the case that institutional representatives were reluctant to turn to Wiesel to take the lead on the Auschwitz controversy. Wiesel speaks from the authority of his own experience and his significant accomplishment. He is also "uncontrollable" by the institutions. Too much power would have to be ceded by the institutions to enlist Wiesel's leadership.

Part Two

The Psychology of Memory

6

The Controversy over the Convent at Auschwitz

Hermann Langbein

When 728 Poles were transferred from the prison at Tarnow to Auschwitz on June 14, 1940, the history of this concentration camp began. It would be one in a series where the Polish intelligentsia was to be isolated, tortured, and decimated. Less than a year after its June 1941 attack on the Soviet Union, all other restraints relaxed, the Nazi regime began "the Final Solution of the Jewish question," the precise name the Germans gave to the racially based, bureaucratically organized mass murder that followed.

There were not enough extermination camps in eastern Poland that were sufficiently prepared for this undertaking. In addition, the armaments industry needed an ever-larger work force. Therefore the Germans found it practical to select laborers from the Jews who were deported for extermination. Whoever was deemed physically fit for work was directed to extermination through work. Auschwitz was fully developed with this in mind.

Beginning in the spring of 1942, as the deportation trains headed to Auschwitz, able-bodied Jews were selected for labor. Those "unfit"—children, older people, the frail and infirm—were immediately escorted to the gas chambers. In this way, the character of the camp evolved: on the one hand, it became the largest of the extermination places; on the other, it became by far the biggest of the Nazi concentration camps. It was not until November 1944 that the mass killings by means of Zyklon B were suspended and the extermination units were dismantled.

When the extent of the mass murder from racist motives became gradually known to the world after 1945, Auschwitz became the symbol of the most extreme inhumanity of the Nazi system. Thus, all those who try to minimize or completely deny the culpability of this system attempt to cast doubts on the facts of Auschwitz.

I was a prisoner in Auschwitz for two years—from August 1942 until August 1944. During this period, the arrival of the deportation trains, the selection of the inmates, and the gassings were daily occurrences. In the hierarchy of the prisoners, which the SS had carefully determined, I stood as a German at the top, for Austrians passed as Germans in all of the Nazi camps. On the lowest level were placed those condemned to death by Nazi ideology's racist reasons—Jews and Gypsies in particular.

My fate cannot be compared with that of those in Auschwitz who had to wear the Star of David, but my life has been stamped by Auschwitz, and I feel myself duty-bound above all to those who are no longer able to testify. Therefore I do not need to explain further why I am not indifferent to the controversies that surround the convent. The building where it has existed is one I saw daily. It stood on "the other side" of the electrically charged barbed wire and was called the "theater building." I knew that canisters of the poison gas, Zyklon B, were stored there.

Already many years ago, the problems culminating in the controversy over the convent were becoming visible. In the fall of 1959, for example, I was asked to investigate the fate of Edith Stein. At that time, I was still the general secretary of the International Auschwitz Committee. According to the Nuremberg racial laws, Stein was defined as Jewish. She converted to Catholicism and entered the order of Carmelite nuns. The sister house in Cologne requested information, since a canonization process for Sister Stein was being initiated.

I was able to determine that Edith Stein had been sent to Westerbork (a transit camp primarily for Jews who were being deported from the Netherlands), along with her sister Rosa, on August 5, 1942, from the Carmelite cloister in Echt, Holland. From there, she was deported to Auschwitz on August 7, 1942. In Auschwitz she and her sister were deemed unfit for labor and were gassed. Edith Stein was fifty-one at the time, her sister fifty-nine. On the deposition of the Dutch Red Cross, it was certified that both had been detained "for racial reasons, and, indeed, because of their Jewish parentage had been deported and murdered."

At that time, the latter finding posed many questions for me. Later I read that Edith Stein had been beatified. I was not aware of her contributions to the Catholic church, and therefore the report of her beatification did not move me. Still later, however, I was to learn that an SS building at Birkenau had been converted into a Catholic church. In it was venerated an image dedicated to the Blessed Sister Benedicta vom Kreuze—the religious name taken by Edith Stein.

This shocked me, because Stein was not killed by the Nazis as a martyr of her Catholic faith. She was choked by poison gas because she was counted among those of the "Jewish race."

That cannot be discounted any more than the fact that the SS building at Birkenau, a place where the extermination of Jews and Gypsies was organized, had been refurbished as a church, while the original purpose of this building remained obscure to the unsuspecting visitor.

These things are known only to a few, for Birkenau lies some distance from the original camp, which is where most visitors to Auschwitz go. I also did little to make these things known more widely, because discussion of such topics can all too easily digress from the main issue of Auschwitz, namely, how far racist ideology was able to lead in the twentieth century.

But then followed the erection of the convent in the theater building next to the main camp, the controversy about it, the agreement to relocate the convent, and the nonfulfillment of the agreement in 1989. The latter brought widely known protests, and then Cardinal Glemp expressed himself in words that were just as evil as they were unmistakable, words which indignation was obliged to challenge.

With the protests appeared that which I wanted to hinder. Auschwitz was discussed and written about the world over—but not the crimes of Nazism, their causes, their scope, and the consequences that subsequent generations would have to bear. The topic was the convent, Polish antisemitism, and who had the principal claim to grieve and pray in Auschwitz.

I mean to say that emotions are not helpful in this controversy, and for that reason I want to remain as objective as possible. Auschwitz had a double character. It was the place of the greatest extermination and, simultaneously, the largest concentration camp. It is symbolized by two memorials: first, the Black Wall between Blocks 10 and 11 in Auschwitz I, where shootings took place continually through those years; and second, the ruins of the gas chambers and crematoria in Birkenau where, for almost as long, people were killed by poison gas.

At the Black Wall, members of all prisoner groups were killed by a shot in the back of the neck—Russians, Czechs, Gypsies, Germans, as well as Poles and Jews. There the largest number of victims were Polish. Those killed in the gas chambers, however, were above all those whom the Nazis had condemned to death because they belonged to a "race" which, according to Nazi ideology, put them on a level with vermin. The SS who discharged the Zyklon B at Birkenau were officially known as "disinfectors," and it was for their victims—Jews and Gypsies—that the gas chambers were built. There was, however, such a vast opportunity for mass executions. More and more prisoners—not only Jews and Gypsies—who had become unfit for work (for example, the sick who were unlikely to recover) were similarly taken to the gas chambers because they could handle a large number.

Who feels qualified to speak in the name of all the victims of Auschwitz? Jewish organizations, because the greatest number of victims by far were Jews deported to Auschwitz to meet a fate that no one, fortunately, no one can imagine who had not had to become acquainted with Auschwitz? I knew more than a few in Auschwitz who had to wear the Star of David on their prison garb, and who were without any religious connection, who had nothing to do with thoughts of Zionism, who as Communists were supported by other convictions. Not only Edith Stein; there were other believing Catholics there, too. Who feels legitimized by them? And in the eyes of the Nazis, Gypsies had a fate much the same as that imposed on those who wore the Star of David. Who speaks for them? Who is permitted, who can stay silent when the so fearfully well-known antisemitic vocabulary is used in reference to Auschwitz?

I have not forgotten that in Auschwitz there were Poles with important functions who themselves gave free rein to their antisemitic feelings—and for that were favored by the SS. And I got to know and treasure Poles who put their moral authority on the line to keep in check the antisemitic tendencies of their compatriots. They knew well how dangerous it was to intercede for someone obliged to wear the Star of David next to his prisoner ID number. For such intercession, Polish friends of mine were shot or hanged in the camp at inspection.

Who is the spokesperson for the Russians, the Czechs, the French, the Yugoslavs who never returned home from Auschwitz? People from twenty-two nations were prisoners there.

On invitation from the editors of this book, I am taking an official position on the issue that has evoked such a broad discussion: the controversy over the convent in Auschwitz. To the Poles, I want to say: Build churches and convents wherever you want, but not in the theater building of Auschwitz and absolutely not in SS buildings in Birkenau. Be considerate of others' religious feelings. I know from conversations and letters that Polish ''Auschwitzer'' (Polish survivors of Auschwitz) support this view. Even the museum director at Auschwitz, Kazimierz Smolen, who was himself a prisoner there and to whom we should be grateful for his decades-long contributions, has officially taken a position against the convent next to Auschwitz I.

To the Jewish organizations, I want to say: Demonstrate and protest wherever you consider it necessary—just not in Auschwitz. It goes against my grain to use big words, but, in my feelings, Auschwitz is a place where no demonstrations should take place.

To the Polish clergy, I would like to shout: Really hold finally to the 1987 agreement—no ifs, ands, or buts. It is up to them to put an end to this embarrassing discussion.

The meaning of the international memorial of Auschwitz lies in reminding us of the mass murders of the Nazis. It compels us to contemplate how they were possible, and why so few sought to restrain them. It compels us to contemplate the consequences, what can be done and what can be relinquished so that a repetition can be avoided. The controversy over the convent digresses from these issues. Who can wish that?

I became acquainted with some of the countless people who eventually perished in Auschwitz. They wore various triangles, which designated different types of prisoners. They varied from each other, just as all people vary. I would not rise to speak for those persons, apart from one thing: the necessary struggle against the roots, racist insanity, and wholesale condemnations of Nazi ideology. Is it one-sided for me to encourage us to concentrate on those for whom Auschwitz is more than a geographical concept? And should it not be possible to find one's self in the process?

Translated from the German by John D. Poynter and John K. Roth.

7

Auschwitz and Oswiecim: One Location, Two Memories

Emanuel Tanay

Auschwitz is the German name for the Polish town of Oswiecim, which is located about thirty-five miles west of Cracow. During World War II it was the site of a German concentration camp for Poles and an extermination camp for the Jews. The name *Auschwitz* became known worldwide as a symbol of Nazi death camps.

"The Poles feel that the Jews have stolen Oswiecim," I was told in Polish by Ewa Junczyk-Ziomecka, editor of the *Polish Daily News*. "The Jews feel that the Poles stole Auschwitz," was my response. Within twenty-four hours of this exchange, I had lunch at the Caucus Club in Detroit with Alfred Lieberman, a prominent Jewish lawyer. The conversation turned to the Carmelite convent in Auschwitz. Mr. Lieberman expressed in moving words his indignation that the symbol of Jewish martyrdom is being violated. "Poles are insensitive to our painful memories," was his final comment.

I told Mr. Lieberman about Oswiecim and its significance for Polish memories of the dreadful German occupation. "This is all news to me," he said with genuine astonishment.

The next day, December 20, 1989, I drove to Albion College to pick up my son, David, and his friend for Christmas vacation. During the drive back, the two young men joyfully declared that they were free from any type of work for the next two weeks. I commented that in contrast I had various obligations, including writing a contribution to a book on the Auschwitz convent controversy. Neither David nor his friend, who is not Jewish, had heard about the subject.

Within forty-eight hours, I had encountered significant elements of the Auschwitz convent controversy—emotional reaction, ignorance of historical realities, and indifference.

In 1960, the Cracow chapter of the Polish Medical Society began to publish an annual volume dedicated to "scientific studies of medical and related aspects of the Hitlerite occupation, Hitlerite prisons and concentration camps, among them the largest and most gruesome annihilation camp, *Oswiecim-Brzezinka*, which became famous under the name "Konzentrationslager *Auschwitz-Birkenau*" (emphasis added). The front page of each issue has the word "Oswiecim" printed diagonally in bold red letters linked by black barbed wire. The twenty-ninth volume was dedicated to the "thirty-fourth anniversary of liberation of the concentration camp Oswiecim-Brzezinka." It contained an appeal to physicians all over the world to contribute to scientific and humanitarian study of concentration camps. There was also a listing of the 644 articles published in prior editions—they ranged from "Consideration of the Psychology of Mass Murder" by T. Bilkiewicz, to "Medical Problems During Nazi Occupation" by J. Maslowski.

Why should scientific study of a whole era appear under the name of one camp? In Poland the answer is obvious: Oswiecim is a symbol of the German occupation of Poland, just as Auschwitz is the symbol of the Holocaust. Oswiecim is part of Polish consciousness. History and individual memories of World War II are inextricably involved with Oswiecim. I lived in occupied Poland on Aryan papers and remember that being sent to Oswiecim was a constant danger for Poles.

A careful reader of the many volumes of *Oswiecim* would never suspect that there were ever Jews in that camp. Jews are not mentioned in the hundreds of articles dealing with the experience of the prisoners of the Nazi concentration camps. Jews are conspicuous by their absence. In fact, one can say that, in general, the distinct fate of Jews under German occupation received relatively little attention in Poland until the 1980s. Meanwhile, in the United States and Western Europe the Holocaust became the object of tremendous scholarly and popular interest.

Ewa Junczyk-Ziomecka, who spoke above about Jews' appropriating Oswiecim, had visited that camp as an elementary school pupil and once again as a high school student. When she saw the piles of hair and spectacles on display, she believed them to be remains of "Polish martyrs." It never occurred to her that these items had been collected from Jews before they were placed in gas chambers. She knew little about Jews until she entered the university, even though she was born and raised on Francziskanska Street, which was once part of the Warsaw ghetto.

In 1987 I went to the Oswiecim-Auschwitz museum. I joined Polish- and English-speaking tour groups. I listened as the guides explained the meaning of various exhibits. The English-speaking guides talked about Jews. The Polish-speaking guides never did. The 1986 edition of the official guidebook to the *State Museum Auschwitz-Birkenau* published in Polish, English, German, and Russian, does not have the word *Jew* in it.

Marian Krzyzowski, editor of *Studium Papers*, a Polish quarterly published in Ann Arbor, Michigan, was born in the United States to Polish immigrants. As a teenager he was taken to Poland by his mother. They naturally visited the

Oswiecim museum. The young Marian asked why there had been no Jews in Oswiecim, and his mother corrected his perception. It seems to me, however, that Marian was right: Jews were not sent to Oswiecim; they were sent to Auschwitz.

Jerusalem is defined geographically the same way in Hebrew and Arabic textbooks, but it represents a different historical entity for Jews and Arabs. Oswiecim and Auschwitz are clearly not the same for Poles and Jews,* either.

The Carmelite convent was established in Oswiecim, a proper place for Polish nuns. The trouble is that Auschwitz, a death camp for Jews, existed at the same location. A Christian establishment at a site of Jewish annihilation offends memory.

The Auschwitz convent controversy centers on memory and memories. To cite only some of their dimensions, they involve relationships between two religions, coexistence of the two nations on the same soil, and victimization by a common oppressor in the same location.

Napoleon's dictum—geography is destiny—is confirmed by the Auschwitz convent controversy. Judaism and Christianity are inextricably involved by having originated in the same setting. Poles and Jews have lived together on the same land throughout the existence of Poland. Poles and Jews were inmates of the same Nazi facility that became a symbol of their martyrdom. The Auschwitz convent controversy is a nexus of these three sets of memories.

Catholic-Polish-Jewish problems, in particular, also involve more than memories. They have to do with identity and self-image. The Catholic church and the Polish nation are no longer identified with coercive evangelism. Hatred of Jews has largely ceased to be an official expression of piety and patriotism, and the few Jews remaining in Poland no longer have to adapt to oppression and persecution as they once did. Facing new realities requires change of beliefs and attitudes, but these needs should also alert us to the dangers of the psychic mechanism known as denial, which often produces questionable shortcuts from the past to the present. The Auschwitz convent controversy demonstrates the futility of denying the past as a method of adjusting to new realities. The amazing fact about this controversy is not that it occurred but that it took so long to erupt.

Like everything else in life, the attitudes of a majority toward a minority are in constant flux. In the last 200 years, the predominant attitude of Poles toward Jews has been hostility. During its short existence, interwar Poland considered the *Kwestja Zydowska* (the Jewish question) to be a crucial social problem. At the outbreak of World War II, antisemitism was a major sociopolitical force in Poland, and it continued to play a significant role during and after the war.

*Editors' note: From time to time, in this volume and elsewhere, a distinction is made between "Poles" and "Jews," as though one could not be *both* Polish *and* Jewish. For one explanation about the assumptions underlying such a distinction, see further, in this volume, the comments of Judith Hershcopf Banki, "Historical Memories in Conflict," chapter 12.

Occupied Poland was the site of extreme Nazi brutality toward the Polish population and the location of the death camps dedicated to implementation of the "Final Solution of the Jewish question."

The universality of religion among all nations and the variability of particular religious beliefs exacerbate conflict between nations. From the beginning, warfare based on religion has plagued humankind. Americans used to religious and ethnic diversity have difficulty appreciating the significance of religion as the cause of clashes between ethnic groups.

In the United States, Catholicism has been a minority religion and a promoter of interreligious tolerance. This is not the traditional role of the Catholic church in Europe, particularly in Poland. The significance of the Catholic church in Poland has no counterpart in the United States. The political power of the church in Poland has always been particularly strong. In interwar Poland, Catholicism was the state religion. Not only has the Polish sense of national identity been inextricably involved with Catholicism, but historically Catholic theology has been the ideological basis for hostility toward Jews, and the Catholic clergy has been in the forefront of antisemitic agitation in Poland.

Antisemitism falsely blames Jews for a variety of social evils—usury, capitalism, and communism, to mention only a few. Let us assume that Jews have made significant contributions to undesirable social developments. What should the world's response have been? The antisemitic answers have included the following:

1. Make the Jews suffer for their misdeeds. (Nongenocidal antisemitism.)

2. Eliminate the Jews from the society by assimilation, conversion, and expulsion.

3. Eliminate the Jews by killing them. (Genocidal antisemitism.)

The Nazis' antisemitism was consistent. As the Jews were the source of all evil, it was only self-defense to "exterminate" the Jews. The nongenocidal antisemites found this drastic solution of the "Jewish question" unacceptable. They agreed that Jews are evil, but as Christians they did not want to be associated with killing them. Nevertheless, the nongenocidal antisemites cannot escape responsibility for the Holocaust. The Holocaust could not have occurred without hundreds of years of "nongenocidal" portrayal of Jews as evil. Christianity cannot avoid responsibility for the Holocaust since it has preached for hundreds of years that Jews are wicked. It is no accident that the Holocaust occurred in Christendom and was carried out by many who would have identified themselves religiously as Christians.

Franklin H. Littell, a historian and a Christian theologian, makes explicit this connection between Christianity and the Holocaust:

The cornerstone of Christian Antisemitism is the superseding or displacement myth, which already rings with the genocidal note. This is the myth that the mission of the Jewish people was finished with the coming of Jesus Christ, that "the old Israel" was written off with the appearance of "the new Israel." To teach that a people's mission in God's providence is finished, that they have been relegated to the limbo of history, has murderous implications which murderers will in time spell out. The murder of six million Jews by baptized Christians, from whom membership in good standing was not (and has not yet been) withdrawn, raises the most insistent question about the credibility of Christianity.[1]

The Canadian Catholic theologian Gregory G. Baum expressed a similar view when he said, "What Auschwitz has revealed to the Christian community is the deadly power of its own symbolism."[2]

Antisemitism should be differentiated from dislike or even hatred of people who are different. The Irish have been the objects of bias, prejudice, and discrimination, but that is no reason to claim the existence of anti-Gallanism. The Romanians have intense bias against Hungarians and vice versa. The Poles have an age-old antagonism toward the Russians. The Germans for centuries have been contemptuous of the Poles. Yet inter-Christian ethnic antagonism is not the equivalent of antisemitism. Antisemitism is a view of the world (*Weltanschauung*). It is an ideology of evil that "explains" most social problems as being caused by the Jews.

From a historical perspective, Polish antisemitism needs to be examined phenomenologically. What were its manifestations and consequences? The significance of an agreeable relationship between Poles and Jews has varied depending upon the historical period of Polish-Jewish coexistence. For nearly 700 years, Jews have been highly dependent upon Poles. It was vital for Jews to be in their good graces or at least not to provoke their antagonism. Before World War II the attitude of Poles determined the quality of life for Polish Jews. During the war the attitude of Poles toward Jews played a significant role in survival for some; for the majority, Polish empathy would have eased the agony of the "Final Solution" imposed by the Germans. After the war, a sympathetic attitude would have eased the pain of the survivors and forestalled the murder of nearly 2,000 Jews in postwar violence on Polish soil.

Polish attitudes and behavior before, during, and after the war are matters of historical record. Before the war, Jews were persecuted; during the war, antisemitism was rampant. There was no collective empathy for Jews in our greatest hour of despair. Individual acts of heroic helpfulness do not contradict the absence of collective empathy for the fate of the Jews during the war. After the war, antisemitism continued and assumed murderous forms. As late as 1968, Polish citizens who had Jewish backgrounds were victimized by a vicious campaign. The Holocaust remained essentially unacknowledged in Poland until the mid–1980s. Blonski's 1986 article in the *Catholic Universal Weekly* is the first public expression of shame for the "un-Christian" attitude of Poles toward their Jewish neighbors.

As we enter the 1990s, Poles and Jews face each other in new circumstances. Poland is a country nearly without Jews; Israel is a country without Poles. In the United States, Poles and Jews have virtually no active involvement with each other. It may seem, therefore, that there is no need for Polish-Jewish dialogue. Nevertheless, the Polish-Jewish relationship has, at this point, both historical and psychosocial significance. That significance should not be underestimated. The majority of European Jews have some historical roots in Poland. Jews are part of Poland's past. The working out of the Polish-Jewish historical relationship is important for the sense of identity for Poles and Jews alike.

A major obstacle to Polish-Jewish reconciliation is the age-old problem of forgiveness. It is difficult for Poles to forgive the Jews for having been "the cause" of shameful Polish behavior. Guilt and shame are painful emotions that give rise to denial and resentment. Jews have difficulty forgiving past wrongs when faced with Polish denial and resentment. At the end of the twentieth century, the Auschwitz convent controversy is a rare practical situation requiring Polish-Jewish interaction. Like a couple divorced a long time ago, Jews and Poles relive their failed marriage and fight over the custody of a gravesite. The custody dispute cannot be resolved without reaching an understanding about the failure of the past union.

The nature and extent of antisemitism in Poland can be determined in a variety of ways. One way is to reconstruct what it was like to be a Jew in Poland before, during, and after World War II. What kind of expectations and experiences would a Jew have in those relatively short segments of history? "Before the war" begins in 1918 with the establishment of the Second Polish Republic and ends in September, 1939, with the invasion of Poland by Germany. The wartime segment lasts until the end of 1944 and the beginning of 1945. "After the war" must be divided into subsegments. The first period ends in 1946 with the Kielce pogrom during which forty-two Jews were killed. It is estimated that roughly 1,500 to 2,000 Polish Jews were murdered in the period immediately following the end of the war.[3] The second subsegment of "after the war" extends to the so-called "1968 events" when the "last Jews" were forced out of Poland. I put the phrase "last Jews" in quotes because some Jews remained even after March 1968. Alina Perth-Grabowska puts the second subsegment "after the war" into perspective:

How many people fell victim to the anti-Semitic campaign of 1968? A precise answer is very difficult to come by, since after 21 years party archives remain closed and only a few 'licensed' historians have access to them and even they have only partial access. . . . We don't know the scale of repression in the provinces where the situation was often worse than in Warsaw. However, the overall figure—20,000—for the number of individuals who left Poland as a consequence of anti-Semitic repression through mid–1969 is reliable. They left behind apartments, jobs, belongings, and professions. They were allowed to depart with only a limited number of personal possessions according to regulations governing those who desire to 'resettle outside the country's borders.' . . . They were also stripped of their citizenship, having to sign a renunciation. The waiting period for departure normally stretched to several months during which time they were avoided by past friends on the streets who often quickly ducked to the other side of the sidewalk.

... Those who were forced to emigrate typically did not belong to Jewish religious or cultural communities in Poland. They lived steeped in Polish matters, spoke Polish, and most often raised their children without instilling in them a sense of difference from "native Poles." Some of these children found out that they were 'different' only when they had to depart. And this was the cause of numerous family tragedies. Many Polish Jews changed their names or kept the names they adopted during the Nazi occupations. There were also many mixed marriages. And finally, there were those families from the intelligentsia which had for generations been Polonized. It turned out, however, that the documentation as to "who is a Jew" had been secretly maintained for years.[4]

In 1968, Poland, a country of 35 million people, had a small Jewish population. Most of them were not even identifiable as Jews. Their names were Polish, and they were thoroughly assimilated. Nevertheless, they were ferreted out as Jews, deprived of work, and forced to leave their country. Even when they went to Western Europe or the United States, some of these Jews remained thoroughly identified with Polish culture, including attendance at Catholic churches.

Ironically, the so-called 1968 events had a positive side reaction. They dispelled the myth of Jewish dominance of the Polish Communist apparatus. They also showed that assimilation, lack of which was frequently given as a cause of antisemitism, was not a solution. The cause of antisemitism in Poland is not the Jew but the antisemite. Antisemitism survived longer than the Jews.

The explanations for antisemitism advanced by some serious Polish commentators lack elementary persuasiveness and are often contradictory. Cardinal Hlond, then primate of Poland, "explained" (justified?) the 1946 Kielce pogrom, for example, as resulting from "overrepresentation of Jews in the Communist apparatus." On the other hand, Polish opposition groups claimed that the pogrom was instigated by the Communists to divert attention from a referendum held shortly before, which the government had won.

It is outrageous that a Catholic cardinal would try to excuse barbaric behavior by such flimsy explanations. The Kielce pogrom occurred after a number of murderous assaults on Holocaust survivors. These assaults were called to the attention of the clergy and other Polish authorities. Upon returning to Kielce, their hometown, survivors found no access to their homes and had to live in a group home—a two-story building at Planty Street 7. Two hundred of them occupied this small structure.

On July 4, 1946, an eight-year-old Kielce boy returned home after a three-day absence. He had visited an uncle in a nearby village. To avoid a beating, he told his parents that Jews had kept him in a cellar. It was assumed by parents and police that the boy was held at Planty Street 7, even though the building did not have a cellar. A menacing crowd gathered outside the building. Frantic telephone calls for help to police and church leaders produced no meaningful response. Men, women, and children were brutally beaten and killed. Jerzy Slawomir Mac comments instructively on the scene:

It is impossible to read these descriptions of the bestiality of a crazed mob, massacring old men, women, and teenaged children, without a feeling of terror, as before the greatest cruelties of war. Children were thrown from the third floor cheder to the street; the wombs of pregnant women were ripped apart; the bodies of the dead were beaten with stones, boards, and pipes. Due to the disfiguration of corpses, eight victims of the pogrom were never identified. One of them is remembered on the plaque on the common grave in the Jewish cemetery not by his name, but by his identification number from Auschwitz— B2969—tattooed on his arm.[5]

Jews were persecuted in Poland before and after the Holocaust. Polish behavior in relation to the Jews during the Holocaust, therefore, could not have been free of antisemitism.

Now I would like to pose a simple question: What did the Germans need from the Poles in order to achieve "the Final Solution"? Ideally, from the Nazi perspective, upon the German entry into Poland the Poles should have engaged in a massacre of Jews. This did not occur in occupied Poland in 1939, but when Hitler invaded Soviet Russia in June of 1941, Lithuanians and Ukrainians did engage in mass killing of Jews. Short of active killing of Jews, however, the Nazis needed noninterference from Poles with respect to anti-Jewish measures. Interference could take a variety of forms ranging from moral support of the Jews to armed resistance and widespread hiding of Jews. Ordinary citizens could provide moral support for the Jews or disapproval of Nazi behavior. It required heroism to offer active resistance.

As a generalization, one is on solid ground in saying that an overwhelming majority of the Polish population provided neither support for Jews nor active resistance against the Nazis' anti-Jewish policies. Mere moral support of Jews was disapproved of. Anyone who lived on Aryan papers remembers widespread expression of support for the resolution of the "Jewish question."

Such subjective impressions are confirmed by more objective sources such as the underground press, official dispatches of the commander-in-chief of the underground Polish army, and communications from the underground officials to the Polish government in exile. The prevalence of antisemitism among Poles during World War II has been recognized by fair-minded people. In a wartime dispatch, the commander of the Home Army, General Grot-Rowecki, cautioned against expressions of sympathy with the Jews in Poland because such statements "create the worst possible impression in the country and facilitate propaganda directed against the government. . . . Please accept it as a fact that the over-whelming majority of the country is anti-Semitic. Even Socialists are not an exception in this respect. The only differences concern how to deal with the Jews."

On the eve of the 1944 Warsaw uprising, when the majority of Jews had already been killed, the political emissary, Celt, upon his return from a mission to Poland, reported as follows to the Polish government in exile: "The government delegate asked me to inform you that according to him 'the government exaggerates in its love for Jews.' The delegate understands that such moves may be necessary for the sake of foreign policy, but he advises prudence and restraint. Both under General Sikorski and now, the government is too forthcoming in its philo-Semitism, because the country does not like Jews.'"[6] Czeslaw Milosz captured the spirit of indifference in his "Campo DiFiori" poem. Indeed for Jews, the practical implication of Polish antisemitism during the war was not absence of rescue efforts but interference with help and escape. I and my family never lacked Polish helpers. We needed only one at a time. Our primary problem was facing the countless people willing to denounce us if they suspected that we were Jews. The Germans got all the help they needed from Poles in their effort to exterminate Jews. This is a shameful chapter in Polish history that cannot be erased by shrill voices claiming "anti-Polonism."

Until the mid–1980s, the dominant Polish attitude toward the Holocaust has been revisionism of the first order. Poland did not acknowledge the Holocaust; therefore no need to refute it existed. There was no dispute that the Jews were killed by the Germans, but then so were Poles, Russians, and others. The annihilation of Jews did not become a reality for these Poles, because Jews continued to be a presence in their mental lives. If Jews no longer controlled retail business, they now ran the Communist government of Poland. Other Jews went to America where, it was imagined, they controlled industry, banking, and the media. The generation born and raised before World War II continued its antisemitic view of the world even after the virtual disappearance of Jews from Poland. The persistence of antisemitism in Poland after the Holocaust should not be surprising. Attitudes and beliefs will continue even when the object of these attitudes and beliefs has disappeared. As contrasted with religious anti-semitism, political antisemitism has existed in Poland for over a hundred years. The persecution and killing of Holocaust survivors after the war was not the bizarre activity of extremists. It continued a long and well-established effort to resolve the "Jewish question." The popular Polish term for Jewish survivors has been "Niedopalki." Although this colloquial term is difficult to translate, it means "those who have not been completely burned."

The Kielce pogrom of July 4, 1946, was not an isolated incident but part of widespread violence against Jews in liberated Poland. Jews the world over should demand from Poland the establishment of a commission to investigate the postwar persecution and murder of Jews in Poland.

Nazi oppression was a cataclysmic event in Polish history. Word-of-mouth, extensive literature, museums, and monuments commemorate those fateful years. For nearly forty postwar years Jews were nearly excluded from Polish memories of World War II. In the 1980s the postwar generation of Poles, free of the antisemitic past, rediscovered Jews and the Holocaust. In December 1989, my friend, Stefan Jagodzinski, sent me a newspaper clipping from the Polish town of Radom. A monument had just been unveiled in the city in memory of its 30,000 Jews killed by the Nazis.

A book by Richard C. Lukas, *The Forgotten Holocaust* (Lexington: The

University Press of Kentucky, 1986), focuses on the victimization of the Poles under German occupation from 1939 to 1944, and it is quite popular in Poland. One could also write a book entitled *The Second Holocaust* dealing with the effort to eradicate Polish memory of "the Final Solution of the Jewish question." The first Holocaust was the "extermination" of Jews; the second Holocaust, albeit unsuccessful, was the attempted eradication of the memory of the first one. Nowhere in the Western world has the denial of the Holocaust been as successful as in Poland and in Soviet Russia.

Poles have had great difficulty recognizing the uniqueness of the Holocaust. In Evanston, Illinois, during the summer of 1989, I visited with two prominent journalists from Poland. They were a cultured and refined couple. I enjoyed being a guest in their American home. "What brings you to Evanston?" they asked. I explained that I was attending a Northwestern University conference on the Holocaust. "After forty-five years," they asked, "is there anything new that can be said about the Holocaust?" I replied, "Yes! A hundred years from now scholars will be gaining new insights about the genocide of the Jews." With some embarrassment, my hostess observed, "You are right; we still study the Middle Ages." Like these journalists, most Poles have failed to recognize that the Holocaust is an "orienting event" for humankind.

The Holocaust is unique not because a certain number of men, women, and children identified as Jews were killed. The singularity of "the Final Solution" was declaring Jews nonentities. The rest was the mere technicality of killing them and disposing of their bodies. The annihilation process rendered Jews dead, nonexistent, even before they were killed.

In June 1944 a Jewish underground group from Budapest attempted to cross the border from Hungary to Romania. I was among them. We were arrested by Hungarian authorities and thoroughly interrogated. A sizeable file was created on each one of us upon completion of the investigation. We were then transported to the Gestapo headquarters in Szeged and, with some ceremony, turned over to the Gestapo. A box containing the investigative files was handed over to the Germans. When the formalities were concluded and the Hungarians had departed, the Germans threw the files in the garbage. We were ordered to yell out a count, whereupon the German noncommissioned officer reported to the *Sturmbann-fuehrer*, "fifteen Jews." Next we were placed in a makeshift prison to await deportation to a camp. The Hungarians who worked with the Germans did not comprehend the meaning of the "Final Solution." They beat us to extract confessions, they created files bearing our names and life histories. The Germans did not need the files, nor did they want to know our names. We were living nonentities to be disposed of expeditiously. The number of "pieces" mattered for logistical purposes only.

After the war, a sense of Jewish nonexistence persisted in Poland. The elimination of Jewish traces went on there until the early 1980s. The failure to acknowledge Jewish existence in life and death offends the memory of the dead and the living. In the last few years, Poland began to rediscover Jews. Books, exhibits, lectures, and monuments now acknowledge more fully their past and present existence.

Like those of individuals, the true histories of nations are rarely, if ever, glorious accounts of progress. Poland's is no exception. The treatment of Jews by Poles over the last few hundred years has varied from tolerance to oppression. Yesterday's virtues can become today's vices. In medieval times, Poles were criticized by the Catholic church for their tolerance of Jews. A papal encyclical was even devoted to this deviant Polish attitude. In the second half of the twentieth century, acceptance of diversity has become a virtue, and Poles are criticized for having been antisemitic.

Poles are justifiably proud of the democracy and tolerance which existed in Poland before the partitions of 1773–95. They are reluctant to acknowledge that interwar Poland was intolerant of minorities. Persecution of Jews was state policy and a national pastime. This aspect of Polish history should give rise to feelings of shame. Instead, the reactions have all too often been denial and blame cast elsewhere.

Whenever people are killed, there are feelings of guilt and shame. My interest focuses especially on the ways in which survivors of killing events engage in self-blame. In more than thirty years of psychiatric practice, I have examined hundreds of Holocaust survivors and at least as many Americans who were soldiers during World War II and the Vietnam war. In my forensic practice I have evaluated countless victims of crime, casualties of plane crashes, train wrecks, hotel fires, and automobile collisions. I do not recall a survivor or bystander of a killing event who did not experience feelings of guilt. Survival guilt is one of the most prominent clinical features in the treatment of Holocaust survivors. The presence of guilt and shame in Holocaust survivors and the absence of guilt and shame among perpetrators and bystanders of the Holocaust have not received sufficient recognition. After the war the culpability of Germans for the Holocaust was taken for granted by the rest of the world. The denials of guilt by individual Germans were presumed to be spurious efforts to avoid punishment or shame. There is little doubt now that an overwhelming majority of Germans who were adults during World War II did not feel (and still do not feel) guilt or shame.

The Holocaust bystanders range from those who had the opportunity to see the "Final Solution" being carried out to those who had occasion to know about it. Poles had the misfortune to live in the country where the Germans chose to locate the death camps. Poland also had the largest concentration of Jews in Europe—they constituted about 10 percent of the country's 35 million people. Among the bystanders, Poles were in a unique situation.

The presence of guilt among survivors and the absence of guilt among perpetrators and bystanders are a clinical and historical enigma. Survival guilt has been studied as a psychiatric phenomenon by Niederland, Krystal, and others. The absence of shame among the perpetrators and bystanders has been neglected by science and public opinion. The Auschwitz convent controversy is at least partly the result of a failure to confront the absence of shame among the by-standers of the Holocaust.

When reminded of past mistreatment of the Jews, the postwar generation of Poles, which neither adopted antisemitism as an ideology nor engaged in such mistreatment, feels itself unjustly accused. Remembrance of the past is experienced as an accusation in the present. This chronological confusion is the result of a failure to renounce the past explicitly. Jews should recognize, however, that behaviorally, if not completely explicitly, Poland has broken with its anti-semitic past. Visits to Poland, accounts by Jews of their recent experiences in that country, and encounters with young Polish visitors and immigrants to the United States convey the extent of the historic changes that have taken place in Polish attitudes toward Jews. An expectation of overt condemnation of the past may seem intellectually reasonable, but it is emotionally possible for only a few unique individuals. Meanwhile the behavioral changes should be welcomed.

In 1987, I visited Poland and wandered throughout the Polish countryside. In an unpublished account of my first visit after nearly forty-five years, I expressed satisfaction about being able to feel safe and secure in Poland. Mariusz Ziomecki, an editorial writer for the *Detroit Free Press*, seemed offended by this observation. He was troubled by the implicit expectation of Polish violence toward a Jew. Mr. Ziomecki is a young Polish journalist who came to the United States at a time of martial law in Poland. From the perspective of my past, the instinctive expectation of violence was equally natural. Imagine a neighbor, upon visiting your home, complimenting you for not being a hooligan.

A French historian said, "Tout comprendre, c'est tout excuser" (To understand everything is to excuse everything). Assuming that this questionable proposition is true, it is necessary to know what is to be understood and excused. An excuse should not be confused with justification. Neither is synonymous with forgiveness. Many a sin is forgiven even though it is neither justified nor understood. There can be, however, no forgiveness without acknowledgement of sin. The essence of a confession is the sinner's recognition of his or her transgression. That recognition entails shame. Shame is an emotion essential to civilized behavior. Gershon Kaufman makes the points as follows: "Shame alerts us not only to transgression but also to any affront to human dignity. By motivating the eventual correction of social indignities, shame plays a vital positive role. In the history of peoples, shame has always been associated with honor and pride. Even risking death may be preferable to suffering the intolerable indignity of shame."[7]

Shame is the emotional element in the concept of sin. *Whatever Happened to Sin?* is the title of a book written not by a theologian but by America's foremost psychiatrist, Karl Menninger. Without the concept of sin and the emotion of shame there is no conscience. The decline of conscience made the Holocaust possible. Antisemitism is a defect in conscience that Christianity has sanctioned for centuries. I doubt that many priests in Poland have been called upon to grant absolution for the sin of antisemitism.

Like the Bitburg affair (see this book's chronology entry for May 5, 1985), the Auschwitz convent controversy has been a memory crisis. It was belatedly discovered that the Bitburg cemetery had Waffen-SS soldiers buried in it. It has been belatedly discovered by the church in Poland that Oswiecim was the burial ground of millions of Jews. In view of Christianity's implication in the Holocaust, it is offensive to establish a convent on the grounds of the Auschwitz death camp. It is offensive to dedicate the convent to the conversion of "our errant brothers" and have it operate under the leadership of an antisemitic mother superior.[8] Better ways to remember the deaths at Auschwitz—Jewish and non-Jewish—can and should be found.

In 1943, Stefan Jagodzinski was a stranger to me, but his kindness and courage saved my life. In 1987, on a rainy November day, he and I visited Oswiecim-Auschwitz together. Stefan purchased flowers, and we took them to the execution wall where two of his brothers had been killed. A devout Catholic, Stefan prayed while I stood with him in silence. We then went to the gas chamber–crematorium area where my "brothers and sisters" had been killed. We wept together in both places. Stefan and I have attachments that no resentments, real or imagined, can undermine.

Poles and Jews have historical attachments and resentments. We are bound together by our best and our worst memories. We need to cope with our past, which is part of our individual and collective identity. As the Auschwitz convent controversy can teach us, memory offended is still memory shared.

NOTES

1. Franklin H. Littell, *The Crucifixion of the Jews: The Failure of Christians to Understand the Jewish Experience* (Macon: Ga.: Mercer University Press, 1986), 2.

2. Quoted by A. Roy and Alice L. Eckardt, *Long Night's Journey into Day* (Detroit: Wayne State University Press, 1982), 71.

3. See Jerzy Slawomir Mac, "The Kielce Pogrom, 1946," *Studium Papers* 13 (April 1989): 44.

4. See Alina Perth-Grabowska, "A Country Without Jews," *Studium Papers*, 13 (April 1989).

5. Mac, "The Kielce Pogrom, 1946," 46.

6. Quoted by Jan T. Gross in a 1985 lecture at Oxford University. The transcript is in my possession.

7. Gershon Kaufman, *The Psychology of Shame* (New York: Springer, 1989), 5.

8. In an interview (29 September 1989) at Auschwitz, Sister Maria Teresa, the superior of the Carmelite convent, expressed antisemitic views. See the *Polish Daily News*, 1 November 1989, and the Appendix to this book. She blamed Poland's misfortunes on Jews, labeled them "anti-Semitic" for their mistreatment of Arabs, and compared present attitudes of Jews to those of "Hitler and his henchmen."

8

An Interview, August 29, 1989

Elie Wiesel and Carol Rittner, R.S.M.

RITTNER: Frankly, if I were a Polish Catholic who suffered in Auschwitz or lost members of my family there, I don't think I would understand why you object to Carmelite nuns praying in Auschwitz for the victims of the Nazis. After all, you've often said, ''Not all victims of the Nazis were Jews, but all Jews were victims.'' How are we to deal with still unreconciled views about how the victims of Nazism should be memorialized?

WIESEL: First, you must know that I do not differentiate among the victims of the Nazis. All must be remembered. All are *worthy* of being remembered. But as a Jew, I cannot forget that among Hitler's principal goals was the total annihilation of the Jewish people. Six million men, women, and children were isolated, humiliated, hunted down, starved, gassed, reduced to ashes only because they were Jews. And I cannot forget that most of the victims murdered in Auschwitz were Jews.

How do we remember a tragedy of such magnitude? True, there is a problem about how to memorialize the victims of the Nazis, but this is not just a problem in Poland. Human memory is too weak to include so many faces, so many names. God alone can remember everybody and everything. To cheaply universalize the Holocaust would be a distortion of history. The universality of the Holocaust lies in its uniqueness. We must remember the particularity of the Jewish tragedy, without neglecting the suffering of others.

To build a convent on the invisible graves of Jewish people who were murdered in Auschwitz is wrong and offensive. Auschwitz is not the place for a convent. Convents should be among the living, not the dead.

RITTNER: But, Elie, why a Carmelite convent on the site of Dachau and not at Auschwitz?

WIESEL: Dachau was different. It was not primarily a death camp for Jews. Many anti-Nazis from all over Europe—resistance fighters, labor leaders, Jehovah's Witnesses, intellectuals, clergy, including many Catholic priests, and others—were imprisoned there, suffered there. Many died there. There were also Jews in the Dachau concentration camp, but almost always they were sent east, to the death centers.

True: in the beginning, Auschwitz was for Poles, Gypsies, Russian prisoners of war, partisans, others. But when we remember, we must remember the entire past, not only before 1941. Between 1941 and 1945, most victims in Auschwitz—especially Birkenau—were Jews. Nearly two million Jews were murdered in Auschwitz. To establish a convent there, where so many Jewish people were murdered, is simply not acceptable.

Please understand: I respect the Carmelite nuns. I respect their piety, their generosity of spirit, their intent. But since you mention Dachau and the convent there, let me ask you: I heard the Carmelite nuns want to build convents in all the camps, in Belzec, Treblinka, Sobibor, Chelmo. Is this true? If it is, I have only one word, ''scandalous''!

I believe in prayer, but not there. It would cause offense and suffering to too many people. This must not be allowed to happen.

Prayer should not offend others, it should help to console them. Surely, these nuns know that the way to God leads through other people, not away from them. Their work of prayer should be a witness to the living, not an insult.

RITTNER: What about the idea of establishing a synagogue *and* a convent at Auschwitz?

WIESEL: I am against it. No religion should build religious institutions at Auschwitz. Not a church, not a synagogue, not a convent. God is God. He listens to all prayers everywhere, from wherever they come. What's the matter with praying to God from five miles away, or ten?

Build the convent outside the area of the camp, as was agreed. Build it in the city of Oswiecim, but not in Auschwitz itself. Nothing should be built there which would further divide people. We have been divided enough.

RITTNER: Is Auschwitz a ''holy'' place?

WIESEL: I don't like to use the word ''holy'' when speaking about Auschwitz. It is a *special* place. A unique place.

If one speaks of Auschwitz as ''holy,'' it is because it has been sanctified by the victims, but there also were killers in that place. How do I combine the holiness of the victims with the unholiness of the murderers? How do I deal with the problem of God in Auschwitz? Where was He? Among the victims? Among the killers? And God's silence? Was He, or was He not silent? And— what about man? Where was his humanity? Why didn't their Christian faith serve as a shield to protect the SS men from engaging in such evil acts? Surely these are also questions within the question you ask.

RITTNER: Would you comment on the behavior of the Jewish students who climbed over the wall into the Carmelite convent courtyard?

WIESEL: I do not believe in bad manners, and I surely do not believe in violence. There are other ways. One does not have to offend someone's religious sensitivity to be heard. We must use words: write letters, use arguments, make speeches, talk to people. Surely, at some point, the nuns must listen to what is being said. At least, I hope they will.

RITTNER: What impact does Cardinal Glemp's words about the Auschwitz convent controversy have on Jewish-Catholic relations?

WIESEL: His words are unworthy of a "prince of the church." They are irresponsible. Cardinal Glemp's speeches have helped deepen the crisis. It's not only a matter of theology but of propaganda as well. What he said at Czestochowa is what antisemites used to say: That Jews control the media, that Jews want to dominate everything, that Jews set impossible conditions. And he went further. He said a "squad of seven Jews from New York" wanted to harm the nuns.

Can you imagine if fifty years ago, at the beginning of the war, a cardinal had said such things in Poland, when there were still 3 million Jews? There would have been pogroms.

That other church dignitaries in Europe, in the United States, and also Solidarity, which is, after all, a Polish Catholic movement, have spoken up, disassociating themselves from Cardinal Glemp's statements, is good and encouraging. It satisfies me. Still, I find it troubling that in 1989 a cardinal would make such statements during a religious service.

RITTNER: What about Pope John Paul II's recent comments that God's covenant with the Jewish people was broken by the Jews and is superseded by the Christian covenant?

WIESEL: Really, what does the pope want? Does he want us to convert? Then, let him say so, but he will be disappointed. We will remain Jewish.

We Jews have always believed there is more than one way to God, more than one gate open. We have had problems with the God of Israel, but never have we allowed someone else to interfere in our relations with God.

As for the pope's idea that the prophets of Israel came to preach conversion to the new covenant, that is totally wrong, and baffling. Do you think that Jeremiah, Amos, Habakkuk, or others wanted us to convert to Christianity? They wanted us to mend our ways. They wanted us to be *more Jewish*, not less Jewish. This pope wants us to be less Jewish, or to stop being Jewish.

The pope's remarks do not contribute to understanding between Jews and Christians. After Pope John XXIII's spirit, Pope John Paul II seems to be going backward.

RITTNER: What practical steps can Catholics in the United States take to repair Jewish-Catholic relations?

WIESEL: We must deepen our friendships. We must continue to build bridges of understanding among ourselves and strengthen those that exist. We cannot wait for the initiative to come from above. We must create a foundation from below. And we must find ways to work together, to show respect for one another.

Catholics who are offended by the comments of certain church officials should make their views known. Support those cardinals, bishops, and others who have spoken for respect and understanding. And we Jews should let our friends and allies in the Catholic church, and in Poland, know how grateful we are.

Catholics must understand Jews *as Jews*, respecting our tradition and beliefs. Priests, and rabbis too, should preach to encourage understanding and respect. Teachers should teach in the same way. And Christians must respect Jewish sensitivity and memory about the victims of the Holocaust.

RITTNER: Given all the problems facing humankind, where on the list of priorities do you place the controversy over the Auschwitz Carmelite convent?

WIESEL: No people can live alone today, neither Jews nor Christians. The damage done was done to us all. The dangers that face us, face us all. But right now, for Jews, and I think for Catholics, too, the controversy over the convent is a priority, because it is so full of tension and anger. If it continues, it could deepen beyond repair, and we can't allow that to happen.

Of course there are other problems, other priorities which need our attention: Epidemics. Famine. Terrorism. Lebanon, an anguished country committing suicide. Apartheid. In our own country, the ugly face of racism. Refugees. Torture. Drugs. AIDS. Children beaten and killed. Fanaticism. And always the somber threat of nuclear annihilation.

What is so agonizing is that we live in a time when there is more than one *number one* priority. We cannot ignore any of them. And yet, for Jews, the events of the past weeks and months in Poland remind us of other words, other events, still vivid in our memories. We must find a way to resolve the crisis between Catholics and Jews, without neglecting the needs of our anguished world. It is up to us, after all, to prove that humanity's fate is not sealed, that everything is still possible.

9

The Controversy over Carmel at Auschwitz: A Personal Polish-Jewish Chronology

Stanislaw Krajewski

Being a Polish Jew in Warsaw—a Jewish Pole and not just a Jew from Poland—since my birth after World War II, I could not help feeling that the Auschwitz convent controversy was aimed at me personally.[1] The culmination of the controversy constituted a series of blows to the relative stability of my doubly focused identity and also to the modest achievements of the work of reconciliation and mutual understanding in which I have taken part. Not surprisingly, I found myself explaining to one side the point of view of the other. This has been an extremely difficult job, because the controversy amounted to something like a war. But who was fighting with whom? Jews with Catholics? Christians with Jews? Or, even worse for me, Jews with Poles? The fronts have been many and mixed, which does not make it easy atop the barricades.

Fortunately, I share this position with many other people: Polish Jews similar to myself, Polish-Catholic intellectuals who do their best to understand the Jewish experience, non-Polish Jews whose approach is so broad that they understand all other points of view, and many non-Polish Christians who really would like to render justice to all sides. We all share one thing: We reject the idea that we really are at war.

Although there are important differences between average Polish and average Western perceptions of the background of the controversy, those of us who do not treat the other side—whether it is Christian, Jewish, or Polish—as the enemy see, instead, partners who have varied approaches. True, a person atop the barricade has climbed there from a particular side. Good intentions do not eliminate differences in approach, and different approaches can lead to misunderstandings. Nevertheless, it is our belief that there is no reason for not reaching a fully satisfying solution to the controversy.

To understand the Auschwitz convent controversy, and eventually to overcome it, it is necessary to grasp Polish perceptions of Auschwitz as much as it is imperative to understand Jewish sensitivity about the *Shoah*. For most Poles, the Polish and nationalistic aspects of the controversy seem more important than the universal ones. In Poland, therefore, the conflict is automatically perceived in terms of Polish-Jewish rather than Christian-Jewish relations. That outcome puts a person like me in a problematic position: It is assumed that Poles are in Poland and Jews are, say, in America. There seems to be no place for me and other Polish Jews similar to myself—the very ones who probably have the greatest interest in reaching a real solution.

THE POLISH APPROACH

Points 1–4 below illustrate the Polish perception of the situation. They express attitudes that are part of my own background, which I fully accept despite the fact that these attitudes often give rise to one-sided, defensive views.

1. For us in Poland, Auschwitz is a symbol of Polish martyrdom under the Nazis.

For me, of course, Auschwitz is such a symbol in addition to being a symbol of the *Shoah*, a unique tragedy. The sad fact is that most Poles do not recognize the exceptional character of the Nazi project to wipe out the Jewish people. They either poorly understand or ignore altogether the Jewish significance of Auschwitz.

At the same time, the non-Polish world does not sufficiently understand Polish suffering and its connection to Auschwitz. The historical fact is that the Nazis tried to crush the Polish nation. They not only introduced bloody terror but also murdered Polish elites and did their best to destroy Polish culture. The Auschwitz camp was employed for these purposes, especially during its first two years of existence when this anti-Polish activity was its main function. Poland is probably the easiest country in which to find non-Jews who could truly testify, ''I was sent to Auschwitz.''

The Auschwitz convent controversy runs deep because it concerns symbolic significance, even sacred symbolisms. There are enough facts to support both symbolisms: Auschwitz = *Shoah* and Auschwitz = Polish martyrdom. Few people are aware of the double identification, however, and that ignorance needs to be dispelled. Symbols are not invented or postulated; they emerge from facts and become facts themselves. The two identifications are realities that cannot be changed. They should, moreover, be respected because they represent a means of remembering real tragedies. Of course, I do not mean that the tragedies symbolized are equivalent, although in Poland they are often taken to be equivalent or even to be the same tragedy.

In Western Europe the fate of Jews was so clearly different from the fate of non-Jews that the singularity of the *Shoah* can be easily accepted. In Poland, however, the difference was not so immense, and the popular attitude is that "we all suffered." In addition, one often hears that 3 million non-Jewish Poles lost their lives alongside 3 million Polish Jews. The implication is that the losses were comparable. They, of course, were not. Ninety percent of all Polish Jews perished, and only Jewish (and Gypsy) children were killed in Auschwitz. Poles tend to disregard even the simple fact that some Jews tried to survive by posing as Aryans—there were such cases even in Auschwitz—while there were no attempts in the opposite direction.

This difference in status is often denied. The argument is usually that the Poles were second on the Nazi list of peoples to be destroyed; there was not time to accomplish this task, but the future of Poles was to be the same as that of the Jews and so, in essence, the fate was the same. Of course, no Jew and few outsiders could accept this argument, which would equate a *possibility* with the *reality* of Jewish children condemned to death. Many sensitive Poles have recognized the difference and testified to it. Already in 1943, for example, Czeslaw Milosz wrote "A Poor Christian Looks at the Ghetto," a well-known poem in which he reflects on the fear that he could be counted "among the helpers of death."[2] In September 1989, Tadeusz Mazowiecki, the first non-Communist prime minister in Eastern Europe, echoed Milosz by observing that "the tragedy and sacrifice of the *Shoah* defy any comparison."

Nazi antisemitism, I believe, had a unique, deeply metaphysical dimension. In the Nazis' diabolic vision, Jews were the source of evil. Murdering the Jews meant purifying the world. Anti-Polish policies were not so "metaphysically" motivated. Frightening as they were, the Nazi plans to convert the Poles into slave labor forces were more "rational."

Why, then, is it so difficult for average Poles to see the differences between the fates of Jews and Poles under Hitler? Significantly, suffering itself is one reason. The dominant Polish tradition is that Poles are the most suffering people in the world. Indeed, according to romantic imagery from the nineteenth century, Poland is "the Christ of the nations" who suffers for the sake of humankind. In this light, it is difficult to accept that others suffered more. It is even more difficult to accept that others could be victimized by Poles. On the other hand, Jewish self-perceptions run parallel. Jewish messianism is, in fact, the source of the romantic Polish vision. Yet, while it is possible for Christians to accept the chosenness of the Jewish people and to consider the victimization of Jews in Christian countries, it is not accepted in Christianity, let alone in Judaism, to perceive the Poles collectively as a "suffering servant." A "generic" Christian approach would be rather different from the Polish one. This difference, however, puts the convent controversy in bold relief. We may say that the controversy became peculiarly sharp in Poland because one "sacred" place is related to two chosen peoples.

In Poland it requires special effort and sophistication to think about Auschwitz in terms of Christian-Jewish rather than Polish-Jewish relations. Not only Polish suffering and Polish messianism but also a psychological tendency to impose dichotomous divisions causes distortions of both popular Polish and popular Jewish perceptions of the realities of occupied Poland. Those realities make bipolar models inadequate.[3] For there were three groups involved—Germans, Poles, and Jews—and their mutual relationships were not only different but also complex and interrelated.

The principal relations were as follows: (1) between Germans and Jews: extermination; (2) between Germans and Poles: subjugation; and (3) between Poles and Jews: witnessing. But tendencies to perceive situations in dichotomous terms produce inabilities to understand the real situation. If the relations are reduced only to a two-sided image—Germans vs. Poles, for example—then distortions naturally follow. In this case, at least from the Polish point of view, there is no other way than to identify the Polish and Jewish positions and to equate subjugation with extermination. Or, if we take a Jewish view that is simply dichotomous, there is no choice but to identify the Polish and German positions and to confuse the role of Polish witness with that of German murderer.

A third example of distortion will be mentioned below, but for now suffice it to say that the result of these considerations points toward my second main point about Polish perceptions.

2. As far as Auschwitz is concerned, Poles perceive their bond of common suffering with Jews to be stronger than their bond of common Christianity with Germans.

This point constitutes one reason why arguments to the effect that in Auschwitz Christians were murdering Jews sounds very strange in Poland and also for me. There are also other more objective reasons for that strangeness. For one thing, Christians were killed in Auschwitz, too, and there were, moreover, antisemites among the victims. For another, Nazis attempted to revive paganism, not to foster Christianity—priests imprisoned in Auschwitz, for example, were treated with special cruelty. Finally, as Jews were killed because they were Jews, homosexuals were persecuted and imprisoned in Auschwitz because they were homosexuals. Yet to say that homosexuals were victims of heterosexuals in Auschwitz, seems to be most inappropriate. The moral is that in looking for the answer to the question who was killing whom in Auschwitz, we should take the facts at their face value. Nazis were the perpetrators, and it is of supreme importance to see that they saw themselves, first and foremost as Germans. That is why Germans, not Christians, have to share the primary responsibility for Auschwitz and the *Shoah*. Most of the Nazis simply neglected their nominal Christianity, but they never underplayed their German identity.

A frequent consequence of my second major point about Polish perceptions, and even more of the competition for the title of "most suffering people," is the tendency to subsume the Jewish deaths under the general category of Polish martyrdom. For me this calculation is, of course, unacceptable. It is ironic that antisemites, who were denying the Polishness of Polish Jews before the war, are most eager to Polonize the Jewish victims. It is the pro-Jewish Poles who understand the fact that Jews were being killed as Jews and not in the framework of more general repressions.

The truth that Jews were killed only because of their Jewishness has rarely been explained to Polish children. Nevertheless, the awareness of the destruction of the Jews is now quite widespread. Many, if not most, Polish school children visit the camp at Auschwitz. Hence, another key point emerges concerning Polish perspectives on the Auschwitz convent controversy.

3. In Poland, unlike Western Europe and the United States, it would be unthinkable to find "revisionist historians" who deny the historical fact of the gas chambers.

One reason is that Poles often have believed that the gas chambers were built for them. There exists, however, a more general and objective reason for my third point. In Poland, World War II, which is known simply as "the war," is part of our lives, part of every family's memories. It is much more real and concrete than in France, Belgium, Britain, let alone in the United States. Auschwitz is a real, physical place, not just a name or a symbol. The German occupation of Poland was total, especially ruthless, and incomparably more brutal than Nazi rule in Western countries. In occupied Paris, opera was performed, with the sole difference that Jews in the audience were replaced by German officers. In occupied Warsaw, opera was forbidden. The occupying German authorities, moreover, could disregard the reactions of Poles because, in contrast to other European countries, there was in Poland no local pro-Nazi government. Incidentally, this fact alone, together with the ruthlessness of the occupation and the concentration of Jews on Polish soil, explains why the death camps were located in Poland. In spite of a popular Western image, there is no documentary evidence that the consideration of local antisemitism played any role in Nazi preparations for the *Shoah*. Given the nature of the occupation in Poland, nobody there could prevent Auschwitz from functioning, even in the first period when it contained mostly Polish political prisoners.

One more difference in perceptions about Auschwitz concerns the meaning of martyrdom. The word is not neutral. In both Jewish and, subsequently, Christian traditions it means suffering for the sake of one's faith. For Jews, it has been observed many times, Auschwitz, or the *Shoah* in general, does not have this redemptive quality. It is an ultimate horror: Jews were condemned independently of their willingness to defend their faith, indeed independently of their behavior. For most believing Jews, Auschwitz must have meaning, but that meaning seems totally hidden. In contrast, from the Christian point of view, the redemptive interpretation is natural. Even Pope John Paul II, whose sensitivity to the Jewish fate is obvious, expressed remarks to the effect that so great a suffering must bring great fruits.[4] This has, of course, nothing to do with antisemitism but infuses the *Shoah* with more meaning than the great majority of

Jews would accept. Such steps are the subtlest way of "Christianizing" the *Shoah*, and they need no physical presence of the church at Auschwitz.

There is one more special aspect to our Polish approach to the problem. Not only Polish Catholics but also the Polich church suffered under the Nazi occupation. In addition, after the war the church's suffering continued under the Soviet occupation. The Communist regime was based on terror, and the church faced at least severe discrimination. Soon it became the only independent institution. For most Poles any pressure to vacate a church building has associations with Communist attempts to eliminate religion from public life. That pressure is also reminiscent of earlier limitations imposed upon the church by foreign non-Catholic powers who ruled over Poland in the nineteenth century. To sum it up:

4. In Poland, the Catholic church represents not only religion, and not only an important part of the national identity, but also resistance against foreign domination and, in particular, Communist totalitarianism.

A PERSONAL CHRONOLOGY

The Early Tension

The Auschwitz convent was established in 1984. When I learned about it, I thought this establishment was all right because of the general factors expressed above. I have always believed that the church has an undeniable right to a presence in Auschwitz. On the other hand, I have always shared Jewish concern lest the triumphalism of the church be displayed there. I thought, however, that the convent was sufficiently discreet. I also had more specific reasons: I knew that many things at the Auschwitz complex had to be changed, including the monument in the Birkenau part of the camp, the minimization of the Jewish tragedy in the camp's exhibits, and the generally unsatisfactory quality of the "museum." I assumed, too, that at least some of the church people who wanted to be present at that place were likely to be among the most sensitive to the *Shoah* and to the Jewish aspect of the camp. I thought they could be our allies in attempts to improve the Auschwitz museum. I still think I was basically right.

Also, no Jewish voice was raised in Poland against the convent. Partly this happened, I know, because Polish Jews were unaware of the project. They also knew, however, other dimensions of Auschwitz, such as I have expressed in my first point above, and their reactions were similar to mine. I am not aware of consultations with Polish Jewish organizations, but a most illuminating illustration of the innocence of the church initiatives to be present at *Shoah* sites is provided by the appeal for funds to build a church-mausoleum in Sobibor, a death camp with no Polish part or symbolism (but situated in a place where a small church had existed before the war). That appeal was published in Warsaw's only Jewish paper *Folks Stimme* in February 1984, shortly before the Auschwitz convent opened. Nobody protested.

Protests about the Auschwitz convent began in late 1985 and early 1986. They were absolutely unexpected by Poles. On the contrary, Polish Catholics were rather expecting the Jews to be grateful for the effort to have prayers said on that dreadful site. They drew comparisons with the former concentration camp in Dachau, Germany, where in the very center there is a synagogue side by side with Catholic and Protestant churches. A Carmelite convent, moreover, has existed there since 1964, and it has never been opposed.

The Polish church did not take part in the specific initiative that triggered Jewish protest. It was provoked by an appeal of the Western organization Aid to the Church in Distress to raise funds for the convent as a "spiritual fortress" that would guarantee "the conversion of strayed brothers." Some Belgian Jews protested, and others followed. While the triumphal tone of the appeal certainly seemed unreassuring, I believed that the controversy was based on misunderstandings. I knew that the Carmelites, a purely contemplative order, did not engage in spreading their religion. I also knew, however, that conversionism remains a principal part of the Christian tradition and is perceived by Jews as a threat. More specifically, the convent was to be named after Edith Stein, a Jewess who had become a Carmelite nun herself, perished in Auschwitz, and later was beatified. That Edith Stein did not become the official patron of the convent was a concession. I wrote that the concession should be welcomed by Jews, and that goodwill would remove other misunderstandings.[5]

I was soon to learn that the main reason for the controversy was Jewish mistrust of the church. An additional element was resentment against Poles. My approach was much more balanced on both planes because of my background: I had friends not just among non-Jewish Poles but also among Catholic activists.

I had, and in principle I still have, three main arguments in favor of the convent's original location at Auschwitz. First, by no means is Auschwitz an exclusively Jewish place. Second, the camp has become a major tourist attraction, and it is most important to have a religious dimension represented there. Third, the original convent stood outside the barbed wire fence. Let me explain these three points more carefully.

In Auschwitz I, the main camp (*Stammlager*), next to which the convent has been situated, thousands of non-Jews, primarily Poles, were murdered. How many nobody knows for sure. It is very confusing that the estimates of the total number of victims of the whole Auschwitz complex often vary from 1.6 to 4 million. At the Cracow postwar trial of Rudolph Hoess, the Nazi head of the camp, the number was estimated at about 2.5 million. Serious scholars quote lower estimates, while journalists and memorials usually cite much higher figures.[6] This discrepancy is unfortunate because the diverging figures contribute to a lack of confidence about the overall truth of the camp and can be exploited by "revisionists." In addition, the proportion of Jews in the total number of victims cannot be exactly established. This can lead to distasteful arguments about numbers. It is difficult, though, to avoid numbers. It seems to me beyond doubt that the large majority of the victims were Jewish. According to the statistics quoted in an official document of the Polish church commission for the dialogue with Judaism, Jews constituted 90 percent of them.[7]

One thing is sure. The overwhelming majority of deaths at Auschwitz occurred in the gas chambers of Birkenau or Auschwitz II. And there the overwhelming majority of the dead were Jewish. In addition, thousands of Gypsies, plus Polish, Soviet, and other prisoners, were killed. The Birkenau death factory, however, was specially established to murder countless transports of Jews.[8] Thus, I thought Birkenau, rather than Auschwitz, should serve as another name for the *Shoah*. Treblinka, where at least 700,000 Jews were killed, also could do so. But it turned out that, for most people outside Poland, Auschwitz is one undifferentiated place. I accept this, because the whole system—consisting of Auschwitz I, Auschwitz II-Birkenau, and Auschwitz III—was indeed administered as one complex.

The second argument touches a deep and controversial point: How are we to remember that horror? An oft-repeated Jewish argument says that Auschwitz must remain empty and silent.[9] The silence is to parallel the nonintervention of God, who allowed the ultimate horror, the industry of death. An interesting theological explication of this attitude was given by René-Samuel Sirat, the former chief rabbi of France.[10] Quoting Jeremiah 7:32, he writes that "the valley of slaughter" is now Auschwitz, even more than Tophet or Gehinnom, where offerings of children were given to Moloch. Thus to offer prayers in Auschwitz would mean to join "the most horrible idolatry."

But whatever the merits of the appeals for "absolute silence, no prayer, no speech," they suffer from two principal defects. One is the fact that almost all Jews (and, of course, Christians, too) come to Auschwitz to pray. Saying the Kaddish is precisely what most Jewish visitors want to do. Initially, I thought that the opposition against any prayer was mainly the rationalization for a spontaneous rejection of the Catholic presence. Then I realized that some—but only some—Jewish survivors of Auschwitz react spontaneously against traditional observances. One of them told me: "I saw my family perish there, but I just can't say Kaddish when I am there."

A second weakness of the theory that only silence can match the death of God's chosen people, or even—to use Elie Wiesel's image—the death on the gallows of God himself, is that Auschwitz is simply not a silent place because so many people visit it. It has become a major tourist attraction. For years, it has functioned as a museum. In order to serve crowds of visitors, kiosks and other facilities were established. I find this "banalization" inappropriate, close to desecration. Yet ill-will is definitely not its source. I do not blame the directors of the museum. They had been Auschwitz prisoners themselves before they devoted their efforts to preserving remnants of the camp.[11]

The flow of visitors, Polish and non-Polish, is the best chance to save the memory of Auschwitz. The problem is how is it possible to change the atmosphere and induce tourists not to behave as in any other museum of torture? Appropriate patterns of behavior have not been established. I have seen merry-making Polish teenagers there. I have also seen a Jewish group who, after a solemn ceremony, made a picnic in the camp, chatting casually. In Birkenau, a much worse desecration took place in the summer of 1989. An American film company made its studio there and built concrete props among which groups of extras were running and having fun. In my view, the best way to stress the exceptional character of the place is to introduce a religious dimension there. I believe that intention was among the main motives for establishing the convent at Auschwitz.

My third argument in favor of the convent was based on the fact that it was located outside the camp's perimeter. I also thought that Jewish protests were partly caused by misunderstanding. People with no idea of the camp's topography could have thought that the convent was in the center of the camp and that Jewish visitors would have to enter a church establishment. In reality, however, no visitor is likely to find the original convent building without seeking it out specifically. True, there is no single definition of the camp's area. The original camp's sphere of interest (*Interessen Gebiet*) was larger than the area inside the present barbed-wire fence. Yet how big a chunk of Poland can be considered to be a cemetery, a prohibited soil? Similar to other Jews, I also would not accept crosses on Jewish graves. But where are those graves? Auschwitz is not really a cemetery. The corpses were incinerated in crematoria, and their dust fertilized a far larger area than that included in any formal boundaries. I would oppose proliferation of crosses in the area of the camp. But where is it? Boundaries of the hallowed—or cursed—soil have to be postulated. I think that the only sensible idea is to take the barbed-wire fence as their definition.

I know that the present building of the convent served as a storehouse in which the deadly gas, Zyklon B, was probably kept. That makes the building relevant to the Holocaust, but after the war, when it was abandoned or served as a storehouse—it did not belong to the Auschwitz museum, even though it was included in the complex as determined for Unesco's World Heritage List—nobody protested. The protests were raised when the church came there. This tells me that the real Jewish emotions pertain to the church. Dr. Yitzhak Arad, chairman of Yad Vashem and a survivor himself, expressed such feelings a few years ago: "Where were these churches when we really needed them?"

The Agreement

Important meetings between Catholic leaders and key European Jewish representatives occurred in Geneva on July 22, 1986, and February 22, 1987. These talks resulted in agreement about the Auschwitz convent. I was very glad, and all people in Poland with whom I was in close contact were relieved and hopeful. Misunderstandings that had been the most visible components of the controversy seemed to be overcome. It was agreed that the convent would be relocated. Rather than being a mere rejection of the nuns' presence, the agreement incorporated the convent into a positive project: building in the vicinity of the camp a new interfaith center "for information, education, encounter, and prayer." In that way, I felt, not only would the nuns find an acceptable place for their service of good intentions, but a broader religious presence in connection with Auschwitz would provide a much needed counterbalance to the tourist character of the place and its "banalization."

Although critics said that only Catholics made concessions, the weekly *Tygodnik Powszechny*, the leading Polish exponent of open-minded Catholicism, was quick to observe that, in the agreement, Polish suffering was specially acknowledged and singled out several times side by side with the *Shoah*.[12] But the agreement, which was a bold step, also revealed a deep division in the Polish church. Cardinal Macharski of Cracow, who signed the agreement, and other persons supporting it met opposition within the church hierarchy and even more among the parishioners and the nuns themselves. The depth of the division inside the church is seen in two statements issued in the spring of 1989. In an official communiqué dated March 9, the Polish bishops wrote how "greatly important" was the building of the new center. But on May 17 the heads of Polish monasteries officially reaffirmed that the convent belongs to the Carmelite sisters, is in its "proper, honorable place," and "harms nobody"; they opposed the relocation and stated their solidarity with the nuns.[13] The debate was reflected in the press, but, in a way, it was all out of place. According to the agreement reached in Geneva, the new center was supposed to be built in two years, that is, by February 1989. Nothing, however, was done by that time.

I felt very uncomfortable that the Geneva agreement seemed forgotten in Poland. Whatever my arguments in favor of the original location of the convent, I was convinced that the agreement was binding and, indeed, provided an excellent solution to the controversy. My friends thought the same. I knew very little about the internal church controversies. In Poland, red tape has often been cited as a major reason for the lack of a perceptible change. It does exist, but I do not believe that everything was done to meet the "deadline." There seems to have been a hope that the admittedly unrealistic date for relocation simply would not be taken seriously either at home or abroad. But that outlook, of course, also meant not taking quite seriously the signatures on the relocation agreement. Sadly, no Polish church leader apologized. It was Cardinal Decourtray from Lyons, one of four cardinals who had signed the agreement, who just before the February 22, 1989, deadline wrote an open letter to Theo Klein of the Council of Representatives of French Jews, who cochaired the 1987 Geneva meeting. In the letter, Decourtray deplored the delay and reassured Klein that the agreement would indeed be honored. He mentioned also how delicate it was to convince the Polish people that there would be no mistreatment of the nuns and no neglect of the memory of Polish suffering.

In Poland, hardly anyone understood why Jews were offended. Even active supporters of the Geneva agreement were using indirect arguments declaring that, if the presence of the convent could provoke so much bitterness, then it should be relocated. The syndrome, "let us defend our innocent sisters from Jewish calumnies," became stronger and stronger. According to one competent opinion, the nuns themselves, who had begun their prayer convinced that it was the only way to fight the Devil, the creator of Auschwitz, became convinced that the campaign against their presence was itself the Devil's work. To my mind, this approach was frightening; it signified religious war. This attitude seems to have been the source of another conspicuous fact: the placement of a tall cross in the convent's garden. It was explained that the cross—it was originally produced and utilized for Pope John Paul II's 1979 visit to Auschwitz-Birkenau—marked the site of executions of Polish Catholics, but its size indicated that the cross was supposed to play a part in the convent controversy. To defend a cross may easily amount to a holy war.

This background explains why I was so happy when I saw a lone article by Father Stanislaw Musial, S.J., published in the official bulletin of the Polish Episcopate.[14] The author is the secretary of the Episcopate's Commission for Dialogue with Judaism. His voice represents the dialogue-minded people in the church. Musial's idea was not only to defend the Geneva agreement but also to explain Jewish emotions to Polish readers. In addition, while citing a lower estimate of the number of Auschwitz victims than is typically the case, he stressed the high proportion of Jews among them. If he opposed dividing the Auschwitz complex into parts, he also emphasized the *Shoah*'s uniqueness.

Not all the notes in Musial's articles rang true. He mentioned some theological differences, although not without oversimplifications. Musial stated, for example, that Jews, unlike Christians, do not make supplicatory prayers, and yet, for instance, "*El Mole Rachamim*" is a traditional Jewish supplication. He stressed that even nonreligious Jews do not oppose prayer at Auschwitz. True, in recent years we have witnessed shared pilgrimages with rabbis and bishops praying at Auschwitz, but *institutionalized* prayer at Auschwitz remains offensive to many Jews.[15] Whatever the shortcomings of Musial's essay, he did present, above all, the main root of different Christian and Jewish reactions to the convent: dissimilar attitudes toward the cross. For Christians, the cross represents the highest good and reconciliation. Humility, however, requires the recognition that it is not necessarily so for others. Musial explained that for Jews the cross and institutions representing the cross call persecutions to mind. Finally, Musial underscored an especially important point: To agree to relocate a legally functioning Catholic institution because of Jewish feeling is an historic decision, with no precedent in the history of the church in Poland or elsewhere. I regret that this side of the problem is not fully grasped and appreciated by Jews.

It is a pity that this basically praiseworthy document was not circulated and popularized but remains unknown to the larger public in Poland and elsewhere. The main reason was that a series of dramatic events in the summer of 1989 strengthened hardline approaches.

The Crisis

That summer it became clear that even the postponed date, July 22, 1989, would not be met. Protests were inevitable and fully justified. I had not anticipated, however, Jewish provocations. In July, Rabbi Avraham Weiss and a few students climbed over the convent's fence and trespassed on the convent's property. After a few hours, they were forceably removed by workers there. Weiss later explained that he only wanted to talk with the nuns, but this does not sound credible to me. Journalists had been invited; the provocation looked staged. I was affected not so much by the removal of the intruders as by a remark in the crowd: "Pity Hitler didn't finish with them."

What made the intrusion particularly intolerable for Poles was the generally known fact that the Carmelite sisters are a cloistered order and do not meet strangers without special permission. Catholic tradition, it is worth noting, has had strict provisions regarding male presence in convent cloisters, including their gardens. Historically, for example, a Catholic man who entered such a place without permission could be subject to excommunication, the severest penalty the church can exact. Apparently Weiss did not care or know about these matters, and in the case of such a carefully prepared action, the latter amounts to the same thing as the former. I was angry principally because of his lack of respect for the nuns. The most sensible argument to use to convince the nuns that they should move, or should have moved, is that by doing so they would show respect for the feelings of many Jews. But, unless one wants only to dictate or force the other side to withdraw, one may demand someone's respect only when one shows respect for the other side.

Psychologically, Weiss's action struck many Poles and Catholics as an act of war. Predictably, it provoked emotions and reactions that shattered years of effort toward mutual understanding and reconciliation. Yet the action obviously did not intend bloodshed—Cardinal Glemp's comments to the contrary notwithstanding. His slanderous remarks at Czestochowa on August 26 showed how high the tension had become. They did not express, however, an entirely consistent approach. Although his entire speech reflected the conviction that Jews are at least suspect, the cardinal admitted that there are good Jews, and he qualified his confrontational rhetoric by admitting that "we have our faults with respect to Jews."[16] Yet conciliatory phrases and an appeal to dialogue could not diminish the impression left by his antisemitic remarks. He condemned Jews for behaving as if they were "elevated above all others," he reproached the media for being "easily at the Jews' disposal," and he proclaimed that "if there is no anti-Polishness, then there will be no anti-Semitism." Antisemitism was presented as a legitimate self-defense. This shocking statement showed how deeply offended he felt by the Jewish protests about the Auschwitz convent.

The feeling that Jews are oppressors may sound absurd to most Western ears. As far as Polish circumstances are concerned, that claim's only sense derives from two sources: from Jewish participation in Poland's oppressive Communist rule; and, in particular, from the fact that many Jews looked favorably at the Soviet occupation of eastern Poland in 1939, which resulted from the secret Ribbentrop-Molotov, that is Nazi-Soviet, pact of cooperation and friendship. This background experience, it occurs to me, provides the most credible explanation for Cardinal Glemp's linking of "Germans and Jews" in connection with the trauma World War II created for Poles. In this way, a version of the third false dichotomy I described early on made its appearance in the Auschwitz convent controversy. When the Soviet Union is added to the picture of occupied Poland, Germans and Jews are lumped together, and Poles become the victims of all three.

As a Polish Jew, I was shocked by Glemp's analysis. Significantly, the cardinal spoke as though he were a Polish king defending his Catholic nation against infiltrations and attacks. I knew the cardinal expressed deep Polish feelings, but I also knew that his attitudes irritated many, including many devout Catholics. It soon became clear that he caused tremendous shock and consternation among serious thinking Poles such as the Catholic prime minister, Mazowiecki. Many persons expressed their outrage in private, but to do it in public is another matter. For many years, it has been bad taste in Poland to criticize the primate in public because the church was oppressed and played a key role in opposing Communist totalitarianism. I hoped, however, that liberal Catholics would say something. So I was very happy that in the most popular daily, Solidarity's recently created *Gazeta Wyborcza* ("Election Newspaper"), a well-known Catholic activist, Krzystof Sliwinski, expressed feelings of shock and pain.

That criticism of Cardinal Glemp, and some later articles, provoked many letters from the readers of *Gazeta Wyborcza*. I have read dozens of them. A majority criticized the paper for defending "other than Polish" interests but a sizeable minority backed the paper's line. Among the former, a confrontational mentality was common. According to this outlook, Jewish attacks and slanders require a firm defense, the defense of "the sanctuary of Polish martyrdom . . . concerning primarily the Polish nation and the Polish state, and only in a secondary way . . . the Jews and the Church."[17] The letter of the provincial head of the Carmelites, Father Dominik Wider, O.C.D., is notable: There the 1987 Geneva agreement is called "a Jewish monologue."[18] Letters supporting the editors were usually softer and expressed real concern. The problem for them was not how to continue the "war" but how to take into account the emotions of all sides involved in the controversy. These writers also stressed the necessity of implementing the Geneva agreement, and often they worried about the rise of antisemitism. A Ms. Brach-Czaina, for example, wrote that she was ready "to thank Weiss for cutting open the ulcer" of latent antisemitism.

The overall impression, however, was quite depressing. I knew that Polish elites genuinely wanted to overcome the dark sides of Polish-Jewish history, but it was difficult to remain optimistic when so many letters exhibited the opposite attitude. Their potent source is the widespread identification of Polishness with Catholicism and of Jews with Communism. Both identifications were reinforced by postwar developments: the imposition of communism, in which Jewish activists played an important role, and the official anti-Catholic policies which were the most visible part of the Communist project to suppress or redefine all national traditions. Cardinal Glemp's declaration frightened Jews in Poland. One Catholic activist, a recent convert from a nominally Jewish family (most Jews in Poland are Jewish by origin only), told me that his mother wondered whether she had been right not to emigrate in 1968. Antisemitic graffiti appeared on walls, and windows were smashed in Jewish buildings. Probably it was natural to connect these actions with the cardinal's homily, although I am sure that it is unfair to assume that his intentions were to unleash antisemitic actions. ''I suddenly felt somewhat less at home,'' wrote Konstanty Gebert, a Polish-Jewish journalist whose background and approach is very close to mine and with whom I used to participate in Jewish-Christian dialogue.[19] In an important article, he expressed his disenchantment with the church, an institution with which he had good contacts while he had been working for the underground press. He also recalled that one of Cardinal Glemp's closest collaborators is Professor Maciej Giertych, who apparently wants to build a nationalistic Catholic movement backed by the church.

Both Cardinal Glemp's rejection of the 1987 Geneva agreement and, a few days later, his questioning of Cardinal Macharski's ''competence'' as a signer of the document called for action. As of this writing during the winter of 1989–90, however, little decisive action has occurred in Poland. Apart from individual voices, support for the Geneva agreement could be found in a letter, signed by forty-six Polish intellectuals, which contains an appeal for ''mutual understanding, reconciliation and Polish-Jewish brotherhood.''[20] Prospects for a solution, however, still seemed grim. Therefore it was especially encouraging to read Jacek Wozniakowski's *Tygodnik Powszechny* interview with Cardinal Glemp.[21] In this interview, published before the intellectuals' letter appeared but after it had been written and signed, the primate said that he had been misunderstood and that renegotiation of the Geneva agreement could well reinstate its original conclusions. This prompted me to write that ''the possibility of a settlement was seen'' and that in order to avoid future problems an international advisory council should be created.[22] I also stressed that overcoming the controversy would encourage Jewish groups—the American Jewish Congress, for example—to support democratic change in Poland.

The partial change in Cardinal Glemp's position reached a kind of fulfillment a few days later. After meeting in England with Sir Sigmund Sternberg, Glemp wrote him a letter agreeing that the convent should be moved to the new interfaith center, according to the Geneva agreement.[23] This reversal of Glemp's earlier views anticipated, I believe, a Vatican declaration that appeared the next day. In that declaration, Cardinal Johannes Willebrands officially endorsed the new center. He also quoted with approval the September 6, 1989, statement by Bishop Henryk Muszynski, the president of the Polish Episcopate Commission for Relations with Judaism, which reaffirmed the possibility of fulfilling the agreement and stated that the tension caused by the July protests had only postponed work on the center. "Rome has spoken; the matter is closed," we exclaimed in relief. Outwardly, at least, it appeared that the controversy had ended, especially when ground for the new center was finally broken in February 1990.

Deeper levels of the controversy, unfortunately, have not disappeared. A dramatic example was the prejudiced approach of Israel's prime minister, Yitzhak Shamir, who suggested in September 1989 that Poles take in antisemitism with their mother's milk. This gross generalization provoked Polish fury, including that of Polish Jews. I was appalled to witness a Jewish leader referring to such stereotypes, especially when we Jews have so often been targets of such stereotyping.[24] Whatever must be said about antisemitism in Poland, I know that antisemitism divides rather than unites Poles.

A specific reaction to Shamir came from Cardinal Glemp. It was not slanderous, but it did show very little understanding and sensitivity. In a November 2, 1989, interview he said there is no antisemitism in Poland and urged everyone to come and see for themselves. It was hard not to become depressed all over again, especially when Rabbi Weiss went on to sue Cardinal Glemp for libel. Although I grant Rabbi Weiss a point—arguably, the cardinal's remark about Weiss's alleged intentions to kill the nuns is libelous—I cannot trust Rabbi Weiss and treat his behavior as anything other than another stage of "war." In Poland his action was taken that way, and, unfortunately, it is not clear to the average Pole that Jews differ in opinions and approaches to the convent controversy. The difficulties are compounded because Weiss represents no serious Jewish organization, and he did not even bother to consult Polish Jews.

Fortunately, the fact that he represents only himself was made slightly more clear to the Polish public during the December 1989 visit of the American Jewish Congress.[25] I was happy to see the Congress, as well as other individuals and serious institutions such as the American Jewish Committee, move beyond the clichéd equation that "Poland = antisemitism" and look instead with sympathy toward Poland's efforts to achieve freedom, democracy, and prosperity.

In summary, I have been amazed how strong the controversy became and how the logic of "war" pushed people to take part in the conflict against their wills. I have encountered many Jews who press for relocation of the convent, but who feel that as far as they are concerned it could stay where it is.

Above all, I have been depressed by the thought that the evil contained in Auschwitz is somehow still active. It seems to be this evil that stimulates in so many people the worst inclinations—Jewish exclusivism and Polish exclusivism, Christian triumphalism and Jewish triumphalism. May God help us to avoid those perils.

NOTES

1. An earlier version of this essay appeared in *Christian Jewish Relations* 22 (Autumn/Winter 1989): 37–54.

2. Quoted in English in *My Brother's Keeper?*, ed. Antony Polonsky (London: Routledge, 1989), 59.

3. In my attempts to grasp the implications of ignoring the "triangular" image of the situation, I was helped by the paper of Andrzej Bryk, "The Hidden Complex of the Polish Mind: Polish-Jewish Relations during the Holocaust," in *My Brother's Keeper?*

4. I personally heard such remarks during the pope's visit to Poland at a meeting with Jewish representatives on June 14, 1987.

5. I published my arguments in Polish in the most influential Catholic weekly, *Tygodnik Powszechny*, 22 June 1986, and in English under the title "The Convent at Auschwitz." See *Moment* (December 1986) and *Sh'ma* (31 October 1986).

6. Even in otherwise good articles, it is often written that there were 4 million victims, among them 1.5 million non-Jews (see, for example, Deena Metzger, "Pilgrimage to Auschwitz," *Los Angeles Times*, 19 August 1989) or 1.5 million "Catholic Poles" (see, for example, Lisa Palmieri-Billig, "Lights and Shadows," *Jerusalem Post*, 27 March 1989).

7. This document is also quoted below. I reviewed it for an earlier article requested by the Wilstein Institute. This article, "Carmel at Auschwitz: On the Recent Polish Church Document and Its Background," has been recently published in *SIDIC* 22 (1989): 15–19. An abbreviated version appeared in *Manna* 25 (Autumn 1989): 6–7, 28.

8. The camp at Birkenau was initially meant as a camp for Soviet POWs. Auschwitz I was created for political prisoners, and for two years, beginning in June 1940, they were mostly Polish. None of these facts seem to be taken into account by Ady Steg, who, during the first Geneva meeting in July 1986, said that the murder of non-Jews there "was a matter of subjecting non-Jews to facilities which were installed for the working out of the Final Solution. In truth, Auschwitz, with its gas chambers and its crematoria, was conceived, constructed, and put to use *solely* for the extermination of the Jews" (see *Christian Jewish Relations* 19 [March 1986]: 48–49). The camp was in existence with mostly Poles as inmates for one and a half years before the Wannsee Conference. We certainly do not have to distort history to justify Jewish claims to Auschwitz.

9. Of course, there are also Catholics who appeal for silence. A well-known Polish Catholic writer, Halina Bortnowska, wrote in *Tygodnik Solidarnosc*, 29 September 1989, as follows: In that place, in which "the smoke of the Holocaust could still be felt," one should not "live or put his signs."

10. "Respecter la douleur à l'état pur," *Le Monde*, 29 July 1989.

11. The recent political changes in Poland made possible serious work toward reshaping the Auschwitz museum. A special committee, headed by Stefan Wilkanowicz, was formed under the auspices of the prime minister and the minister of culture. I, too, am a member of it.

12. See *Tygodnik Powszechny*, 15 March 1987. The exceptional character of the *Shoah* was strongly stressed, too. The author of the article, Father Stanislaw Musial, S.J., as well as Jerzy Turowicz, editor-in-chief of the weekly, took part in the Geneva talks.

13. I quote from an extensive article, "O Karmelu bez emocji" ("About Carmel without Emotions"), by Father Waldemar Chrostowski. See *Tygodnik Solidarnosc*, 29 September 1989.

14. *Biuro Prasowe Episkopatu Polski, Pismo Okolne*, 29 May–4 June 1989. See also note 6 above.

15. Rabbi Leon Klenicki from the Anti-Defamation League of B'nai B'rith in a "pray-

erful reflection'' about his participation in the Catholic-Jewish Tyniec Conference in 1988 wrote: At Auschwitz ''together, we prayed and that prayer was an expression of hope for the future of Jews and Catholics in Poland.'' See *Studium Papers* 13 (April 1989): 73.

16. I quote from the text published in *Zycie Warszawy*, 28 August 1989.

17. This is actually a fragment, quoted in a letter, of a text by S. Borkacki published in a Cracow newspaper, *Gazeta Krakowska*, 5–6 August 1989.

18. Partially published in *Gazeta Wyborcza* (24 July 1989), together with a few other letters, including my own.

19. See the article with this very title, ''Troche mniej w domu,'' *Polityka*, 9 September 1989. Konstanty Gebert uses the pen name Dawid Warszawski.

20. Dated September 12, it appeared in *Tygodnik Powszechny*, 24 September 1989. I signed it, too.

21. See *Tygodnik Powszechny*, 17 September 1989.

22. See *Gazeta Wyborcza*, 18 September 1989.

23. See the statement by Clifford Longley in *The Times*, 21 September 1989.

24. Together with Andrzej Friedman, a friend who serves with me on the board of the Polish-Israeli Friendship Society, I wrote a letter of protest—dated September 15, 1989—to Prime Minister Shamir. The letter is reprinted in this book's appendix.

25. See *Gazeta Wyborcza*, 5 December 1989. Henry Siegman was quoted as saying that Weiss was behaving ''in a destructive and irresponsible way.''

10

The Psychological Point of View

Leo Eitinger

In order to understand, from a psychological viewpoint, the nature and strength of people's reactions to the present situation at Auschwitz, one needs to know something about the development of grief—what reactions occur, both normal and repressed; the special impact that a disaster or a catastrophe makes on the minds of survivors; and the therapeutic efforts possible to reduce their dangerous psychological consequences. Some of these points will be discussed in the following pages.

Psychiatric/psychological research has taught us that grief reactions usually pass through several stages in a rather typical succession and duration. This does not mean that the phases are clear-cut, starting and finishing according to a strict timetable. As with everything in real life, there are many variations, many overlappings, many relapses, and so on. On the whole, however, there is a certain phasic course which a bereaved person has to go through, or rather to work through.

The initial reaction to the loss of a dear and loved person is usually an experience of shock, lasting from a few hours to several days. The bereaved person either feels dazed and helpless or may give the impression of being hyperactive or even completely disorganized. This usually rather short period gives way to a phase in the mourning process where the emotions, the distress, and the awareness of the loss become very conscious. Denial and despair, uncontrolled and uncontrollable weeping, and intense preoccupation with the fact of loss and its irreversibility, preoccupation with the deceased and everything that has any connection with him or her are the most outstanding features in this phase. The preoccupation can be so massive that anything without relation to the deceased temporarily loses its interest and significance, be it family, music, nature, and so on. The bereaved gives the impression of being introverted or completely withdrawn. Self-reproaches are rather frequent. They often and quickly turn into reproaches against others like doctors, nurses, the hospital, but also against members of the family, friends who want to console the bereaved, and sometimes even against the deceased him/herself: "How could he/she do this to me just now when I needed him/her so much?" Sleep disturbances, feelings of hopelessness, and other symptoms of depression are also very common at this stage.

But fortunately this "reactive phase" does not last forever. Usually after a few weeks, more or less, the bereaved starts to accept the changes in the new situation and learns slowly to understand not only intellectually but also emotionally that the lost person cannot be recovered. Step by step the interest in social activities returns and the former relationships are reestablished. The bereaved has to learn that in a way he or she has got a new identity; the memories of the beloved are not so vivid anymore, and while they are fading very slowly, reintegration into a new way of life is developing. This process of adaption through mourning is probably universal and found in practically every culture. It makes a substantial difference, of course, if the deceased has been a husband or wife during a good marriage of many years' duration, the only child of young parents, or an old aunt with a rather loose relationship to the bereaved. What is important in the actual context is that the course of grief usually takes months, sometimes even years, and that the bereaved has to go through a relatively long-lasting psychological work, very painful in the beginning, but rather rewarding and strengthening after a long period. After a crisis, one has overcome a difficult period of one's life, gained a victory over it, grown stronger because of one's own psychological efforts and work.

This is the normal or rather the ideal development after bereavement, the successful adaption to the loss-change with resolution of the disruption and restoration of a new equilibrium one can live with. Not all cases, however, follow the same course. The grief responses to a significant loss, the normal reactions of shock, despair, and recovery, are often distorted, exaggerated, prolonged, inhibited, or delayed. In some cases the bereaved is not able to leave the depressive stage of grief and remains continuously under its spell for years on end. In the present context, however, other forms of pathological grief are of greater interest. In cases where the bereaved is not able to express any signs of grief immediately after the bereavement (i.e., the grief work cannot be done immediately), a distorted form of the grief work will appear sometime in the future. Grief reactions may be inhibited and mourning responses uncompleted for various reasons and in the most different situations. It might be the "last wish" of the deceased ("Don't grieve, do not weep, please just behave as always," etc.). Or it might be other moments which make a normal grief reaction impossible. The repressed inhibited grief reactions will then manifest themselves in later life under different symptomatology without obvious connection with the now consciously forgotten bereavement. These new psychopathological reactions, apparently unrelated to the grief, may be a rather atypical depression or in some cases slight behavior disturbances that are not understood immediately.

Most psychiatrists and psychologists agree, therefore, that grief work is essential to the resolution of grief. Going through the task of working with one's grief is thus necessary to the normal regeneration of the survivor; otherwise the danger of a pathological development of grief with long-lasting and disturbing symptoms can be overwhelming.

Mourning behavior, that is, conventional structured rites at funerals and after, is determined by the customs of society and will very often help the bereaved through their shock and sorrow and back to normal activities. These structured rituals are very different from culture to culture. In the present context it is important to stress the fact that the mourning rituals of Orthodox Jews are probably among the most highly prescribed and considered among the most consoling and supportive in the Western world. According to Jewish tradition every bereaved person must be assisted both by the family and the community to face the loss. The mourners are united and usually gathered in one dwelling for the first seven days after the funeral, and friends are expected to visit. The mourners are greeted with a standard phrase expressing condolence and are not supposed to reply. The visitors share their sorrow, express their concern, and give consolation and companionship. During these first seven days the mourners are not expected to have any other social obligations. In the next thirty days they are supposed to return slowly to community life, but they continue to recite a special prayer for a whole year. After that the deceased one will be remembered by his family on anniversaries of the day of death and ceremoniously on all holidays during the official services. This ensures that a member of the community will not be forgotten, will be remembered at times of joy and sadness as long as his community exists.

When we try to compare the psychological grief reactions and the loss and mourning with the realities of the Holocaust, one must acknowledge that this event is in every possible way far beyond human intellectual or emotional comprehension. This applies to the unimaginable number of victims killed during the Holocaust, to the extent of the disintegration and devastation of all interhuman and psychosocial connections, and to the destruction of practically the total Jewish settlement in Europe. In order to demonstrate the limitations of our psychological possibilities and to understand the dimensions of the Holocaust and its impact, it suffices to look at the stereotype of human reactions to huge numbers. We are completely unable to differentiate in our consciousness and in our emotions between, let us say, 6 million and 7 million or 5 million people killed. The numbers become sterile statistics, and statistics do not awaken feelings.

Therefore if we want to understand the psychological impact of a disaster experience, we must study situations that are surveyable, catastrophes where one still can count the victims, where one is able to see, talk to, and understand the survivors and their families. One of the disasters that has been studied very intensively and extensively and has aroused international interest shall be reported here as a kind of paradigm. It is the so-called Buffalo Creek disaster, which has had far-reaching theoretical and practical consequences.

On February 25, 1972, a large slag dam collapsed and 132 million gallons of water and debris-filled mud roared through the Buffalo Creek Valley in West Virginia. The mud wave destroyed everything in its way; 125 were killed and 4,000 lost their homes. The disaster did not last more than fifteen minutes, but the flood hit the entire twenty-five-kilometer, narrow valley with undiminished force. The inhabitants had been worried about the make-shift dam for a long time. This apprehension of the mountain of slag looming above their homes was one reason the catastrophe did not become even worse. Most of the survivors were not seriously hurt physically, because they had managed to flee to higher levels of the valley before the wave appeared.

Public opinion was directed toward those who were regarded as responsible for the poor condition of the dam. The surviving 654 persons from 160 families filed a lawsuit against the company. It was not only a question of lost homes and property, which the company was willing to compensate without a lawsuit. Mental health problems and psychic impairment were, according to the litigants, effects of the disaster. The court decided that all survivors should be examined individually by a group of prominent psychiatrists and sociologists. The results were striking. In the beginning the examiners wondered whether all the sufferers had been poorly integrated persons with many chronic mental diseases, and whether the catastrophe now was considered a means of obtaining a large amount of compensation from the company. But after thorough investigations of the survivors' earlier life and after numerous discussions it was concluded that this was not the case. All of them showed signs of anxiety and uncertainty of long duration, set off by the disaster. They also had made attempts to regain equanimity and to develop new mechanisms to master their problems. The investigators—independently and without knowledge of comparable studies—diagnosed a clearly delimited clinical syndrome in practically all the survivors. This syndrome could be traced to two experiences. First the immediate effect of the catastrophe on each individual. Second, the effects of the destruction of the local society, the loss of its internal organization, solidarity, and mutual support.

As previously mentioned, most of the survivors had suffered no physical harm. Some few had not even been in the valley during the calamity. Nevertheless, the court's decision was that all survivors, even those who had been absent, were entitled to compensation on account of the psychic trauma. The court stated that the permanent loss of dwellings, and the destruction of the protective and supportive influence of the local society, were of decisive importance. The sociological examination concluded that the survivors had suffered individual as well as collective traumas. They had lost the traditional human interrelationship of this small mining society based upon close kinship and neighborhood. The compulsory transfer from familiar places and people resulted in a loss of habitual human relations and support. In some cases this led to apathy, lack of interest in others and in oneself. Apparently, this small society had been much stronger as a unit than the separate parts of it turned out to be without connection with and assistance from the rest.

It was evident that the effect of the catastrophic event was not brought to a close when the wave had passed the valley. This was only the first phase. In ordinary natural disasters the frightened inhabitants will as a rule be able to return to their familiar surroundings, to rebuild their homes and their environment. In such cases the psychological supportive instrument will be present to assist also the internal recuperative processes. In Buffalo Creek this was not possible. The dazed survivors did not return to the well-known places but had to settle in a strange and uncertain environment. They were exposed to further stress in the period when their situation should have been relieved and when they should have had the opportunity to adapt themselves to a new existence.

After most environmental catastrophes the victims will understand the presence of enormous elemental forces against which man, in spite of all his technology, is powerless. In Buffalo Creek human failure, carelessness, and imprudence were evident. This produced bitterness and vindictiveness in addition to the despair, mingled with the realization that retribution could not change the situation.

In all disaster situations the families will regularly have many questions about how the dead persons were found and about the manner of death. Therefore they should be given an opportunity to meet possible survivors who have something to tell, the rescuers who found the body, and the nurses and doctors who tried to resuscitate the victims, and so on.

Studies of survivors of catastrophes and especially of the surviving members of the families have shown that the latter need psychiatric/psychological help and that this help correctly applied reduces the risk of negative and long-lasting grief reactions. It has also been demonstrated that the family is the unit providing the most important source of strength before and during the outcome of a disaster loss. There is furthermore strong evidence that sudden and violent death causes more pathology in the bereaved than normally expected losses. The main reasons for this are the untimely and often tragic and terrible circumstances, the periods of waiting and uncertainty, the unexpectedness of the sudden death, which often is a shock experience in itself. Further complications for grief work are the difficulties in connection with retrieving the body or identifying the remains of the disaster victims. Disaster psychiatrists have learned that it is one of the most important tasks to take measures which alleviate the consequences of the sudden loss.

Perhaps the most important is to help the family fully to grasp the death of the victim and to help them start on the difficult path of accepting the loss. The full realization of the loss, the reality aspect, seems to be closely identified with the dead body, the physical aspects of death, as well as the circumstances in which it happened. It is therefore important to make arrangements for the families to see the dead bodies. The problems connected with this are very complicated, and the arrangements must be scrupulously planned. Each family must be evaluated in detail and the state of the body must be taken into consideration. Meeting the dead gives the family a chance to see, say goodbye to, and touch the beloved for the last time and to comprehend fully that the loss is real, that the uncertainty is over, and that they must make a final farewell. It was important to learn that in cases where the face is too mutilated to be seen, other parts of the body may be recognized and serve as a kind of symbol for the deceased. A hand will be caressed for instance.

In this situation of extreme helplessness every symbol that has any kind of connection with the deceased acquires the greatest importance. This has been proved by the fact, for instance, that viewing the scene of the disaster is one of the most important parts in the coping strategies for the surviving members of a family whose nearest members have been hit by a disaster. If this viewing can be carried out in (small) groups it will be natural that the visit is combined with memorial ceremonies of a rather intimate character. The emotional impact of being confronted with the scene of a disaster for the first time is usually so strong that the families prefer to be shielded as much as possible from the intruding gaze of outsiders or the media. One has learned from experiences of the most different post-disaster situations, whether war, industrial disasters, natural catastrophes, or the like, that the survivors attach many emotions to the scene of the disaster and that the importance of it does not diminish with time.

Social support is always a very salient factor in promoting recovery after loss. Public memorial services after catastrophes are therefore considered an important means to demonstrate to the bereaved that they are not alone, that the whole community and in some cases even the whole nation is feeling with them and trying to console them in their loss.

These are only a few points in the complex range of therapeutic efforts which are used today in order to reduce the impact of catastrophes on the bereaved.

If we consider what has been said about bereavement, loss, grief, and mourning, whether from an individual or psychological point of view after a disaster, and compare this with the situation of the survivors after World War II, we see that the differences concern dimensions which are completely unfathomable. Here it is necessary to stress the difference between survivors of the Holocaust who have been in the camps themselves and "survivors," that is, members of families, relatives, and friends who survived outside occupied Europe.

The former, usually having been transported together with their beloved to Auschwitz, learned often in the most inhuman way, very quickly, what had happened to their families immediately after their arrival. Their hunger, unhappiness, desolation, desperation, and emaciation, however, did not allow them any normal psychological reactions to the terrible information. They had to repress and deny everything. Any thought of parents, children, wife, or husband was a luxury they could not afford. They had to use every single grain of energy for the simple task of surviving and to exclude absolutely everything else from their minds.

After the liberation, most of the survivors were numbed and far too weak to understand completely the impact of the event. The awakening from the nightmare of the inferno of the camp was very slow; the lethargy and apathy, which to a certain degree was necessary to everybody to survive, receded only gradually. The awakening to full emotional consciousness was often perhaps more painful than the captivity itself. Most of the survivors had lost so many of their family members that even when the capability of normal reactions returned, they were unable to mourn in a normal way. They never could go through the grief phases described, and were therefore never in a condition to work through their grief. It was thus in accordance with psychological experiences that most of the survivors' grief reactions were "pathological," that they had long-lasting depressions "without obvious reasons" and in some cases behavior disturbances like reclusiveness, tendency to isolation, etc., which "objective observers," who did not know what had happened, classified as changes of personality or other more or less inadequate psychiatric diagnoses.

The families of the Holocaust victims who had lived in free countries and after the war had learned about the catastrophe that had befallen their beloved had as a rule not much better psychological possibilities to work through their bereavement reactions. They too were overwhelmed by the number of the victims, by the immeasurable quality and quantity of the tragedy.

Here the psychological experiences from other catastrophes must be applied, and a comparison with the above-mentioned Buffalo Creek disaster could be instructive to a certain degree.

One has to imagine a flood lasting not only a few minutes, but several years; killing not 125, but 6 million people; a destruction caused not by human negligence, but by deeply fanatical and hateful monomania and by the reckless determination of a destructive and paranoiac dictator and his blind and obstinate followers. Furthermore, the destruction encompassed not fourteen mining hamlets, but hundreds and hundreds of towns, cities, and communities. In addition to this, the survivors are not the greatest part of the total population, but they are only remnants, a handful of hopelessly isolate people, with chronic psychiatric and somatic traumatization and diseases. Like the survivors of the Buffalo Creek disaster, the survivors could not return to their familiar ground, but had to adjust to new and strange surroundings. The survivors' new surroundings were, however, most strange. New countries, new languages, new laws, and new lives were the problems with which they were confronted.

In addition to this, it is important to stress the above-mentioned family disasters and their quite exceptional bearing on the family in an Eastern European Jewish community. In support of this statement, it might be appropriate to quote a few excerpts from the anthropological study by Zborowski and Herzog:

Family ties continue close even when one is no longer part of the household. Several times each year, aunts, uncles, cousins—the entire family . . . will gather to celebrate some event, or one of the holidays. . . .

Human relations are expected to endure. There is seldom a final end to anything. Certainly a brother is always a brother, a sister always a sister. There may be quarrels and misunderstandings, but in time of crisis a family hangs together and cares for its own. If parents cannot give their children the support and help that is their due, other members of the family are expected to step in. Perhaps an uncle, an aunt, a grandparent, or even a more remote relative will take responsibility. It is always assumed that those who can will do, and those who have will give. . . .

Nothing so strongly demonstrates the sense of family cohesion as the assumptions about the help one can count on as matter of course from relatives. It is taken for granted that if a brother's child is sick and the brother cannot pay for the best of attention, if he has a daughter to be dowered, a son to be educated, a more prosperous brother or sister should shoulder the expense. It is "only natural" that the brother or sister who emigrates to the United States "can't rest" until he brings more of the family over. It may be less that he cannot bear to live without them than that one just "naturally" behaves so. At times, however, extreme personal devotion enters in. . . .

Kinship ties, even distant ones, entitle an individual to food, lodging and support when he comes to visit. In a strange town or city you seek out a relative to stay with, and there is usually one to be found. He may be your uncle, your seventh cousin, or the nephew of your brother's mother-in-law. If a man needs a job, a wealthy relative must give him one if it is at all possible. If not, he must help him to find one.

Again it cannot be assumed that the assistance is always joyously extended. On the contrary. . . . But again, there is no choice. The obligation is real and unalterable.

These mutual obligations act almost as a form of insurance in an economic system as unstable as that of the shtetl . . . For the shtetl, the community is an extended family.[1]

It seems appropriate to quote fully this description of the central position held by family cohesion in the minds of the survivors. It will then be easier to understand that the total disintegration of this cohesion in the community and in the family would necessarily result in radical changes in the individual's apprehension of both the self and the surroundings.

Furthermore, it must be pointed out that none of the psychological helping activities for survivors of catastrophes described earlier was available. This applies both for the families in the free world and in much higher degree for the real survivors of the camps. There was no family present that could act as the most important source of strength; everybody knew that the death had been a sudden one; the circumstances had been more than tragic. There were no bodies left, not even a pile of ashes or a cinerarium. In addition to all that, there was no absolute certainty that somebody was dead or not. There was no proper documentation and usually no witnesses to what had happened. The mass slaughter was performed under the highest degree of secrecy and usually without survivors. Based on facts available, one had to believe and conclude that there were no survivors left from all the huge transports to Treblinka, Majdanek, Sobibor, Auschwitz, and so on. But miracles happened. From time to time some of one's relatives had been heard of or had been seen or even suddenly appeared. In most cases the agonizing uncertainty persisted in the minds of many people for years on end.

There were no funerals, no proper mourning rituals, and no day for anniversaries. What remained for most of the survivors (both concentration camp survivors and other bereaved families) was "viewing the scene of the disaster" as described earlier. And Auschwitz, the camp where a great part of the European Jews had been killed, became the main "scene of the disaster." Though it had been transformed partly into a museum with all the positive and negative attributes of just a museum, other parts of the camp evoke feelings of anguish when entered. There are no graves and no headstones at Auschwitz, but nevertheless the site has become the symbol of a graveyard for millions of people, not buried but burned. It is visited with devotion and awe by thousands of persons who have lost their parents, brothers and sisters, husbands and wives, and last, but surely not least, their children. The visitors are the grieving remnants of hundreds of Jewish communities in Europe now living dispersed all over the world. From a strictly descriptive psychological point of view, one may say that these are people with unresolved, delayed, or inhibited grief responses and that they expect unconsciously some kind of emotional relief when visiting this scene of disaster. A real consolation is of course impossible, and they have to accept the realities of history and life.

But we know what importance is ascribed to symbols by bereaved people. Berge H. Pollock, the president of the Institute for Psychoanalysis and professor of psychiatry at Northwestern University, describes this in a short sketch from a visit to the Washington, D.C., Vietnam memorial, "where I saw children search for an engraved name. 'Is that Uncle John?' The still bereaved grandmother shakes her head affirmatively and they move back to look at their link to the dead soldier, their link to continuity of past, present, and future."

And so how does the situation at Auschwitz psychologically affect many of the bereaved who visit it? This tragic site is in a way holy to many different kinds of people and to many denominations, not only Jewish victims—although their numbers were by far the largest. One does not expect any denomination to appropriate, symbolically, the place of grief. This is particularly true when the symbol of that denomination is one which, for many of the victims and survivors, has been a symbol of hatred and persecution, not of the love and forgiveness it was meant to signify. So the bereaved who arrive hoping to find consolation by identifying the place of death and making some kind of personal memorial ceremony, receive instead something more than a serious shock. They become disturbed, and the unresolved grief that has been a torment through many years, turns into a feeling of new unresolved despair.

NOTE

1. Mark Zborowski and Elizabeth Herzog, *Life Is with People: The Culture of the Shtetl* (New York: Schocken Books, 1967), 303–4, 306.

Part Three

The Theology of Memory

11

The New Road

Claire Huchet-Bishop

Monday June 13, 1960. . . . The great day, the one of the pontifical audience. In the Vatican, the Swiss guards stand at attention, the officer salutes. . . . The pope greets us standing. I bow and John XXIII shakes hands informally with me. . . . Then I submit my request regarding the teaching and, first of all, its historic base. But how was I to convey, within a few minutes, the kind of spiritual ghetto in which the church had gradually and ultimately confined the old Israel as well as shutting him within a material ghetto? Hence was formed what I called the teaching of contempt. Practiced throughout centuries, it impregnated deeply the Christian mentality. Therefore it is essential that a voice be raised from on high, from the "summit"—the head of the church—to point out to all the right way, and to condemn solemnly the teaching of contempt as inherently anti-Christian.

Concretely, how could this be done? Then I present my concluding note and the suggestion that a subcommission be created within the Council in order to study the question. The pope at once reacts: "I thought about it from the onset of our conversation."[1]

Thus reads part of the report that a Jewish scholar named Jules Isaac wrote about his meeting with Pope John XXIII, and which I choose to recall at the beginning of these reflections, because Isaac's action opened the way for respectful memory. Owing to that memorable conversation, John XXIII called Cardinal Augustine Bea, and a subcommission was formed to study the Christian teaching regarding the Jews. In spite of relentless opposition, especially from the Christian Arab hierarchy, a text was finally approved. It cleared the Jews, past and present, of being collectively responsible for Jesus' death.

After nearly 2,000 years, an accusation that had caused untold persecutions was wiped out by the declaration of *Nostra Aetate* on October 20, 1965. Then and there the Catholic church made a spectacular 180-degree turn. Its prime mover, Jules Isaac, could rest peacefully in his grave—he died in 1963—for his accomplishment was to open a door tragically closed for almost two millennia. The opening of that door pointed toward what I shall call the New Road that Jewish-Christian relations ought to take.

Unfortunately, however, twenty-five years after *Nostra Aetate*'s light had pierced twenty centuries of darkness in Jewish-Christian relations, a huge cross, the very symbol for the Jews of Christian persecution, has been raised by well-meaning but poorly informed Carmelites over the ashes of 1.5 million murdered Jews at Auschwitz. Has the door opened by John XXIII and Jules Isaac been closed again?

Those of us who remember the 1948 publication of Jules Isaac's initial study, *Jésus et Israël*, recall its hearty reception by the British pioneers, the Reverend James Parkes and William U. Simpson.[2] In France the book met astonishment at best. It embarrassed many, was hailed enthusiastically by a few, and was dismissed by others who could not stand the truth. Here was a well-known historian—the author of a seven-volume world history, which was a standard text throughout French state schools and universities—a man the Vichy government had shamefully deprived of his high-ranking post as Inspector General of Education on account of his Jewish origin, though he himself was not observant; a man whose reputation as a scholar and humanist was flawless; and now he had written a book that revealed, in 400 uncompromising pages, the Christian responsibility in the extermination of 6 million Jews. Specifically, through impartial study and through analysis of both Catholic and Protestant commentaries on the Gospels, Isaac showed how the Christian mentality has been saturated with a deep contempt for Jews. As a result, it became possible for Hitler and his henchmen to perpetrate Auschwitz without having to face a general Christian outcry, let alone a clear, vehement, effective protest from the Vatican.

At the end of *Jésus et Israël*, Isaac offered practical suggestions—what to do, concretely, to rectify Christian teaching. These Eighteen Points had been brought by Jules Isaac to Seelisberg in 1947.* They served as a base for the famous "Ten Points of Seelisberg." It is instructive to compare the two texts.[3] Both mention the Jewishness of Jesus, his family, and his disciples. They also warn against saying that Judaism was degenerate at the time of Jesus and against using the word "Jews" exclusively to designate the enemies of Jesus. Isaac's language is direct, forceful. The fourteenth point, for example, speaks plainly about the

---

*Editors' note: The Ten Points of Seelisberg were based on Eighteen Points about Jews and Judaism, suggested by the famous French scholar, Jules Isaac (in *Jesus and Israel*, ed. Claire Huchet-Bishop, trans. Sally Gran [New York: Holt, Rinehart & Winston, 1971]) to Christians involved in "Christian teaching worthy of the name." These Eighteen Points formed the basis for the Seelisberg Declaration issued by the Third Commission of the International Emergency Conference of Christians and Jews at Seelisberg, Switzerland, in August 1947. This conference, noteworthy for its early date, included both Catholic and Protestant Christians.

deicide accusation. The Seelisberg Declaration, however, avoids the word "deicide" itself. Vatican II did the same: "Although the Jewish authorities and those who followed their lead, pressed for the death of Christ (cf. John 19:6), nevertheless what happened to Christ in His passion cannot be attributed to all Jews, without distinction, then alive, nor to the Jews of today."[4]

To stick to the word "deicide," as Isaac had done, would have had a much greater impact on the crowds that for centuries, in Poland especially, have hurled it at Jews. As Bishop Stephen A. Leven of San Antonio, Texas, emphasized at the Council, "The word deicide [is] a word of infamy and execration invented by Christians and used to blame and persecute the Jews. . . . It is not up to us to make a declaration about something philosophical, but to reprobate and damn a word which has furnished so many occasions of persecution throughout the centuries."[5] In vain did Father René Laurentin, Rabbi Abraham Joshua Heschel (an observer at Vatican II), and a few others, Cardinal Lercaro (Bologna), Bishop Elchinger (Strasbourg), join with Bishop Leven. They met with opposition, mainly from the Arab group, who argued that to clear the Jews explicitly of deicide was also to suppress the view that exile was the Jews' punishment and thereby to justify the existence of the State of Israel.

It is wise not to forget that the situation that confronts us today in the Middle East is linked also to a theological debate. The fact that reference to that debate is not made now does not mean that it does not color, perhaps subconsciously, the attitude of some Christians. How could it be otherwise? Could we expect the effect of a steady, persistent, centuries-long indoctrination to be erased within a few years? Still, as pussyfooted as it was, the text of *Nostra Aetate* stood as a revelation to Catholics. But questions remain: Does the reversal of the Vatican's traditional teaching strike at the root of the prejudice? Does the acceptance of *Nostra Aetate* help to form a sound judgment in circumstances where Jews are involved? Should we expect *Nostra Aetate* to help people understand Jewish reactions against the Carmelite convent at Auschwitz, the largest cemetery of Jewish martyrdom? Is the New Road, born from Jules Isaac's anguished call and John XXIII's eager answer, taken at all, and if so, how?

Several responses can be discerned. First, as hard as it is to believe, some people know nothing about the New Road. There are still people who, upon hearing that Jesus was Jewish, recoil in disbelief or disgust. Others just refuse to use the New Road. They fear losing their own identity. The old way is their security. Still others are eager initially to take the New Road, because they expect it to be the way of angels. But when they discover that Jews may be less than angelic, they turn away in self-righteous disappointment.

There are also those who declare haughtily that they do not care about the New Road. It is useless to raise with them the shocking question: What about the 6 million murdered Jews? They retort: "Exactly! What did the religious establishment do to oppose that? Nothing. So whatever it does now is null and void." Rejecting that view, some have taken the New Road only to find that the hurdle posed by the Carmelite convent at Auschwitz cannot be cleared: "Why all the noise about the Carmelites living there?'' they say. ''The Carmelites are praying, they are not doing any harm.'' Then, in France at least, there are some who stood with Jules Isaac twenty years before Vatican II and for whom the New Road is hardly new, although it is not naturally smooth because the blindness of other travelers slows up the march and because one is never sure of being wholly free from the effects of the age-old teaching of contempt.

Thus, it seems that there is a gap between the official pronouncements and their application to concrete situations. Yet there is no lack of signs posted helpfully on the New Road, including some twelve guidelines issued by the Vatican and by the pope himself since 1965.[6] Among them is the 1969 promulgation that modified the ''Good Friday Prayer.'' It took twenty years, however, for action to be taken after Jules Isaac raised with Pope Pius XII in 1949 the issue of the prayer's antisemitic references.[7] The Catholic church does move slowly!

In 1974 the ''Guidelines and Suggestions for Implementing the Conciliar Declaration *Nostra Aetate*'' dealt with liturgy, teaching and education, and social action. To intensify the search for a better understanding between Jews and Catholics, the International Liaison Committee was formed, including representatives of the Catholic church and the International Jewish Committee for Interreligious Consultations. The members of this Liaison Committee met yearly in various countries and examined diverse questions created by *Nostra Aetate*, such as the development of dialogue through the use of the Scripture, Judaism's image in Christian education, and Christianity's image in Jewish education.[8] Many prestigious leaders worked in this group. It is not possible to mention all of them here, but those whom I found making particularly helpful contributions include the following: Rabbi Marc Tanenbaum, the late Pierre Dabosville, Rabbi Leon Klenicki, Father Edward Flannery, Rabbi Henry Siegman, Monsignor Jorge Mejia, Rabbi Ronald B. Sobel, Father Marcel Dubois, O.P., Rabbi Irving Greenberg, Father Bernard Dupuy, O.P., Rabbi Emmanuel Bulz, and a host of lay people, professors and writers, André Neher, Eugene Fisher, the late Zacharia Shuster, Joseph Emanuel, Andre Chouraqui, Clements Thoma, Jean Halperin, the late Malcom Hay, Michael Wyschogrod, and many others.

Pope Paul VI's 1975 address to the Liaison Committee emphasized the necessity for Catholics ''to learn now to understand better what are the characteristics, deemed essential, by the Jews themselves, regarding their living religious reality.''[9] At Mainz, five years later, Pope John Paul II outlined ''The Road to Understanding.''[10] Then, in 1985, the Vatican published the important ''Notes on the Correct Way to Present the Jews and Judaism in Preaching and Catechesis in the Roman Catholic Church.'' This document was followed shortly by ''Presentation of the Notes' Intent.''[11]

In 1986, at the Great Synagogue in Rome, John Paul II declared that the purpose of his historic visit was ''to make a decisive contribution to the consolidation of the good relations between our two communities. . . . ''[12] Alas, this impressive first in the church's history coincided with disclosures about the Carmelite convent at the Auschwitz camp.

Something is amiss somewhere. There seems to be a lack of synchronization between the Vatican and national local churches, for we can recall happily many excellent guidelines issued from local churches. They include, for example, the 1969 "Guidelines and Suggestions" from the New York, Rockville Center, and Brooklyn Center dioceses; the 1970 "Recommendations of the Pastoral Council of the Netherlands Catholic Church"; the 1971 "Catholic-Protestant Declaration" from the German Kirchentag; the epoch-making 1973 "Pastoral Orientations for Relations with Judaism" published by the French Bishops Conference; and the 1977 "Réflexions du Conseil de la Fédération des Eglises Protestantes de la Suisse."[13] Many other studies in the spirit of *Nostra Aetate* have been carried on in Europe and the Americas as well.[14]

One should also note Jules Isaac's 1948 founding of the "Amitié Judéo-Chrétienne" (Jewish-Christian Fellowship), the first Jewish-Christian group on the Continent—it later became "L'Amitié Judéo-Chrétienne de France"—aimed at developing "knowledge, comprehension between Judaism and Christianity so that respect and fellowship will replace the centuries-old misunderstanding and the hostile tradition."[15] Among its recent concerns is the Carmelite convent at Auschwitz. Several issues of its monthly periodical, *Sens*, have dealt with it. The "Amitié Judéo-Chrétienne de France" is also a member of the International Council of Christians and Jews (ICCJ). With delegates from nineteen countries, the council has its headquarters at the Buber House in Heppenheim, Germany.

Such a flowering of good-spirited studies and actions did not prepare us for the Auschwitz convent scandal. It is not my purpose here to delve into its history. That has been abundantly written about and discussed in the international press. What should hold our attention as Christians and Catholics is the complexity of the situation and the confused thinking that accompanies it.

Consider that, in the brief survey made above of the various national Catholic declarations issued after *Nostra Aetate* and concerned about revising Christian teaching regarding the Jews, there is no mention of any from Poland. This may result, of course, from the notorious lack—at least until recently—of communication between East and West. Yet, what took place at Auschwitz in 1984—largely unknown in the West—makes one doubt that the Polish Catholic church had made a start on the New Road, if it were even aware of the Road's existence.*

True, if there are discrepancies, there are reasons for them. Poland's suffering during World War II exceeded that of all other occupied countries, with tens of thousands of non-Jewish Poles killed at Auschwitz and 3 million other war casualties. Hitler's aim was to weaken Poland to such an extent that it would

Editors' note: Since this chapter was written, there are signs that the Polish Catholic church has made a start on the New Road. See, for example, this book's Afterword.

virtually become Germany's slave. It is natural that such a national distaste became uppermost in Polish minds. Yet from that tragedy to silence about the *Shoah* creates a gap difficult to cross. Why, then visiting Auschwitz, does one rarely receive an inkling from the guides that this is the greatest Jewish cemetery in the world? Throngs crowd into the place. It is apparent that this is a national pilgrimage site to commemorate Polish martyrdom. And indeed martyrdom it was between 1940 and 1942, but not later, when the gas chambers were installed. Then the number of Jews murdered there was many times greater than that of the Poles. Silence about this is deafening.

Such memory loss about the *Shoah* explains how the plan to establish a Carmelite convent at Auschwitz could have been hatched. For the Poles, this soil is Polish, and it is the center of Polish martyrdom. Moreover, isn't it odiously petty to link the memory of suffering to numbers? It would be if it were not the case that the numerical question is connected with a project that, if successful, would have entailed mortal consequences for the whole of humankind. The Nazi attempt to turn Poland into a slave nation was hideous. But to undertake to wipe the Jews from the face of the earth was diabolical. This determination to stamp out Jewish men, women, and children like vermin—thus making sure of the complete destruction and lasting annihilation of the Jewish people—this project, which nearly came to completion, struck at the root of the tree of human life.

Unfortunately, the killing of a group of people is not new. Such crimes have been perpetrated many times in history. But to the killing of the Jewish people another dimension is added, and it is that dimension which, as Christians, we should have perceived, had we not become blind and deaf through the church's teaching of contempt. To say this does not diminish one's own sympathy for Polish suffering. Only we have to recognize that, at Auschwitz, Polish and Jewish suffering are not on the same level.

The attempt at the "Final Solution" also tolls the bell for the final extinction of humanity's spiritual light. Though not through their own merit, the Jews as a people are the bearers on this planet of God's covenant with humanity. We Christians partake of that covenant's immense promise, which guarantees the meaning of human life, through Jesus, a Jew, and his first disciples, who were all Jews, too. That is the reason why Hitler's second target was Christianity. Once the Jewish root was destroyed, the Christian branches were vulnerable, and the road would be clear for Nazism's worldwide domination. Then the concept of blood kinship would replace "love thy neighbor as thyself," and Hitler's command would take precedence over conscience, the latter being but "a Jewish invention."[16]

In those days of darkness throughout Europe, there were a handful of people— Christians, humanists, atheists—who had, consciously or not, assimilated the Judeo-Christian message and who, at their own risk and peril, saved Jews. Today why cannot we perceive that to plant a cross over the place where Jews met the paroxysm of Hitler's hatred is an act of insufferable appropriation? That it was done with the best of intentions is precisely what makes it lamentable. That fact points to a lack of recognition of and sensitivity about the Christian responsibility for Auschwitz. Such blindness led Father Werenfried van Straaten to declare that "the Carmelites will bear witness to the victorious power of the Cross."[17] It makes Cardinal Macharski explain that "Auschwitz should not be only a monument of hatred, but . . . the Carmelites will make it also a monument of abetting love."[18] Considering the New Road in Jewish-Christian relations taken by many in the Catholic church since 1965, one might have at least expected consultation with Jewish representatives regarding the Carmelites' project. When Pope John Paul II visited Auschwitz in 1979 and expressed the wish that "a high center of prayer, reconciliation, and penance" be established there, did he take for granted that the Jews would be consulted?[19] Or was that question and its legitimacy totally absent from his mind? Two thousand years of walking roughshod on the Jewish community leaves deep marks on the subconscious. The theology of supersession and the habit of hegemony are ingrained, especially, it seems, in the Catholic hierarchy. With disarming—and appalling—"goodwill," a second killing of the Jews was initiated at Auschwitz.

That the attempt at erasing the memory of the *Shoah* has been stopped through the joint effort of Jewish and Catholic representatives is a matter worth further reflection. Before we pursue it, however, consider the lesson we can learn from our injurious Christian behavior. The conscious effort to accept the Jews as they understand themselves, a path recommended by the Vatican, has not been too evident in Poland. Awareness of the New Road established by Pope John XXIII has not occurred evenly in all countries. It is known that there were practically no Jews left in Poland following the *Shoah*, and yet there were pogroms and purges, and, as Claude Lanzmann's film so painfully shows, Polish antisemitism still exists. The effect of the traditional indoctrination survives any new Vatican directives. It is evident that the young Poles who are trying earnestly to fight this popular inclination need all our sympathy and encouragement. That statement, of course, must not imply superiority. In France, for example, though the last pogrom dates back to 1321, though Dreyfus was rehabilitated in 1906, though 230,000 out of the 300,000 Jews who lived in France at the outbreak of World War II escaped deportation mainly through the dangerous secret connivance of the non-Jewish population, still we can hear today some French people saying, "I am not antisemitic, some of my best friends are Jews," or describing the Jews as grasping, possessive, and domineering. Desecration of Jewish cemeteries and the politics of Jean-Marie Le Pen testify that antisemitism still lives in France. It is because we know the disease that we can understand the Poles' predicament.

Christian antisemitism is a contradiction in terms. Wondering, with Jules Isaac, how the *Shoah* could have taken place in a Christianized Europe, we have to conclude that a large part of the European population, laity and clergy alike, was never Christianized. It is not surprising that some of us, their descendants, take more willingly to the pagan deities of racism than to Judeo-Christian ethical values. We know ourselves how very difficult it is to follow Christ. But follow we must, unless we declare, like Peter, "I don't know him"—what a warning to all the popes!

It is important to understand that the Carmelite scandal did not occur through ill-will. Ignorance was the culprit—ignorance of the Jews' long history of persecution at Christian hands, ignorance of the Jewish people's particular vocation, namely, "the sanctification of the Name," which "makes of the life and the prayer of the Jewish people a blessing for all the nations of the earth."[20] Their faithfulness to the covenant should have brought about our admiration, especially after the *Shoah* during which God seemed to break the covenant. It is they, the Jews, who resolved even after Auschwitz to continue the covenant, to live deliberately as Jews in the diaspora and throughout Eretz Israel, the third part of the triune Jewish command, Torah-People-Land.[21]

Our deadly ignorance of Jews and Judaism should be dealt with here and now. Nicolas Berdyaev used to say that "antisemitism testifies to Christianity's unfinished task." We should work at this task concretely and not only through reading. We should strive to form small diocesan groups of priests, rabbis, lay people, Jews and Christians, to learn about each other from each other. Controversy avoided, proselytism banned, declarations of faith accepted—these are some of the criteria we need. Study of Jewish history should be pursued: What is 1942 to the average Christian, what is it to a Jew? We should invite each other to the celebrations of our respective communities. We should organize reciprocal visits to our places of worship and schools. All these urgent endeavors are recommended in the various "guidelines" and "orientations" mentioned above. We must also reject the old theology that conceived itself only by denying the other, by spurning the validity of the other's identity.[22] Gradually, through all these efforts, esteem can take the place of contempt.

Paradoxically, the unfortunate Carmelite affair may have broken new ground for such relationships. At Geneva, for the first time in history, representatives of both the Jewish community and the church worked out together the practical resolution of the conflict. That it amounted to a compromise on both sides does not lessen its value. On the contrary, it shows that the old road of nonnegotiable antagonism can be abandoned. To do so required humility from the Christians and generosity from the Jews.

This kind of attitude should be maintained as we continue to work for the undelayed relocation of the convent. That we "do not grow weary of any weariness" is of the greatest importance in today's world.[23] Soon no living witness of the *Shoah* will be left. Yet the memory of the *Shoah* should never be erased, lest the crime be repeated. Let Auschwitz I and II remain Auschwitz, bare of any sign of human life. Nothing. Horror. And Silence.

The convent affair is not a marginal question, as some might think, considering the magnitude of the recent East European political upheaval. The Jewish-Christian reconciliation is not apart from history. The New Road of understanding and esteem is a necessary condition for the evolution of the human spirit. Referring to the passionate pages on deicide in *Jésus et Israël*, Jules Isaac said that he wrote them "under the imperative of a sacred duty: commemoration."[24] He meant commemoration of the death of his wife and daughter at Auschwitz. Let the *Shoah* be commemorated, today and all the days to come, by Christians and Jews walking hand in hand on the New Road—each in his or her own identity and yet together, proclaiming in deeds, and not only in words, that the human being is not a thing but the responsible partner in the project of the God of Abraham, Isaac, Jacob, and Jesus.

NOTES

1. Jules Isaac, "Notes sur huit jours à Rome, Juin 1960," *Combat pour la vérité* (Paris: Hachette, 1970), 265–70. In the body of this essay, the English translations from the French are mine.

2. Jules Isaac, *Jésus et Israël* (Paris: Albin Michel, 1948). The English edition, *Jesus and Israel* (New York: Holt, Rinehart and Winston) was published in 1971.

3. To compare these items in detail, see Isaac's "Appendix and Practical Conclusion," *Jesus and Israel*, 489–95.

4. See "Declaration on the Relations of the Church to Non-Christian Religions," in Arthur Gilbert, *The Vatican Council and the Jews* (New York: World Publishing Company, 1968), 271–88.

5. Cited by Gilbert, *The Vatican Council and the Jews*, 154.

6. Mention should also be made of the Protestant documents, also triggered by Jules Isaac, that emerged from meetings of the World Council of Churches in Amsterdam (1948) and New Delhi (1961).

7. See "Modification de la prière du Vendredi Saint," in Marie-Thérèse Hoch and Bernard Dupuy, *Les Eglises devant le Judaïsme: Documents officiels 1918–1978* (Paris: Cerf, 1980), 350–52.

8. See *Fifteen Years of Catholic–Jewish Dialogue 1970–1985* (Libreria Editrice Vaticana, 1988), xv–xix.

9. See "Déclaration du Pape Paul VI, 10 Janvier 1975," in Hoch and Dupuy, *Les Eglises devant le Judaïsme*, 365–67.

10. See "The Road to Understanding," in Eugene J. Fisher, A. James Rudin, and Marc H. Tanenbaum, *Twenty Years of Jewish-Catholic Relations* (New York: Paulist Press, 1986), 212–15.

11. See *Fifteen Years of Catholic-Jewish Dialogue*, 315–18.

12. Ibid., 321–25.

13. See Hoch and Dupuy, *Les Eglises devant le Judaïsme*, 120–29, 197–207, 42–72, 171–79, and 236–43.

14. Two very helpful brochures along these lines have been published. See "Within Context" for the catechetical presentation of Jews and Judaism in the New Testament (U.S. Catholic Conference and Anti-Defamation League, 1987) and "Guidelines on the Presentation of Jews and Judaism in Catholic Preaching" (U.S. Bishops' Committee on the Liturgy, 1988).

15. See the Statutes of Amitié Judéo-Chrétienne de France, Article 2.

16. The first quoted material is scriptural. See Leviticus 19:18, Matthew 19:19, Mark

12:31, and Luke 10:27. The second quoted material is a comment by Hitler cited in Yves Chevalier, *L'Antisémitisme* (Paris: Cerf, 1988), 440.

17. See *Regards: Revue juive de Belqique*, December 1985.

18. Correspondence of the International Jewish Committee on Interreligious Consultation, 27 May 1986.

19. See *Regards*, 21 March 1986.

20. See Hoch and Dupuy, *Les Eglises devant le Judaïsme*, 175.

21. See Irving Greenberg, "Penser Auschwitz," *Sens*, November 1989.

22. See Chevalier, *L'Antisémitisme*, 369.

23. Edmond Fleg, *Le Juif du Pape* (Paris: Rieder, 1925), 182.

24. Isaac, *Jésus et Israël*, xxiii.

12

Historical Memories in Conflict

Judith Hershcopf Banki

From the beginning, the conflict around the Carmelite convent at Auschwitz had some of the surreal and inexorable quality of a nightmare, in which seemingly mundane events are invested with awesome significance.[1] There was a pervasive sense of some advancing menace and of powerlessness to stop it. To a number of Holocaust survivors, the menace was the convent itself—seen as both a threat and a provocation. To those actively involved in the field of Jewish-Christian relations, who had been cheered by—and in many cases had contributed to—the substantial progress toward mutual understanding and rapprochement achieved in recent decades, the menace was the unraveling of that progress, as incomprehension and resentment hardened into anger and outrage on both sides. This dreary-looking building, made sinister by the uses to which it had been put by the Nazi overlords of the Auschwitz death camp, became sinister again as a symbol of conflict and confrontation.

In the end, the controversy became a kind of witches' brew, threatening to boil over and poison the surrounding atmosphere. This potent stew had much in it: clashes of historic memory; conflicts of religious and ethnic identity, particularly between Jews and Polish Catholics; unreconciled views on how the suffering of these victimized peoples should be memorialized. Every issue of potential conflict between communities whose past interaction was remembered very differently by each side, every possible clash of identity and self-perception, came together on this issue. In short, just about everything that could go wrong went wrong.

That is, almost everything. In fact, after a series of escalating conflicts, we were pulled back from the brink, as it were, by a combination of forces: first and foremost, by a core group of Catholic, other Christian, and Jewish leaders on both sides of the Atlantic who had come to trust one another over the years and who worked diligently and faithfully to keep the channels of communication open and the dialogue going during the most difficult of moments, among them members of the American hierarchy and a number of Roman Catholic sisters; second, by some courageous voices in Poland; and ultimately, by the public intervention of the Vatican itself.

These developments have given all parties some welcome breathing space. During this period, it is important to examine the crisis around the convent at Auschwitz as a kind of case history. We must make an effort to learn from this crisis, both for the sake of the past, to honor the memory of the innocent men, women, and children murdered at Auschwitz—over 90 percent of them killed for the "crime" of being born of Jewish parents—and for the sake of the future, to establish bonds of kinship and communication and to summon the courage to confront a painful history together.

A brief review of the events as they developed may provide a framework for understanding why the convent set off so much passionate argument on both sides. Even at this stage, not all the facts about the installation of the convent in its present location are known. Even were the facts agreed upon, total objectivity might not be possible: each community will look at the convent from the perspective of its own history. With every effort toward fairness, this review will perforce examine the developing crisis through Jewish eyes.

The precise origins of the convent remain unclear. It has been frequently noted that the present pope, when he was still archbishop of Cracow, expressed the desire that there be a place for prayer and meditation at Auschwitz. Apparently, the Carmelites of Cracow were given permission by the Polish government to occupy a building on the outer edge of the camp some time in 1984. Originally intended as a theater but never used as such, the building was used by the Nazis to store supplies, particularly the Zyklon B gas used in the gas chambers.

Jews were neither consulted nor informed about this decision and only learned about the convent the following year, through the circulation, in Belgium, of a fund-raising brochure produced by an organization called Aid to the Church in Distress. The brochure called the convent Catholics' "gift to the Pope," claimed "the Carmelites do penance for us who are still alive," referred to "the victorious power of the Cross of Jesus," and predicted the convent would become "a spiritual fortress, a token of the conversion of brothers from various countries who went astray." The reference to the conversion of "brothers who went astray" was probably aimed at lapsed Catholics and was not intended to convey conversionary intentions toward Jews, but regardless of intentions, the language was so triumphalistic and insensitive that its negative impact was predictable. The brochure also described the convent as a compensation for the "outrages" which had been visited upon the pope. Again, neither the "outrages" nor the pope were specified. Some Jews assumed the author was aggressively defending Pius XII against any possible criticism of his actions during World War II. More likely, the author was expressing his own anger at a less-than-enthusiastic reception accorded John Paul II during a papal visit to the Low Countries in 1985. But again, the language was provocative and its effects predictably unfortunate.

This fund-raising brochure had an explosive effect on the Jewish community, first of Belgium and later throughout Europe. There was no mention anywhere in the document that Auschwitz was the primary place of systematic murder of Jews during the Holocaust. In fact, there was no mention of Jews at all. The impassioned nature of the conflict which ensued is partly explained by the way in which the presence of the convent became known on the public scene. And since the language of the brochure was future-oriented, it was not clear to those who began protesting the installation of the convent that it was already in place, that the nuns were already there and had been there for over a year.

It must be noted that the tone and content of the fund-raising tract drew intense criticism from a variety of Christian sources, as well as from Jews, including the Christian members of the Amitié Judéo-Chrétienne of France. Criticism of the installation of the convent itself was more measured, but Cardinal Albert Decourtray, archbishop of Lyons, declared: "It is the attempt to totally exterminate the Jews that we call the *Shoah*,[2] of which Auschwitz is the symbol. Such affliction and suffering has conferred on the Jewish people, through its martyrs, a particular dignity that is quite properly its own. And to construct a convent at Auschwitz would, for me, impinge upon that dignity."

The intensity of the Jewish response—which was virtually unanimous—apparently caught Cardinal Franciszek Macharski, archbishop of Cracow, in whose diocese Auschwitz-Birkenau falls, off balance. A church leader sincerely interested in Christian-Jewish rapprochement who had visited Yad Vashem, the Holocaust Memorial Museum in Jerusalem, he viewed the convent as a token of reconciliation. He was apparently astonished to discover that Jews viewed it as an act of appropriation. In an article in the Polish Catholic weekly *Tygodnik Powszechny*, editor Jerzy Turowicz noted that Auschwitz "is also a symbol of the martyrdom of the Polish people during the Nazi occupation" and asked, "Do these two symbols really have to divide our two nations?" Turowicz had previously demonstrated sensitivity to the feelings of Jews and had called for an examination of Polish antisemitism; his was a friendly question with no hostile intentions. Nevertheless, it was on this very question that the struggle was joined. From a Jewish perspective, the Polish church had acted unilaterally to stake out a claim to the place that both summarized and symbolized the destruction of European Jewry. The Jews' sense of bewilderment and betrayal was very real. Their protests mounted in intensity.

Efforts to resolve the conflict led to a "summit meeting" held July 22, 1986, in Geneva, Switzerland, between members of the Roman Catholic hierarchy from France, Belgium, and Poland and rabbinic and communal leaders of French, Belgian, and Italian Jewry. Out of this meeting came a moving recognition of the special significance of Auschwitz for Jews and a promise that reconstructive work on the convent would be halted. Jewish leaders interpreted that promise as the first step in relocating the convent, but when additional nuns were reported to have moved into the building and when workmen and supplies were seen entering the building on a regular basis, they feared a resolve to keep the convent at its present site.

The protests, both Jewish and Christian, continued, leading to a second Catholic-Jewish "summit meeting" (Geneva II) held February 22, 1987, which appeared to have ended the impasse. A nine-member Catholic delegation that included four cardinals and members of various national bishops' commissions for relations with Judaism, and a nine-member Jewish delegation which included the chief rabbi of France and European representatives of national and communal Jewish organizations, agreed on a declaration and a program of action.

By calling Auschwitz "the symbolic place of the *Shoah*," reflecting the Nazi aim of destroying the Jewish people "in a unique, unthinkable, and unspeakable enterprise," and at the same time calling attention to "the sufferings of the Polish nation" during the same period, sufferings which demand "profound respect and devout meditation," the Catholic and Jewish leaders wished to honor the feelings of both Jews and Polish Christians and still point to the uniqueness of the "Final Solution"—the Nazi program to annihilate all Jews.

The program of action called for the creation of a center for "information, education, meeting and prayer" to be established "outside the area of the Auschwitz-Birkenau camps." The center, a Christian initiative, was to be carried out by the European churches, with Cardinal Macharski overseeing the implementation of the project in Poland and the bishops of other countries undertaking the fund-raising to realize the project within a two-year period. (Since the project was later mislabeled an "interfaith center," with the implication that the Jewish community had first assumed and then abandoned responsibility for supporting it financially, it is important to stress that it was assumed by all present and described at the outset as entirely a Christian-sponsored project.)

The aims of the new center, spelled out explicitly in the appended document, were basically to encourage exchanges on the *Shoah* and on the martyrdom of the Polish and other peoples during World War II; to combat trivialization and revisionism regarding the *Shoah*; and to encourage Jewish-Christian dialogue. Two points of the agreement were particularly salient in view of later developments: one, albeit expressed in very recondite language, that the Carmelite sisters would be housed in the new center upon its completion; two, a clear commitment that there would be "no permanent Catholic place of worship on the site of the Auschwitz and Birkenau camps."

As noted, this agreement appeared to have resolved an increasingly tense and painful controversy, which had tempers flaring on both sides. It was greeted with enormous relief in the Jewish community. A conference between representatives of the Vatican Commission on Relations with the Jewish People and representatives of Jewish organizations—once postponed because of uncertainty regarding the relocation of the convent at Auschwitz—was rescheduled for February 23, 1989, the day after the new center was to have been completed.

Needless to say, the so-called deadline came and went without so much as the breaking of ground for the new center. The approaching deadline prompted a flurry of correspondence between some of the parties who had signed the "Geneva II" declaration in an effort to show some indication of progress toward the implementation of the agreement, but without success. For some in the Jewish community, the failure to implement the agreement was regarded as a deliberate rejection of a solemn commitment; others, who still retained confidence in the goodwill and good intentions of their Roman Catholic cosignatories, nevertheless found it hard to swallow the lack of concrete results, and even harder to restrain the activists in their own community.

On July 14, 1989, Avraham Weiss, an activist Orthodox rabbi from Riverdale, New York, and six rabbinical students scaled the wall of the convent garden in a protest demonstration; the group was attacked, roughed up, and forcibly ejected by Polish laborers working within the convent. The incident received major press coverage and further exacerbated already bruised feelings on both sides. On August 10, Cardinal Macharski publicly announced that he was suspending the project, and that the delay was due to "a violent campaign of accusations and defamation" on the part of "certain Western Jewish circles."

Cardinal Macharski's retreat from the agreement to build the new center occasioned additional criticism. The American Jewish Committee termed it a "unilateral rejection of the very process" through which Catholic-Jewish understanding had been achieved in recent years. Tension was brought to a head by the Roman Catholic primate of Poland, Cardinal Jozef Glemp, in a sermon delivered at the Polish national shrine in Czestochowa on August 26. Cardinal Glemp issued an attack on the Jewish community which, to Jews, seemed laced with the themes of traditional antisemitism. He claimed that Jewish protests against the convent were an "offense to all Poles and a threat to Polish sovereignty"; he accused Jews of talking down to Catholics as if from a position of superiority; he suggested that the protesters had come to physically attack or murder the nuns; and he accused Jews of power over the world media. (Subsequently, he claimed that the Geneva II agreement should be renegotiated because its original signatories were not "competent," a claim that obviously offended Cardinals Decourtray, Lustiger, and Danneels; they responded by defending the agreement and asking, "If four cardinals, including the archbishop of Cracow, are not qualified to represent the Catholic side, who might be?")

The responses by other Roman Catholic church leaders to Cardinal Glemp's intemperate outburst may well have been unprecedented in recent history. Officials of the American hierarchy were quick to disassociate themselves from his remarks. Cardinal John O'Connor of New York called Glemp's remarks "distressing and harmful"; Archbishop Roger Mahony of Los Angeles associated himself with that criticism; Cardinal Bernard Law of Boston urged the Carmelites to move from the present site; Cardinal Edmund Szoka of Detroit called for the honoring of the original agreement. Moreover, within Poland itself, Glemp's comments were criticized by the newspaper of Solidarity, and the Polish episcopate's Commission on Dialogue with Judaism called for the honoring of the agreement and the building of the new center. Finally, on September 19, the Vatican ended a long silence by endorsing the 1987 accord, supporting the idea of the new center and volunteering its own funds toward its construction. Since that time, Cardinal Glemp himself has endorsed the agreement.

On February 19, 1990, ground was broken for the new building. Cardinal Macharski and representatives of the Polish government attended the groundbreaking ceremony. In March 1990 an American Jewish Committee leadership delegation visited the construction site. Despite remaining uncertainty about when the Carmelite sisters will move to their new quarters, and despite some remarks attributed to the superior of the convent which are replete with traditional anti-Jewish stereotypes, the black mood of the summer of 1989 has been lifted. Both sides have been granted an opportunity for bridge-building. Can we learn something from the bitter struggle around the convent at Auschwitz?

Some elementary observations come to mind. First, the Jewish people did not deliberately choose Auschwitz as the sign and symbol of the Nazis' "Final Solution" out of some conscious desire to deny the suffering of other peoples. If Jews had wanted in some conscious and systematic way to find a place whose name would not have competed with the tragic memory of Poles or other victim communities, they would have chosen another death camp. Alas, there were more than one: factories of horror, conceived, designed, and built entirely or largely to murder Jews. Had the choice been deliberate, Belzec, Birkenau, Treblinka, or Majdanek could have served as well. But the name *Auschwitz* gradually came to represent the Holocaust, through the recorded memory, the literature and poetry of powerful writers, through repetition, the sanction of time, and the determination of the Jewish people not to forget. It is a terrible irony that the same place and the same name also came to represent for Polish Christians their own suffering and martyrdom under Nazi occupation and that for Poles Auschwitz is a national shrine.

The other side of that proposition is also true. Polish Catholic authorities did not deliberately install the Carmelite convent at Auschwitz in order to deny or usurp the uniqueness of the Holocaust for Jews. They may be faulted for insensitivity, for failure to anticipate the impact of the convent on the minds and hearts of the Jewish community or even to think about Jews in connection with Auschwitz. Their decision undoubtedly revealed a failure of imagination and empathy, but it was not based on malice. There was no conspiracy on either side to deny or "steal" the historic experience of the other. As the conflict heated up, other, more nationalistic and antisemitic voices could be heard, claiming Auschwitz for Poles alone. But this was clearly not Cardinal Macharski's original intention.

Second, it has become clear that most Polish Christians still have no idea that over 90 percent of the people killed at Auschwitz were Jews. They are well aware of their own losses, and they learn in visits to the camp that "human beings" were shipped from every corner of Europe to Auschwitz to be gassed there: Dutch and French, Belgian and Greek, Romanian and Hungarian, Ukrainian and Italian. They do not learn that almost all of these were Jews, for many non-Jews were killed at Auschwitz. But only Jews were gathered from every nation in Nazi-occupied Europe as part of the plan to totally annihilate them as a people, down to the last infant.

Third, most Poles were surely not aware that the building granted to the Carmelite sisters was within the confines of the UNESCO "patrimony" of the Auschwitz camp as defined by World War II maps and as agreed to by the Polish government itself in 1972.

Fourth, because opposition to the convent was originally mobilized and led by Jewish civic or communal groups, including Holocaust survivors, there was a widespread misconception among Christians that religious Jews had no problem with the location of the convent, that it was the activism of "secular" Jews that was responsible for the mounting agitation. As late as the summer of 1989, a distinguished professor at a major Roman Catholic university in Europe commented in a private conversation, "It is the secularist forces in the Jewish community who are opposed to the Carmel. If we could only have a dialogue with rabbis or with representatives of the Orthodox community, I'm sure we would see eye to eye." The incursion of (Orthodox) Rabbi Weiss and his students may have put an end to such speculation, but in any case the comment itself represented a serious misreading of the Jewish community. In his assumption that the convent would be accepted and welcomed by all "religious" people because it was a place dedicated to prayer, the speaker showed that he gravely misunderstood the nature of the Jewish community and underestimated how deeply European Jews had been offended by the establishment of the convent at Auschwitz.

Did American Jews react the same way? At the outset, no. News about the convent's establishment and the circulation of the fund-raising brochure did not arouse the same instantaneous and near-unanimous protest among Jews in the United States that it did in Europe. The issue was slow to surface. Several reasons have been advanced for this difference in reactions. For one, European Jewish communities, decimated and demoralized after World War II, had grown in strength and self-confidence in the intervening years, and wished to resolve what they considered to be an essentially European problem. Moreover, they wished to show themselves as an effective third force in the world Jewish community, along with the Jewish communities in the United States and Israel. (It is interesting to note, for example, that no American Jews were invited to participate in the Geneva Catholic-Jewish "summit meetings," and no American Jew was a signatory to the 1987 agreement.)

Another reason for the lesser impact of the convent controversy in the United States may well have been the relatively benign history of Catholic-Jewish relations in this country. Despite a pre-Vatican Council II legacy of anti-Jewish teaching and preaching and despite pockets of Catholic antisemitism in the recent past—the radio broadcasts of Father Charles Coughlin are an instance—the

Roman Catholic church in the United States has never persecuted Jews, as contrasted with the situation in Europe, where the church used its power to oppose civil and religious rights for Jews, including the basic right of citizenship. A memory of the sporadic, but intense, hostility of the church to Jews and Judaism is part of the historic consciousness of Jews who are aware of their history, but in the United States that remembered hostility has been partly offset by a more positive experience of interreligious understanding. The United States never had a national religion or an established church, and Jews had the right of citizenship from the beginning of American nationhood.

Moreover, Roman Catholics, as a minority within the nation as a whole, had themselves been targets of prejudice and discrimination. Mutual victimization does not necessarily guarantee mutual sympathy, as Jews and Polish Catholics discovered in their own conflict over the Auschwitz convent, but the American experience of constitutional protection of religious liberty, separation of church and state, and the multiplicity of religions, cultures, ethnic groups, and languages succeeded in defusing or at least moderating some of the prejudices and hostilities that sometimes intensified into group violence in Europe.

Given these differences, and given also the progress in Christian-Jewish relations achieved in recent decades through the burgeoning interreligious dialogue, the Jewish community in the United States was not particularly excited about the convent when the story first came to light. Concern grew slowly, but it did grow. And when it became apparent that the terms of the Geneva agreement had not been fulfilled and that the promised center had not even been begun, the issue became a salient one in the United States as well. The meeting between Vatican and Jewish organizational representatives (most of the latter from the United States) scheduled to begin on February 23, 1989—one day after the supposed completion of the center—was canceled. A strong sense of betrayal, of mistrust based on broken promises, surfaced in the Jewish community.

What, after all, were the underlying issues? Why did the establishment of a convent at the edge of the Auschwitz death camp send shock waves through much of the Jewish community of Europe? As several well-meaning commentators asked, what was wrong with a dozen or so nuns praying for the souls of *all* the victims, and for peace and reconciliation for all humanity? What, indeed? How can one understand a nasty "turf" battle over a place where so many people suffered and died?

The critical issue for those who opposed the convent in its present site was the ultimate question of how the Holocaust would be remembered. In essence, they argued along the following lines: It is some forty years since the gates of the death camps swung open and revealed the horrors perpetrated there. There are very few witnesses left and even fewer survivors. Forty years from now, when there are none left, who will be seen as the primary victims of the Nazi ideology of hatred—Jews or martyrs to Christian faith?

This passionate concern about whether the story of the Holocaust would be told without Jews seems, on the face of it, paranoid, but it is rooted in somber realities. Both in Europe and in the United States, we have seen the growth of an entire industry of denial. Ideologues claiming the title of "historians" have claimed that the death camps were not death camps, that the gas chambers were used to fumigate, not to kill. One-half of the Jewish people of Europe died during the Nazi period, the overwhelming majority by systematic murder, torture, and starvation. It is difficult to imagine the rage and agony of a people who, having sustained these losses, are now told that it didn't happen.

Beyond the deliberate denial, based quite clearly on antisemitism[3] is another layer of denial, not intentionally antisemitic, but almost as destructive to Jewish morale—obfuscation of the fact that Jews were targeted for annihilation only because they were Jews. Until very recently, it was possible to visit Auschwitz, see the facilities, learn how many "human beings" were gassed and burned there, and not be informed that almost all of them were Jews and were killed for that reason. It is reported that the informational plaques have now been changed.

The sense that their own history had been denied them was compounded for the survivors by the fact that Catholic devotion at Auschwitz has tended to focus on two figures of great significance for the church, St. Maximilian Kolbe and Edith Stein. Without denying their profound importance to Catholics, these figures of necessity send an ambiguous message to Jews. St. Maximilian, a Roman Catholic priest who offered his own life in exchange for that of another prisoner in Auschwitz and who perished in the other man's stead, was an authentic martyr. During his lifetime, however, he was also the editor of a journal which published antisemitic articles, and the revelation of this information understandably created some consternation among Jews. Was it not possible, some asked, to find a Polish hero to canonize who offered a more positive role model for Catholic-Jewish relations?

The other figure was and is even more problematic for Jews. Edith Stein, a Jewish woman who converted to Christianity, became a Carmelite sister and perished at Auschwitz after being deported from a convent in the Netherlands, has been beatified by the church as a "martyr to the faith." Yet she was dragged away from the convent, shipped to Auschwitz, and gassed there not because she was a Carmelite or a Catholic, but because she was born a Jew. The authenticity of her conversion is not at issue; Edith Stein was a conscientious convert to Christianity. It should also be noted that the Nazis had stepped up deportations of Catholics of Jewish origin because the Dutch bishops refused to be silent about these deportations. Still, she was killed as a Jew, and thus seems to Jews a particularly inappropriate symbol of Jewish-Christian reconciliation.

And after all this, and after the agreement to relocate the convent had been signed in Geneva, the erection of a large (over twenty-feet-high) cross near the site of the convent added fat to the fire. Its defenders were quick to point out that the cross marked the place where a group of Polish partisans had been machine-gunned by German troops during the war. Yet they never questioned why a cross seemed the self-evident symbol of heroic Polish resistance to military occupation. Was it not possible that the German soldiers who carried out this execution also considered themselves Christians? Certainly to Jews, the cross is pre-eminently a religious symbol, representing Christianity. It is precisely this identification of Christianity with Polish patriotism and national pride that has made the controversy around the Auschwitz convent so painful to both sides. Cardinal Glemp's comment that Jewish protests against the convent offended ''all Poles'' and jeopardized Polish ''sovereignty'' were instructive in this regard, revealing how closely religion and national identity were intertwined in his thinking. Indirectly, he appeared to be saying that to be a Pole, one needed to be a Christian—presumably, a Catholic—and that Jews could not be ''real Poles.''

Demonstrably, more than one agenda was discernible in the convent controversy and more than one history needs to be explored and understood. There is a history of Christian-Jewish—more cogently in this case, Catholic-Jewish—relations to be honestly faced. The Reverend Edward Flannery, first secretary of the United States Bishops' Secretariat for Catholic-Jewish Relations, has observed that Christians have ''torn from their history books the pages the Jews have memorized.'' Despite substantial progress in mutual knowledge and understanding, this is still true. Most Christians remain largely unaware of the church's record of hostility to Jews and Judaism. They have never been taught that many of the measures they associate with secular antisemitism such as confining Jews to ghettos, forcing them to wear distinctive clothing, denying them certain professions and livelihoods, and limiting their access to education through quotas, all had their precedents in church legislation. They are probably also unaware that the use of the cross as a logo by political movements, parties, and organizations before World War II usually had deliberate antisemitic intent.[4] Innocent of this history in both deed and knowledge, they tend to interpret Jewish protests against the Auschwitz convent as a kind of gratuitous animosity against the Christian faith.

There is also a Polish-Jewish agenda which needs to be explored free of rancor and mutual recrimination.[5] A Task Force on Polish American-Jewish Relations, cosponsored by the American Jewish Committee and the Polish American Congress, has conducted a dialogue along these lines for over ten years in the United States and has made admirable progress in overcoming stereotypes and suspicions. Yet pockets of mutual ignorance and resentment remain, partly rooted in vastly different recollections of the relationship between the two communities in prewar Poland. Polish-American ethnic leaders may recall how well the Jewish minority fared and how well the two groups got along. Jewish participants may remember discrimination, persecution, and violence. These memories must be reconciled.

Healing the wounds torn open by the bitter conflict around the Auschwitz convent will require the recovery of a common history and a common memory. It will require patience and goodwill on both sides, and a capacity for identifying with the experience and memories of others. Jews should realize how fragile is the sense of Polish sovereignty and for how brief a period of recent European history Poles were allowed to control their own destiny. Jews should also question for themselves whether a historical memory based only or primarily on recollections of victimization—what has been termed the "lachrymose theory" of Jewish historiography—serves the interest of truth or wise communal policy. For their part, Polish Christians should realize that in addition to and separate from their own very real agony under German and Soviet occupation, there is a legacy of Polish antisemitism that needs to be acknowledged and addressed on its own terms.

Addressing these issues is at the heart of the reconciliation process. Nothing can replace or make up for the innocent lives lost during the Nazi Holocaust. For Jews those losses include a million children murdered and the destruction of entire communities, centers of learning, scholarship, and spiritual creativity. But at least something would be gained if out of this senseless destruction emerged a commitment to finally confront and put an end to antisemitism, the world's oldest and most persistent pathology of group hatred. Rightly or wrongly, the organized Jewish survivor groups came to believe that the convent at Auschwitz, taken together with the tendency to ignore the specificity of Jewish victims in the exhibits and lectures given inside the camp, together with the focus on Catholic martyrs to the faith, signified a de-Judaizing of the Holocaust and thereby a neglect of the underlying issue of antisemitism.

A final observation is in order. There is both hope and irony in noting that the Polish episcopate's Commission on Dialogue with Judaism, headed by Bishop Henryk Muszynski, called for the upholding of the Geneva II agreement and the building of the new center even as Cardinal Glemp was repudiating the agreement. To even appear to take issue with the primate of one's country, particularly given the popularity and influence of the church in Poland and the highly volatile nature of the convent issue, constituted an act of courage. It should be acknowledged as a powerful affirmation of hope. The irony—with absolutely no reflection intended on members of the Polish Bishops' Commission, who have demonstrated goodwill and good faith—is that such a commission should have come into existence now, after the Holocaust. A few thousand Jews, mostly aged and infirm, remain from what was previously the largest, most creative, intellectually and spiritually vital Jewish community in Europe. One cannot help but ask what might have been the outcome had there been a serious, sustained, church-sponsored Catholic-Jewish dialogue in Poland before the Nazi onslaught. Granted, it was a different time, a different church, a different Jewish community, and speculation along such lines will yield no certainties. But the question itself should spur all involved in this painful controversy to put its resolution to the service of mutual understanding and reconciliation. The new center to be constructed near, but not on the grounds of, Auschwitz will, one hopes, provide a hospitable environment for such efforts. That was its original intention—a place for study, for the exchange of information, for dialogue and encounter, a place for Christians and Jews to work together to combat trivialization or denial of the Holocaust. Is it not a goal worth all our efforts?

NOTES

1. The author wishes to express appreciation to Bishop Henryk Muszynski, president of the Polish episcopate's Commission on Dialogue with Judaism, for his careful reading of this article in draft form, for his thoughtful suggestions, and his enthusiastic endorsement; to Sr. Carol Rittner, coeditor of *Memory Offended*, for her encouragement; and to Rabbi A. James Rudin, the American Jewish Committee's director of interreligious affairs, for his always helpful and sensitive suggestions.

2. In Europe, the term *Shoah* is more frequently used; in the United States, the term "Holocaust." Both terms will be used in this article, in accordance with normal usage.

3. Many sympathetic non-Jews are unaware of the extent to which denial of the Holocaust is a deliberate strategem of antisemitic organizations and individuals, and so they may view the determination of the Jewish community to memorialize that history as a kind of neurotic obsession.

4. Milton Himmelfarb recalls the story of a YMCA secretary, sent on a relief mission to Europe after World War I, who was introduced to Admiral Horthy, then regent of Hungary. Horthy asked what the initials YMCA stood for. On being informed the Young Men's Christian Association, he extended his hand warmly and declared, "Delighted to meet another antisemite."

5. Clearly, the responsibility for confronting antisemitism is not addressed uniquely to Poles. The persistence of this virulent pathology is apparent in the recent outbursts of anti-Jewish violence and rhetoric in many parts of Europe, Western as well as Eastern, but it is particularly troubling to see this ancient hostility flourish as an adjunct of the rising nationalisms that have emerged as Soviet hegemony and Communist ideology appear to be crumbling in Eastern Europe. The issue also has special poignancy for Polish-Jewish relations because of the heavy concentration of Jews in Poland until World War II and the fact that a high proportion of American Jews trace their families' origin to that part of the world. To see the old charges of conspiracy rise again, to see Jews blamed for the political problems and economic dislocations in a country where almost no Jews are left—in short, to see antisemitism without Jews—is a sobering reminder of the task before us.

13

Auschwitz: Where Only Silence Becomes Prayer

Mary Jo Leddy

> Auschwitz must absolutely become a place of absolute silence, non-prayer.
> . . . Let us all, together, make ours the words of the psalmist, "For you,
> Lord, the silence alone is prayer."
>
> —René-Samuel Sirat, former Chief Rabbi of France

There is no doubt that the situation of the Carmelite convent at Auschwitz has provoked a crisis in Jewish-Christian relations. It remains to be seen whether this crisis may also present us with yet another opportunity to confront the questions which Jews and Christians in the twentieth century should not avoid.

This incident (which is really a series of incidents) can be discussed on a number of levels that are distinct and yet related. I will refer briefly to two of these levels, the historical and the sociological, before reflecting in a more extended way on the symbolic and theological significance of this controversy. I do not want to diminish the importance of the historical and sociological dimensions of this issue. However, I do want to acknowledge the significant expertise which other writers will surely bring to this collection of essays. They are far more qualified than I to comment on these dimensions of the dispute over the Carmelite convent at Auschwitz.

My purpose in developing a more sustained reflection on the symbolic and theological dimensions of this question is to explore some of the elements within the Christian tradition of spirituality that could facilitate a more genuine solidarity with the Jewish response to the reality of Auschwitz.

In other words, this essay is a preliminary search for the ways in which

Christians can respond to Auschwitz not only out of sensitivity to the history of Jewish experience but also from within the Christian tradition. While it is true that Christians cannot respond fully to the reality of Auschwitz without recovering the Jewish dimension of their faith and affirming the integrity of Judaism in its own terms, it is also true that Christians can only confront this place of radical evil by becoming more rather than less Christian. The Scottish philosopher John MacMurray wrote that friendship means "to become oneself for another." I take this to imply that solidarity between Jews and Christians, substantial and not merely sentimental solidarity, will grow to the extent that Jews become more Jewish and Christians become more Christian.

To anticipate: my sense is that the Carmelite nuns who are now located at Auschwitz do not represent an image of what solidarity between Jews and Christians should be in facing the post-Holocaust world together. However, there are elements within the Carmelite tradition of spirituality that could provide Christians with a deeper, albeit partial, response to the reality of Auschwitz.

THE HISTORICAL CONTEXT OF POLAND

No serious discussion of this dispute can take place without situating it within the context of the particular history of Poland. Many Jews read this history as a particular instance of the abiding reality of Christian antisemitism. (Perhaps for this reason the statements of the Polish pope John Paul II are carefully scrutinized for signs of antisemitism.)

However, the recent and preliminary research of Roman Catholic theologians Ron Modras and John Pawlikowski suggests that a closer reading of this history is called for. There are notable examples of efforts on the part of some Polish Catholics to come to the rescue of persecuted Jews. John Pawlikowski (in a May 1989 public lecture in Toronto) has noted the fact that Roman Catholic communities of nuns were the most significant group that seems to deserve further research into the reasons why this was so. One wonders, for example, why these communities of women were so much more responsive than the communities of religious men. In any case, a fact such as this suggests that the story of the Carmelite nuns at Auschwitz is a rather tragic sequel to the untold story of quiet heroines in Poland.

Nevertheless, the exceptional actions of these and other Christians probably serve to prove the general rule that most Catholics in Poland actively or passively cooperated in the Nazi persecution of the Jews. Whether Poles behaved better or worse than other peoples who were dominated by the Nazis is still a matter of debate among historians.

THE INSTITUTIONAL FRAMEWORK OF THE CONTROVERSY

The dispute over the Carmelite convent offered an unusual opportunity to glimpse the pluralistic reality that exists within the Jewish and Catholic communities today. This pluralism often confounds those who would prefer to deal with a more uniform reality. Jews and Catholics who are familiar with the pluralism within their own communities can still be surprised by the diversity of organization and opinion that exists within another community. The pluralism that is so familiar to the insider is perplexing to the outsider. In Jewish-Christian dialogues there is always the lingering question of who speaks for the Jews, who speaks for the church?

Jews know the wide range of religious beliefs and political positions which exist in the Jewish community: orthodox-conservative-reform, religious-secular, left-right-center, etc. There has never been anything resembling the Catholic effort to define the beliefs that determine membership in the community. Membership in the Jewish community is usually through birth rather than through adherence to any particular belief or position. The principle of unity is peoplehood rather than a particular profession of faith.

This intrinsic diversity is reflected in the wide variety of Jewish organizations and movements—all claiming some legitimacy to speak for the Jewish people. And then there are those Jews who, while belonging to no organization or movement, nevertheless rightly claim their experience as Jewish. Catholics who are unfamiliar with the diverse reality of Judaism are sometimes perplexed by what they see as contradictory statements and approaches within the Jewish community. The situation of the Carmelite monastery at Auschwitz is a case in point. There were Catholics confused by the differing means used, on the one hand, by official Jewish leaders and, on the other hand, by grassroots Jewish activists.

Yet Catholics need only reflect on the diversity that exists within the church to know that this is the creative and sometimes confusing reality of their own faith community. Jews who expect a uniform or consistent position from all Catholics will be confounded by the variegated reality of the Roman Catholic church on a number of issues. Because of the hierarchical structure of the church and the governing principle of papal primacy, it is understandable why non-Catholics would expect a more coherent approach to disputed questions.

My experience of working as a journalist with a Catholic newspaper for fifteen years has given me a vivid sense of how the church actually operates. This apparently highly ordered institution is sometimes disorganized, ineffective, and snarled in its own communications. There are times when those who have official positions have little authority and power. And I have learned never to discount stupidity and ineptness as factors in shaping bureaucratic responses.

A certain organizational confusion was evident in the conflicting and shifting responses given by the various levels of those who were involved in the Carmelite convent controversy: the nuns, members of the local Polish hierarchy, an international group of cardinals, the Vatican officials, and the pope himself. At times there was a great gap between what was being done in Poland and what was being decided elsewhere. One of the factors in this controversy was the unfortunate fact that the Carmelite women themselves were not consulted by the church officials who made the first decision to move the convent. This lack of consultation is not unusual in the church, but it can have the regrettable consequence of further alienating those who were not consulted.

The nuns were not the only ones who were not consulted. The Jewish community was not asked for its opinion when the Carmelite convent at Auschwitz was originally proposed. The Carmelites, no doubt, asked the permission of the local bishop of Auschwitz, but neither they nor he seemed to recognize the importance of discussing the matter with Jewish representatives. One wonders what might have ensued if this had happened.

This controversy revealed a tension between the authority that is exercised at the local and national level in Poland and church officials at a higher international level. This tension is present in many other areas of the world over a variety of issues, for example, the tension between progressive Latin American bishops and the Vatican. At stake is the right of bishops to deal with local issues with some measure of autonomy and the responsibility of the Vatican for the whole church.

The Carmelite convent was not only a local matter; it also became a matter of much broader significance for the relationship between the church and the Jewish people. To reduce the dispute to organizational factors alone is to deny the much deeper questions posed by the presence of the Carmelites at Auschwitz.

THE SIGNIFICANCE OF AUSCHWITZ

The systematic murder of nearly 6 million Jews happened in various times and places during the dark period of the Hitler era. Yet it happened in some places more than others. Within the Jewish community over the last fifty years, Auschwitz has come to symbolize the place of the Holocaust or *Shoah*. Some would say that this is because Auschwitz was the place where the greatest number of Jews were murdered. Others would say that this place is significant because it is the place which clearly exemplifies the systematic and bureaucratically organized nature of this vast crime. Then there are those who would say that Auschwitz entered the imagination of the world because writers such as Elie Wiesel were able to convey the full horror of what had happened there. Auschwitz became the place of "night" in Jewish history and in the history of the contemporary world.

All of these factors may have contributed to making Auschwitz the place of abomination in the memories and imaginations of the Jews and an important number of Christians.

Personally, I must resist the argument that Auschwitz is significant because of the number of Jews who were killed there. This kind of body-count politics has become all too common in our world. Such quantitative thinking numbs people to the infinite value of even a single human life. If only a single innocent child had been murdered at Auschwitz—simply because the child was Jewish—then that death camp should be a place of memory and mourning.

Similarly, I cannot affirm the significance of Auschwitz for the Polish people simply because of the number of non-Jewish Poles who died there. We must not stack up the number of the dead to give more weight to a particular position. All of those who entered Auschwitz were numbered, reduced from being a person with a name to a number. Let us not number them again. The God of the Judeo-Christian tradition calls us to affirm the infinitive value of each person. To kill even a single person is to kill the image and likeness of God in this world.

One of the most regrettable aspects of the discussion of the Carmelite convent was that there was a noticeable increase in body-count arguments to legitimate a "claim" on Auschwitz. Articles written with this kind of argumentation served to numb the far deeper question: How could any human being bear to claim such a terrifying reality?

Auschwitz is significant, I suggest, because of the quality of the evil that was present there. It was a place of radical evil—where evil was done for the sake of evil.

If we ask what purpose was served by the murder camp, we would have to answer that it served no purpose at all. Cruelty has long been present in human history, but it usually serves some interest—economic, political, or even psychological. The systematic destruction of millions of human beings cannot be comprehended within the usual categories of historical explanation. This wastage of life did not serve the Nazis' economic purposes and even diverted crucial energies and resources from the war effort. This was evil done for the sake of evil.

Hannah Arendt has described the qualitative difference between radical evil, which defies our categories of explanation, and the evil that can be comprehended, at least through its motivations.

There are crimes which men can neither punish nor forgive. When the impossible was made possible it became the unpunishable, unforgivable absolute evil which could no longer be understood and explained by the evil motives of self-interest, greed, covetousness, resentment, lust for power, and cowardice; and which therefore anger could not revenge, love could not endure, friendship could not forgive.[1]

It would be tempting to describe Auschwitz with the religious term "hell." Yet, this would be to remove Auschwitz from the realm of human responsibility. The terrifying thing about Auschwitz is that it happened in this world and that it was a place constructed by human beings. It was not the work of the devil but of the demonic dynamic in human society. And what can we say about God—who seemed willing to let human freedom realize its most inhuman possibilities?

The Jewish people were the victims of radical evil. That is the reality they met at Auschwitz. For the Jewish people, this place is not only a cemetery for millions; it is also the place of abominations that endures in memory but beyond the reach of hope.

It is true that there were many non-Jewish victims at Auschwitz. There were many Poles murdered at Auschwitz. Jews and non-Jews suffered from the horrible dehumanizing process engineered by the Nazis. We today should not engage in the dehumanizing process of trying to measure the suffering of one people against another. The suffering of each victim at Auschwitz deserves to be remembered in its uniqueness.

Yet we must remember that many non-Jews were victims at Auschwitz, but we must acknowledge that they were not victims of radical evil. To say this is not to diminish the suffering of these victims, but it is to acknowledge that they were victims of the "evil motives" that have operated in human history—self-interest, greed, nationalism, racism, lust for power. The murders of millions of Poles served some Nazi purpose. Thus, while Jews and non-Jews suffered immeasurably at Auschwitz, it was the Jews who particularly experienced evil as radical.

However, Poles have every right to suspect that they too were vulnerable to a more radical evil. If the Nazis had realized their dark design of eliminating the Jewish people, the next step would have been the systematic destruction of the Polish people. Fortunately, the flames of Auschwitz were extinguished. Memories, however, continue to burn.

The presence of the Carmelite nuns offends the memory of the Jewish community. The offense is most obvious in the form of the high cross that stands as a large, looming presence over the camp. It appears as a symbol of Christian imperialism, an attempt to impose a certain meaning on the suffering of those who died at Auschwitz—including the suffering of the Jewish victims.

Christians must realize that the central symbol of their faith remains in the memory of Jews as a sign of death and destruction. The cross was carried high while Jews were persecuted in pogroms and inquisitions. Many Jews have been placed on a cross for refusing to accept Jesus. The history of the use and abuse of the cross gives Jews little reason to understand the mystery it symbolizes for Christians.

In the best of the Christian tradition, the cross signifies the mystery of redemptive love. In choosing to live by love, Jesus also chose the death that would be the consequence of such a way of life. The cross promises redemption for Christians, not because of the amount of suffering Jesus endured, but because of the freedom and love with which he embraced such suffering. Jesus is the example of authentic martyrdom. Thus, Christians have looked to the cross as a symbol of the meaning of life, love, suffering, and death. The cross does not eliminate suffering and death for Christians, but it does give meaning to those human experiences.

Well-intentioned Christians may genuinely believe that the cross could be a source of consolation in a place such as Auschwitz. However, they should reflect on the profound difference between the suffering of Jesus and the suffering of those at Auschwitz. His was a chosen suffering. Theirs was a humanly imposed suffering. Martyrdom was never a possibility for a Jewish person at Auschwitz. How can there be anything redemptive in such suffering?

There are those who have suggested, in an act of historical imagination, that had Jesus been alive in the 1940s in Europe he would have been wearing a yellow star and walking with his brothers and sisters to the gas chamber at Auschwitz. This makes the point that Jesus was a Jew and that Christians have persecuted his people, but it overlooks the fact that this Jesus would never have become the Christ of faith because his would not have been a chosen death.

I respect the Jewish view that we should not attempt to give any meaning, Christian or Jewish, to what happened at Auschwitz. It is a place that has become a black hole of meaning, a hole of oblivion for human faith and understanding. All prayer disappears into this black hole in the universe.

The Jewish response to Auschwitz often takes the form of action rather than contemplation. The Jewish act of faith after Auschwitz is to create concrete possibilities for hope. Such a commitment obviously gave birth to the State of Israel and continues to give birth to efforts to change the world from a place of peril into a place of promise. Refusing to give meaning to Auschwitz, Jews have responded to its reality by engaging in meaningful action. It is as if in drawing the limits of meaning at Auschwitz, they have set a boundary to meaninglessness.

Christians have everything to learn from the Jewish commitment to changing the world. Since Vatican Council II, Catholics have become more involved in the world and this involvement has opened up new ways of Catholics and Jews being in solidarity together.

Vatican Council II also marked the beginning of a long and slow shift in the church's attitude toward the Jewish people. While there is still antisemitism (practically and theologically) at every level in the church, there is also a new desire to respect the integrity of Jewish religion and experience. Thus there are Catholics (as is evident in the efforts of those who have tried to persuade the Carmelites to move) who would be willing to respect the Jewish refusal to give meaning to Auschwitz.

Yet such an attitude risks becoming mere liberal tolerance if it is not coupled with a serious Christian response to the radical evil of Auschwitz. Obviously this had demanded a re-examination of the antisemitic elements in Catholic teachings and practices and a reinterpretation of some of their central symbols. The Carmelite nuns, who may be very fine women, seem oblivious to such a challenge. Indeed, the financial support they received from Aid to the Church in Distress seems to suggest that their prayers may be not for the conversion of Christians but for the conversion of the Jews.

It is not quite clear from media reports why the nuns are praying and for whom. If they are praying for the conversion of the Jews, then this must surely be rejected. If they are praying to make some reparation for the sins of those who committed such great crimes, then this must be questioned. What would it mean to make reparation for such crimes, what penance could ever serve to lessen the punishment deserved? Indeed, the very idea of contemplation at a place such as Auschwitz seems to belittle the importance of acting so that evil finds less place in the world.

These particular nuns must move from their convent at Auschwitz—and the sooner the better. Yet it would be unfortunate if their departure made us forget some of the remaining dimensions of the Carmelite tradition of contemplation that would enable Christians to respond as Christians to the radical evil of Auschwitz.

Within the authentic tradition of Carmelite spirituality there is a profound sense of what is called "the dark night." This spiritual experience of the abyss of meaning was most eloquently explored by Teresa of Avila and John of the Cross. They described the reality of believers who experience the absence of God and of meaning. In the dark night, words falter and prayers fail. It is a time of unknowing, unfeeling, and disbelief. One can only remain in a vast silence, waiting.

One cannot draw out more from this contemplative tradition than is there. For example, Teresa and John saw this dark night as the inevitable time of passage to a deeper form of contemplation, a passage from the experience of God to belief in the God of experience. It would be irresponsible to suggest that a phase in the development of contemplative prayer can be compared to the concrete experience of Auschwitz. The Hellenistic roots of this contemplative tradition make it more suited to describing an interior, personal experience than the collective experience of history. Nevertheless, the acknowledgement of "the dark night" in this Carmelite tradition of prayer allows Catholics to admit spiritually what they cannot always acknowledge theologically—that there are times that we remain unknowing and uncomprehending in the face of meaninglessness. All we can do is be with the reality of that experience.

Auschwitz summons Catholics to a concrete commitment to acting to change their church and the world. However, I would suggest that there must also be a contemplative moment, a contemplative dimension, to any such action. We must learn *to be* with what we cannot think about or pray about. While we cannot stay with the reality of Auschwitz, we must not flee its darkness. Auschwitz commands us to speak and to act for more justice in the church and in the world. It also summons us to silence.

NOTE

1. Hannah Arendt, *The Origins of Totalitarianism* (New York: Harcourt, Brace & World, 1973), 459.

14

Jewish and Christian Suffering in the Post-Auschwitz Period

Albert H. Friedlander

First, Auschwitz was a satanic idea upon a drawing board. Then it became reality. Eventually it imploded upon itself and became once again an idea. And now it has become a controversy. The heated discussion between Christians and Jews related to the Carmelite convent at the gates of Auschwitz can only be viewed as a tragedy. The editors of this book have presented us with a careful chronology of the events, listing at least some of the blunders that brought Christians and Jews into a destructive confrontation. And they list the efforts that, in effect, brought us back from the brink of a landscape where faith has gone and where ignorant armies clash by night. I am pleased that the European dimension has not been ignored, and that some recognition has been given to the work of Sir Sigmund Sternberg here; his patient dialogue with Cardinal Glemp did produce the conciliatory letter which led, one hopes, to the solution. Yet I am not so much concerned and involved in re-creating the historical pattern that scholars can follow and analyze as a "classic case" where a successful dialogue between religions may be deemed to have taken place. I am still stunned by the fact that a controversy related to Auschwitz has taken place at all.

Auschwitz can never be comprehended. It is the place of broken silence, the dark hole of evil in the world. Those who were there and died took the mystery of its evil with them in order to present it to God. Those who survived can at best give a stammered testimony that the world can respect even when it cannot understand it. It is the testimony of Jews, of Christians, of Communists and Social Democrats, of homosexuals, of the Sinti-Roma, of groups and of individuals. It belongs to everyone; and it belongs to no one. We cannot understand it because our minds cannot encompass the totally demonic; but we must not forget it—that would bring Satan into the world. But when we stare at Auschwitz, we freeze into statues. Auschwitz, Treblinka, Mauthausen—Stheno, Euryale,

Medusa—the eyes of the Gorgons look at us through the smoke of the chimneys that still travels back and forth through the atmosphere. I do not wonder that the good nuns, staring at the hell of Auschwitz day and night, became programmed into a pattern which could not look outside itself, which ignored Jewish thought and feeling. As of old, they had taken the shield of their religion as a mirror through which to see the unseeable. And so they survived. But they were trapped in that mirror image that had coped with evil by contracting it to the point where they thought they could control it. They wanted to pray it away. With all of the love and respect I have for nuns at prayer, I must say that they were only praying for themselves. That is a glorious task. And out of a tradition that believes in the "Thirty-Six Righteous" for whose sake the world is preserved, I can only treat such prayer with awe and respect. Their prayers came before God to be accepted. I cannot speak for God. But the prayers did not come to us; not to the families of the victims; not to the victims. It was not the right place. It was not the right time. They were not the right prayers. The evil has remained in the world and in that place. Auschwitz is not the place where prayers remove darkness. It is the place where one can remember the evil and walk away maimed. Out of that encounter can come good, but not in Auschwitz. The story of the Akedah, of God testing Abraham by demanding his son Isaac as sacrifice, has received different interpretations within Judaism and Christianity. But Mount Moriah became a holy place—with sanctuaries built there by Jews, Christians, and Muslims—because the tragedy did not take place: father and son walked down the mountain hand in hand. Auschwitz is not Mount Moriah, nor Calvary. It is an evil place and will remain an evil place, empty and desolate, salted with the tears of mourners, where no sanctuary can stand. A place of worship there becomes a place of self-deception. And so it is not a matter of politics, of hasty actions in creating a place of worship at Auschwitz without consulting others, which is the issue here. Nor, indeed, would I want to turn this meditation into a piece of political analysis that would see the whole issue in the framework of Polish nationalism.

There *is* that aspect to be considered, of course. Quite apart from all else, the various manipulations behind the scene reached out toward that Polish national pride which wanted to turn Auschwitz into the Polish "Tomb of the Unknown Soldier." Schools are brought to that place; the rightful tale of Polish heroism is told and retold, within the framework of a political faith that had set the secular above the sacred. In a strange way, pushing the plan for the Carmelite convent at Auschwitz was an attack against both church and synagogue. Old traditions were revived at that point. And yet, in these reflections, I would want to separate the religious and political issues, fully aware that they are interwoven in all aspects of Christianity and Judaism. In the end, one must come to terms with the religious differences that emerge out of an honest confrontation. How *can* Jews and Christians hurt one another when they believe they are acting in conformity with the basic teachings of their religions?

The brief of this book requests of its contributors that they address themselves to three key questions. The first one is clear and simple: "How does the recent Auschwitz controversy and its seeming resolution reflect and impact the most important issue(s) in Jewish-Christian relationships?"

This is oversimplification, of course. But one basic issue, clearly, is the fact that we are different religions, with different beliefs. The need for interfaith dialouge has made us stress the important similarities in our conversations. But we misunderstood each other, in the case of the Carmelite convent at Auschwitz, because we have a different concept of suffering. Auschwitz cannot be understood; it remains Arthur A. Cohen's "Tremendum," the totally other evil outside our reach. But human suffering—and God's suffering—play an important role in both religions. Often, this brings us together. In this case, it divided us. Christian and Jewish theology both confront human suffering with compassion. And Auschwitz, before it is anything else, is the ultimate, agonized suffering of the individual human being tortured by an evil society and by an evil neighbor. Both religions want to give comfort to the living; and both address themselves to the situation of the victims who died at Auschwitz.

We move toward confrontation at this point. In the past, both religions have linked suffering with the punishment for evil deeds committed by the sufferer during life. "*Mipney chatta-eynu*": because of our sins did we go into exile, said the rabbis; "*yissurim shel ahavah*": afflictions are sent by a loving God who seeks to purify us, who wants to test us within a process of justice, they add. And Christianity more than concurred with that approach; it intensified it, stressing the totally flawed nature of the human being who was evil from birth, evil through birth itself. Theology judged the human being here and found it wanting. If the Book of Job rebelled against this notion and fought against the idea that the most righteous of persons was punished for hidden sins through suffering, it only succeeded in challenging the severity of the human judgment: Job's friends can no longer speak of his guilt. But God's judgment stands—how can we begin to understand the divine plan?

Auschwitz shattered the theological framework. Traditional theologians within both religions have maintained a rear-guard action here which has led to conflicts between both faiths; and the Auschwitz convent must indeed be seen as an expression of mummified Christian thinking unable to cope with the reality of the situation. Traditional Jewish thought failed as well. Can the million children killed in the camps be viewed as souls tested for purity, or as sinners who were rightly punished? Can *any* of the victims be viewed as recipients of just punishment for their sins? The Jewish community will not listen to rabbis who take that position; and they were grievously hurt to be told by Christians that their families who died in the camps underwent a redemptive process of suffering.

The cup of human suffering overflowed. If Jews and Christians are to talk together about the nature of suffering as seen in Auschwitz, both must first learn to speak a new language. And there is another, specific problem which came to the fore during this confrontation: the nature of *Jewish* suffering. Again, the Book of Job tried to give its answer in its first sentence: "There was a man from the land of Uz, whose name was Job." Job was not Jewish. The question "Why do the righteous suffer?" was, therefore, not seen within the frame of a theology positing Israel as a "Suffering Servant of God." That concept still has a life of its own within Israel, partly as a rationalization for the suffering of Israel: "It is our function to give testimony for God through our suffering; it is our burden, our task!" Applied to Auschwitz, this becomes almost an abomination. And when Jews hear from Christians that the "wandering Jews" fulfill their function of heralding the second coming of Christ, that this is their role in the Christian drama of redemption, they can only react with anger.

We can no longer view suffering as a divine punishment. We can no longer see Jewish suffering as part of the plan for the redemption of humanity. And we cannot, must not view Auschwitz as a restatement of Calvary—a Christian heresy that underlies much of their stance in this situation which separates us from them. Both Jews and Christians have central teachings on the "Suffering God"; but they are also divided by that teaching. In the midrash, God cries and mourns with the Jews as the Temple and Jerusalem are destroyed; and the indwelling Presence of God, the Shekinah, goes into exile with Her people. For the Jews, God is present in their suffering. For Christians, they must share in God's suffering on the cross. The emphasis has shifted, and human suffering is subsumed under the burden of the cross. Jews cannot do this. Auschwitz cannot be explained to them by Calvary. But that, in effect, is what the Carmelite convent at Auschwitz tried to do. Without necessarily wishing to offend the neighbor, the whole issue of Auschwitz was removed from the world, and the non-Christian neighbor was confronted with a triumphalism (which did not necessarily view itself as such, but could only be understood in that light by others).

The nuns—and Christianity as such—have failed to understand the nature of the objections against the convent at Auschwitz as expressed by Jews. Deeply hurt, good Christians have pointed out to the Jews that their actions were motivated by concern and compassion for the Jewish victims; that their prayers were intended as a balm to assuage the wounds of suffering humanity. They saw the wounds of Christ at Auschwitz. They wanted to pray for him and to him; and they wanted to pray for the Jews. How could the Jews reject their prayers? Would that not be, in some ways, a *Jewish* triumphalism?

One cannot deny all aspects of their case. Every religion has a touch of triumphalism within itself, wants to assert itself against the neighbor. But in the matter of mourning for our dead, Jews do not ask others to say Kaddish. We pray as a family, we are remembrancers with a particular need to say Kaddish for the millions who have no descendants left in this world who could fulfill that religious obligation. And we do not wish those who have died to become subjects or symbols for another faith that in some ways challenges their status as *kedoshim*—holy ones who died in their purity. I am touched and moved when nuns tell me that they have prayed for me in their convent. I was overwhelmed when they permitted me and another rabbi to speak at the funeral of Sister Louis Gabriel (Professor Dr. Charlotte Klein) and to accompany her body to the cemetery. But I was invited to pray with them. Auschwitz does not invite the church to establish itself there. I have gone to concentration camp sites with interfaith groups, and we have prayed there together. But we were visitors, an enclosed enclave moving through deserted places where evil had ruled and was still present. We did not set up places of worship to fight evil; we simply wanted to survive the moment by strengthening our memories and our faith. *Cohanim* (Jewish priests) do not enter a cemetery. And we somehow shuddered at the thought of nuns living in Auschwitz, that cemetery of total evil.

The convent could not but express its notion of the Suffering God at Auschwitz. And this separates us. Some years ago, the Protestant theologian Dorothee Soelle examined the story told by Elie Wiesel in his book *Night*: the small boy hung on the middle gallows, with two men hanging on either side of him. This has become the great text of Christianity's attempt to understand Auschwitz, and it is generally related to Calvary. But Soelle's radical theology had a new point to make for Christians: if they *wanted* to see Christ on the cross in that sad figure of the child, they could only gain one specific lesson out of this—God is on the side of the victims, not on the side of the perpetrators. God suffers with the people and is in the midst of Israel. I hope her teaching is a corrective within Christian thought. At various interfaith conferences, I have tried to stress our position: Auschwitz is not Calvary. Calvary is the resurrection. Auschwitz is death. And God's suffering is human suffering.

At a recent Oxford Symposium on the Holocaust, Dorothee Soelle again addressed this central problem of the Suffering God. In a way, she anticipated the controversy of the Auschwitz convent when she said:

As I see it, the great danger of Christianity is in its open or latent anti-Judaism, which distances itself triumphantly from the pain of God and comes down on the side of the victor. This . . . appears everywhere where Christianity makes definitions of itself which are not legitimate, i.e., which are not in accord with God's social, political, and historical will. . . . A Christianity which excludes the Jewish interest destroys itself: it excludes justice from redemption, politics from theology, this world from the presumed other world, recollection of deliverance from individual suffering, and death and any meaning from non-thematized collective suffering.[1]

Both the positive and negative aspects of Christian thought, as they can be applied to this particular controversy, come into play here. Positive Christian thinking brings the teaching of the Suffering God into the human situation, where divine pain can be alleviated by human action that directs itself to the removal of evil in the world. I also heard Dorothee Soelle give a similar talk at the Frankfurt Kirchentag, where she cited a Latin American feminist liturgy used in an evening mass:

Donde esta Dios?
Where is God?

Esta con el pueblo de Dios.
God is with the people of God.

Donde esta el pueblo de Dios?
Where is the people of God?

Esta en la lucha por justicia!
It is in the battle for justice!

Donde Esta la lucha?
Where is the battle?

Esta aqui!
It is here!²

The liturgy breaks away from the theological text here in order to enter life itself. God is not found on the cross but in the suffering people. And in this approach it is the function of Christianity to leave the hallowed place of retreat and to encounter the Suffering God in the midst of suffering humanity. The kind nuns of the Auschwitz convent may claim that this was their intention: every grieving relative coming to Auschwitz would find them ready to give their help! But the idea and the approach were wrong. It was an intrusion into the privacy of grief, together with the mistaken notion that evil could be prayed away at the place of murder. Evil must be pursued and fought throughout the world, and Auschwitz is there so that we may know that the faces of the Gorgons look at us in every place where the worth of an individual life has been negated.

The latent anti-Judaism of the New Testament is recognized by many Christians. Nevertheless, the Auschwitz convent controversy helps us to understand that no dialogue between the open and informed leaders of Christianity and Judaism can control the major misconceptions of the Jewish stereotype that wanders unimpeded through the Gospel classes of the average Christian community, and which resides within the simple nun at prayer. Dorothee Soelle, at the Kirchentag, tried to speak to the motto of that conference: "Ecce homo: Behold the man!" I gave one of the opening sermons at that conference, and used the same text. Other preachers saw it as a chance to preach Christ to the multitude and wondered what a rabbi could do with such a text. But I tried to place it back into the human situation, to deal with the history of Palestine at a time when the Romans were the occupying army. Pontius Pilate, that saint (in the Coptic tradition, at least), was compared by me with Klaus Barbie; and the Butcher of Lyons scored higher! Looking at the text closely, at the scourging of Jesus, at the procurator's attempt to select one of two Roman victims—Barabbas or Jesus—I could point out the similarity between Pontius Pilate and an SS man giving the Jewish mother "Sophie's Choice": "Which one of your children shall I kill? Keep one—and I'll kill the other!" The large church where Goethe had been confirmed was deathly silent when I came to this question, when I asked them to pick out the guilty one. Did the cry "Let his blood be upon our head!" fit this story? If, suddenly, the situation is seen in the context of our time, can the victims become the murderers?

We are actually back in the Auschwitz controversy at this moment. When one takes the concentration camp and makes it a counter in a theological game, it is easy to lose sight of what has happened, to turn death into victory—at least, in the books. In just the same way, the Gospels turned the tragedy of a judicial murder by the Romans into an article of faith which was used to persecute the Jews. But we see the end result of the game: it is Auschwitz. Can we, should we still play that game?

Once more, it is the fixed glare of Medusa, the Gorgon's face of evil, which froze those who wandered into the outer precincts of Auschwitz into a static pattern of belief that tried to exorcise evil with words of dogma and could not break through into the actual life of the victims and the mourners of other faiths. History is not seen as history when it is subsumed under *Heilsgeschichte*, the unrolling of God's will which cannot be challenged or questioned. In that frozen world of belief, Auschwitz could be seen as an aspect of Calvary, just as the Akedah—Abraham tested through his son Isaac—becomes mainly a prefiguration of Calvary. The human dimension is lost. The rich Jewish heritage that entered Christian thought from the very beginning is cut off from its roots. And the Jews who died in Auschwitz alongside the others become symbolic counters in the Christian game of salvation. But this cannot, must not, happen. That is why it is not enough to withdraw from the brink and relocate the Carmelite convent elsewhere as a place for dialogue among religions. We must begin to recognize the wrong that was done out of noble intentions, the naïveté of simple religionists who transgress against others without knowledge (and, in the case of the American rabbi leading a raiding party against the nuns, the wrongs done *with* knowledge).

Somehow, we must not let evil hypnotize us. That is what happened. And the result was more evil and pain in the world.

The second question asked of us tries to formalize the parameters of an enforced confrontation between Christianity and Judaism. It stated: "In both the Jewish and Christian traditions, what assumptions most need to be reexamined, what obstacles most need to be overcome, what pitfalls need to be avoided, and what strengths most need to be utitilized to address the issue(s) in ways that might improve those relationships?"

Pitfalls. Let us think about this first, since we have already begun to discern some of them in the previous section. Mainly, there is the matter of approaching evil. Quite apart from differing interpretations as to the nature of evil, there is also the way we approach it. Judaism and Christianity both talk of exorcism, even though the use of bell, book, and candle has diminished over the years. Enlightened, rational Judaism has tried to dismiss this aspect of the Jewish tradition. The black ram's horn now rests in the museum, and the Leviticus texts read in the synagogue on Shabbat are the foundation of homiletical excursions which explain the curse resting upon the house as wet rot or immoral conduct and explain the purification rites in moral terms. But the film *The Dybbuk* (and the play) frequently reappear on videos or in amateur productions, reminders that we are linked into a secular culture that delights in its "omens" and "demons," its horror films where the protagonists of religion at best win illusionary victories. The world knows of evil in the world and, again, wants to push this knowledge into the harmless level of games, just as "war games" minimize atomic war itself. Religion *is* infected by this. A pitfall does exist, and prayer is misused as a mantric chant which tries to place a wall between us and evil, or which assumes that prayer will destroy Auschwitz. As long as this frozen pattern in the face of evil persists, we will be unable to live—or live together—in the world after Auschwitz.

What are the "assumptions" that need to be re-examined? First, let us say with respect and with pain that most Christians make the false assumption that Christianity had, really, nothing to do with Auschwitz and with the Holocaust. The Nazi plan, it is asserted, rose out of pagan thinking, and was as much an attack upon the church as upon the synagogue. In common with most rationalizations, there are some facts here that are expanded, blown up, and given a prominence that obscures the historical reality. The Nazis tried to destroy the Christian opposition against them by creating a "German National Church" that would support Hitler. There was resistance against this, as we can see in the "Confessing Church." But why did they succeed at all? And why did so many churches maintain their silence in the face of evil? Why were there so few Bonhoeffers, Niemoellers, Kolbes, Lichtenbergs? The few *proved* that there was the possibility, the seed, and the reality of Christianity fighting evil. On the whole, it did not do so. I remember *Kristallnacht* and the burning synagogues— and the silent churches alongside the burning houses of worship where Jews and Torah scrolls did in some places burn and die together in the sight of neighbors. And, when Sister Carol Rittner returned from a visit to Auschwitz where Elie Wiesel had brought a group of Nobel Prize winners to behold the darkness, she told us that she had heard the church bells in the vicinity of the camp. In her mind, she also heard those same bells ringing at times when the chimneys of Auschwitz were strewing the ashes of human beings over that land, ashes carried by the wind to the nearest villages. Can we assume that Christianity, as the guilty bystander, had no share in Auschwitz? And then, one examines the ideology. Certainly, Christian anti-Judaism in the New Testament, and Christian antisemitism through the centuries were very much present in the Nazi teachings. It was a misuse, of course—but a misuse one found within the churches as well. Here is where Christians will have to use their strength to remove the false assumptions, and where Jews have to be strong in reminding themselves that there is an attempt for such a new beginning, and that children are not to be blamed for the sins of their ancestors.

This leads to the confrontation of the assumption that does exist within the Jewish community, based upon the picture which we have just presented. Jews feel that Christians are responsible for the Holocaust—a natural assumption in a world where the majority group defined itself as Christian and benefited initially from the Nazi system: Aryanized Jewish shops, looted homes, possessions taken away—Jews killed and Christians protected. How could one not make this assumption? But it was a false assumption, since the evil did not reside totally within the church and within Christian teaching. Evil exists outside of religion *as well*, and we did not perceive this clearly. It is a false assumption that there is *no* evil within religion, and the fires of fanaticism can be found in both faiths. But one cannot ignore the society that is destroyed by other means, and which sweeps religion along as an accomplice but not as the ultimate protagonist of the destruction of human beings. To overstate this argument in order to clarify our thoughts: Standing before Auschwitz, Christians must no longer assume that they and their religion are innocent in this matter. They must accept responsibility. And Jews must no longer confront the Christian community with the assumption that the neighbor is the guilty one. They must learn to see the complexity of evil and must learn compassion for the Christian plight that involves the next generation in an inheritance of guilt where they were also victims. Jews have faced the dark past. The survivors—the children—have told themselves: "In some strange way, it was better to be one of the victims instead of being among the murderers." I have heard this often and can see the hope and prayer that reside in these words. But when one reads Elie Wiesel or Primo Levi, such a statement is hubris; and it is almost an abomination in the face of the dead. The inmates of the death camps did *not* want to be among the victims; they wanted to live in any possible way; and that was not a moral failing within them. All we can do—and this applies to the next generation—is to enlarge the concept of the victims in order to enclose the children of Eichmann within that definition.

We know and understand so little. We make the false assumption that we can understand what happened in Auschwitz; that we can define good and evil, the victims and the villains, that we can be judge and jury. We must break away from this, but not to the point where we call everyone innocent or guilty. We do believe in justice and judgment, and must at least recognize that there are gradations of evil, that one moves from black to gray and white, and that we cannot simply walk away from this. Recently, the British Parliament debated whether or not war criminals should be tried in British courts for crimes committed elsewhere (if such criminals lived in Great Britain). I wrote to one of the leading Members of Parliament who was against such trials and urged him to change his mind. In his letter to me, he said: "My dear rabbi, leave those old, poor war criminals alone. Leave them to God!" I could not follow this line of reasoning. We have to judge others, as we have to judge ourselves. But it is precisely here that Jews and Christians may come closer together.

There are other, dangerous assumptions. In the matter of the Carmelite convent at Auschwitz, our discussions broke down because we made erroneous assumptions about the nature of the participants who were part of this discussion. We thought, for example, that the bishops spoke for the church. And that the church, led by the pope, spoke for all Christians involved in this matter. I think, incidentally, that Christians worked with the same false assumption. The church was considered a monolithic totality, and it was assumed that the statements made were the authentic pronouncements of Christianity. We believed, with the Vatican, that statements made by the leaders of the church were the final word in this matter. And then, something quite curious happened. The nuns refused to move. How could this be? Had not the Cardinal . . . had not the Pope . . . how could they say "No"? But they did.

As outsiders, we cannot know the internal circumstances. As we have indicated earlier, there may well have been nationalist motives, a strong *vox populi*, which could account for the sometimes strange actions of Cardinal Glemp and of the nuns when they took a stand against the Vatican. And, sadly, one cannot rule out the presence of antisemitism in their actions—the old feeling that "an international Jewish conspiracy" was depriving them of their rights to establish their tomb for the unknown (Polish) soldier. Personally, I would prefer to think that a strong and naïve piety made it difficult for them to accept the fact that they were praying in the wrong place. Whatever the motives, the fact remains that the world made totally wrong assumptions about the nature of the religious structure that included within its framework the Carmelite convent at Auschwitz. The church is *not* monolithic. Decisions made in Rome are not carried out automatically. We are living in an age, dramatically revealed to us by the recent events in the Eastern bloc of the Communist hegemony, where individuals rebel against authority and where local options prevail. The church is in conflict. The ongoing internal struggle within the Catholic church in Germany has seen large-scale rebellion against the appointment of conservative bishops by the pope, who refused to accept anyone on the lists prepared by the German communities. So, too, did Cardinal Glemp listen to the Polish community more than to the Vatican decision. And one must accept this and have a certain amount of sympathy for his actions, particularly since he did, in the end, support the decision to move the convent. In the end, it is significant that he managed to use the intemperate actions of the American "invaders" of the convent to give support to the strong Polish feelings, and that he could utilize the friendly dialogue with Sir Sigmund Sternberg to retreat from what had become an untenable position.

The lesson to be learned here is surely that one cannot rely upon one or even several meetings with "the leadership" on both sides to resolve all issues. There is more democracy within religion than we tend to assume. Decisions are taken home for an informal "ratification" by communities that no longer accept the right of leaders to make important decisions without some kind of consultation. Leaders must still lead, must set goals for their communities and open up these communities for dialogue with the neighbor. But we can no longer assume that a public statement has settled an issue, or that an official proclamation is acceptable to both sides in a controversy. The important declaration of 1980 by the Rhineland Synod said marvelous things about the new Christian awareness of the rights of Jews and Judaism. But counterdemonstrations followed, and a decade later that statement is largely eroded because it does not represent the majority view of the professing German Christians. In the same way, we must not assume that the removal of the Carmelite convent from Auschwitz has settled the issue—more accurately, that it *will* settle the issue. At this time of writing (January 1990) the move has not yet taken place. New problems are certain to arise. The convent may still be in place upon that dark and bloody ground when this book appears; and this need not be ascribed to a "Christian conspiracy" which has subverted the will of church leaders desirous of undoing what they see to have been a wrong action.

The messianic world, or even just the right action to correct a specific wrong, does not necessarily come when we are ready for it. We live in an imperfect world, one in which stubborn, stupid bureaucracy often prevails. Religious dialogue often takes place against a backdrop of apathy and ignorance: "Even the gods fight in vain against stupidity," said Goethe. And so the failure of a move out of Auschwitz is not necessarily the failure of dialogue. And if a successful move has been achieved, it is not necessarily the triumph of the forces of good. There will be new problems: problems of economics, of politics, of religion. The one victory that may have been gained will rise out of the fact that men and women of good will from both camps will have encountered one another with the knowledge that they have shared a problem which has helped them to understand one another.

It is difficult to anticipate the immediate future; perhaps that is why theologians deal happily with eschatology, and make their pronouncements about the end of time. Their statements are beyond empirical verification—unless the physicists are right and time ultimately reverses itself! But anything said about tomorrow still rests upon assumptions that fade away with the next dawn. Nevertheless, I would tend to assume that the convent will be removed from the Auschwitz perimeter, and that some kind of a more ecumenical center will arise some distance from the death camp. Where will it be built? Elie Wiesel has said: "Build the convent outside the area of the camp, as was agreed. Build it in the city of Oswiecim, but not in Auschwitz itself. Nothing should be built there which would further divide people. We have been divided enough."[3]

I would agree totally. But will those who live in Oswiecim agree? Some years ago, at a Hamburg Kirchentag (the national Protestant Church Conference, held every two years and attended by some 200,000 delegates) I was part of a silent march to the concentration camp at Neuengamme outside of Hamburg. As we marched through the nearest village, all the doors closed and the curtains were drawn inside the windows. The villagers did *not* want to be reminded of their silence, their proximity to evil, their passive acquiescence to the murders. Would Oswiecim be different? There may well be a challenge here to our work that could become a positive achievement, if representatives of Oswiecim are involved in the discussions, participate in the plans, have an active share in the educational aspects of such a center. But we must not assume that one can build there without the cooperation of the inhabitants: it must also be *their* attempt to move toward reconciliation. And they are far away from this way of thinking— as can be seen by the fact that the name of Oswiecim was not changed. How can one live within a town by that name if one does not block out the immediate past? Similarly, Dachau outside of Munich spends much money and effort upon reminding passing tourists of the medieval glories of this "quaint" village, and it is difficult to find inhabitants who will give directions to the "museum" of the Dachau concentration camp. Perhaps this aids us in coming to terms with a Polish attitude that has removed that whole landscape of hell, Auschwitz with all of its tributary camps, into an obscured patch of history viewed only through a distorting mirror which will not freeze the blood and confront them with the ultimate evil of which their parents were not innocent. Auschwitz as a museum reflecting Polish resistance and suffering under the Nazis is a passable lesson to be taught to schoolchildren under a carefully supervised excursion which will not confront Jewish suffering but Polish heroism. But, in that context, what will one do with a place of prayer in a town that wants no more reminders? It may well be the greatest challenge of all for the nuns. Their prayers must not only deal with the victims who died half a century ago, but with their immediate neighbors who were silent and did not let those victims intrude into the prayers said in their churches.

Other assumptions could well be examined at this point. What is the nature of humanity caught in the web of evil? Did different types of human beings live outside and inside the camps? A careful reading of the books of Elie Wiesel, of Primo Levi's *The Drowned and the Saved*, supplies the beginnings of answers here. But there comes the point where we are weary of asking questions. We want answers. And at least some of the answers are more accessible to us when we move beyond our own religion and listen to our neighbor; when we move beyond religion and listen to those who struggle with the same problems, but outside the comforts of religious faith. Yet there is one question to which we must give an immediate answer, particularly since it is more often asked from the outside: "Why should one think about the Holocaust at all? When we consider the barbarities, the genocides committed in the past forty years, is it not parochial to keep coming back to this one event of the twentieth century? Can we not let it rest now, and stop tearing our old wounds open to the point where we again sicken unto death? Why?"

Oddly enough, despite our insistence that we must go beyond our own religious tradition in search of answers, the fact remains that we must turn to the theologians here. The Holocaust—the *Shoah*—the Churban—The Tremendum . . . was unique. History and psychology, even the social sciences, will grudgingly acknowledge that nothing quite like it had ever happened before (but will add that this might be said of any event!). Also, they cannot guarantee that another Holocaust may not happen again. But theology here comes to recognize the tremendum of evil that cannot be fully encompassed by human understanding. It comes to remind us of guilt that cannot be ignored, of tasks of alleviation which have not yet been accomplished, of our own confrontation with evil as it exists in the world and in ourselves. And it can fight more readily against the rationalizations that exist in the various scientific answers which try to relativize the evil by subsuming it within their various disciplines and making it compatible with one theory or another. The dialectics of history eat up evil. Psychology attempts to understand all in order to forgive all. Religion can also try to assuage human guilt by letters of indulgence and acts of remission that move the problem of Auschwitz outside the realm of immediate human responsibility. But, in this time and in this place, the sensibilities and concern with human suffering can break through older patterns of dogma and return us to the place where God demands of us: "Where is your brother?" Judaism and Christianity, despite some falterings, have not hesitated to acknowledge that we are our brother's keeper. And, in a time of assertion of individual and of communal freedom, we can also assert our responsibility to deal with a past that is still a trauma, a gaping wound in the world.

Religion has to fight the assumption that Auschwitz was a past event. Auschwitz lives today, and it is the duty of religion to come to terms with the knowledge that the evil of it still spills out into the world, and that we cannot know the nature of current evil if we do not see the relationship between that past darkness and present acts of dehumanization and of destruction. There exists the concerted effort in the world, particularly in politics and in history, to remove Auschwitz from present considerations. But the basic teaching of Judaism (and, through inheritance, within Christianity) is the word: *Zakhor*—Remember. The rites of religious traditions convey this reality of the spiritual life through our emotions. And the centrality of "teaching" within Judaism assures that these emotions are brought into the realm of rational thought where exodus and exile, as well as the return to the land, become areas of spiritual enlargement. In a curious way, the problem of the convent at Auschwitz brings us closer to our neighbor here. We can see that we share a *theologia viatorum*, that we travel upon the same way. And at that point, the shared anguish becomes a doorway of hope.

The final question addressed to the contributors of this volume was "Are there lessons Jews and Christians can learn as a result of the recent controversy?"

I do not really think that I want to answer this. Religionists always tend to be didactic, to leave the scene with a moral trailing behind them. For myself, I have certainly learned something—about myself. I was amazed at the anger I felt against what was certainly the innocent piety of the nuns (and what *may* have been innocence within the American invasion of the convent). I was saddened that so little progress has been made in our work of interfaith. But then I consoled myself with the final words in Spinoza's *Ethics* which assure us that one must struggle greatly to attain what is worthwhile.

I can only suggest that we must continue to work together. Then, perhaps, our prayers will also be joined. And the suffering messiah will move one step closer to a suffering world.

NOTES

1. Dorothee Soelle, "God's Pain and Our Pain: How Theology Has to Change After Auschwitz," *Remembering for the Future*, 3 vols. (Oxford, Eng.: Pergamon Press, 1989), 3:2743.

2. Dorothee Soelle, ''Gottes Schmerz und unsere Schmerzen,'' *Dokumente Deutscher Evangelischer Kirchentag* (Frankfurt: 1987), 261.

3. See Elie Wiesel's interview with Carol Rittner in the *National Catholic Reporter*, 15 September 1989. This interview, which occurred on August 29, 1989, also appears as chapter 8 in this book.

15

Memory Redeemed?

Robert McAfee Brown

That memory can be "offended," as the title of this book reminds us, is clear. Memory is all too frequently offended, and we need to acknowledge offenses whenever they obtrude as discordant notes out of the past that challenge the harmony (such as it is) of the present.

One need not argue that the events surrounding the contested presence of the Carmelite convent at the edge of Auschwitz have offended the memory of Jews and Christians alike. We have all seen deep convictions trivialized, sacred commitments sneered at, and hopes for the future challenged. That is a given. The question that really matters, therefore, is the next question: Can the events, with their ugly spinoffs of evil and misunderstanding, be turned to any good use for the future? *Can memory offended become memory redeemed?*

Whether the answer to that question is yes or no, there are possibilities implicit in it that must be explored, although any answers we discover will remain ambiguous; good is always vulnerable to fresh attack, and evil (we must hope) contains at least potential seeds of redemption, however small they may be and however rocky the soil on which they fall.

What resources, then, can Jews and Christians draw from this as yet unfinished episode that might augur a better future for our relationships with one another?

1. We can be reminded of how close to the surface antisemitism always is and do battle with it wherever we find it.

It is unfortunately necessary to direct attention once again to the homily of Cardinal Glemp on August 26, 1989, at the shrine of Our Lady of Czestochowa, in which, from the admirable affirmation that "a dialogue is necessary" to clear the air between Poles and Jews, he drew the following conclusions among others:

Beloved Jews, do not converse with us from the position of a people raised above others. . . . Do you not see, esteemed Jews, that intervention against [the Carmelite nuns] injures the feelings of all Poles and the sovereignty we gained with such difficulty?

Your power is the mass media, which is at your disposal in many countries. Let them not serve to inflame anti-Polish sentiment.

Recently a detachment of seven Jews from New York attacked the convent at Auschwitz. To be sure, because they were restrained, it did not result in the killing of the sisters or the destruction of the convent.[1]

It is not necessary to call Cardinal Glemp an antisemite (which in any case is not the author's privilege or right), or even to read between the lines, to see how these unfortunate words directly served to fan the flames of antisemitism to new heights by the simple process of dredging up ancient and stock-in-trade antisemitic images: (1) You Jews look upon yourselves as a "chosen people" superior to all other people. (2) You Jews are creating such anti-Polish sentiment that you are threatening the very sovereignty of our nation. (3) You Jews control the mass media worldwide and can use this power to bring discredit on the rest of us. (4) Seven of you Jews who "attacked" the Carmelite convent were unable to kill the sisters and destroy the convent only because others repulsed you.

Summary of the summary: Jewish arrogance and Jewish power are directed against innocent Catholic nuns and against all Poles. As Elie Wiesel remarked, if these words had been spoken half a century ago, there would have been an instant pogrom.

Closer to home, the syndicated columnist Patrick J. Buchanan let forth an incredible barrage in the *Washington Times* on September 25, 1989. After accusing Jews of "a systematic campaign to exclude all others from the honor role of the dead, to write us [Catholics] out," he goes on to insinuate (without checking his sources) that the Holocaust Memorial in Washington will memorialize only Jews who died at Hitler's hand and will exclude all others who likewise died. "What does it take," he asks, "to be a first class victim?" The insinuation is, of course, wrong; from the beginning, the Holocaust Memorial Council has been committed to remembering all of Hitler's victims. But facts are not important if, by their disregard, calumny can be visited on Jews.

At least it can be said of Mr. Buchanan that he is impartial in his hatreds. He excoriates Cardinal O'Connor (who publicly disassociated himself from the remarks of Cardinal Glemp) for admitting "the always irate Elie Wiesel" (Buchanan's words) that "there are many Catholics who are anti-Semitic . . . it's deep within them" (O'Connor's words). Explosively distancing himself from what he calls "the clucking appeasement of the Catholic cardinalate," Mr. Buchanan assures the world that the cardinal does not speak for *him*, and urges the cardinal to step aside so that the real "defenders of the faith" can take command. But, ironically, the tone of the entire column demonstrates that sometimes antisemitism is, in Cardinal O'Connor's words, "so deep within" that those who most blatantly exemplify it are oblivious to its presence.

We will have learned no lessons from the Auschwitz convent episode, unless we realize that expressions of antisemitism have not been exorcised from our common life, but can reappear at any time. It is a hard but necessary truth that we must always anticipate new expressions of antisemitism even as we deplore them. To be forewarned is to be forearmed.

2. We can relearn the importance of keeping promises.

When the convent was first located on the edge of Auschwitz, there was initial dismay in Jewish circles, a dismay that understandably escalated when fund-raising efforts for the convent gave the impression, whether accurate or not, that one of the tasks of the Carmelite sisters would be to pray for the conversion of the Jews—an especially inflammatory theme in Jewish-Christian relations, to which we will later return. The consequence of a number of such episodes was an agreement reached at Geneva in 1987 to relocate the convent at a suitable distance from the death camp, and an explicit date was set for the move. But no steps were taken to implement the agreement, and as a result the church was accused of having acted in bad faith.

The matter was further exacerbated when Cardinal Glemp indicated that he did not feel bound by the agreement, and accused Catholics who had negotiated it of being "incompetent"—a charge that earned him no points in high places (four cardinals were members of the commission) and had the unintended effect of eliciting a stream of Catholic support for honoring the agreement as soon as possible. Only after a great deal of Catholic intramural maneuvering and much off-the-record discussion was the matter finally resolved with a definitive statement from Rome that the convent would, in fact, be moved. *Roma locuta, causa finita*—save that even subsequent to this decision from above, the head of the Carmelite sisters declared that it was the intention of the nuns to remain where they were.

Not only does this dimension of the total episode point to the need for better coordination of Catholic public utterances, but, more importantly, it indicates that public trust is eroded when promises are not kept. Had the plan approved in Geneva in 1987 been acted upon in the observance rather than in the breach, the more recent *contretemps* could have been avoided altogether.

3. We can commit ourselves to seeing events from the perspective of the "other."

This is the central need for the future. It is clear that new sensitivities are needed on all sides, not only for care in formulating what we say, but equally for care in what we do, and for care in the symbols we employ. We need to reflect on how what we affirm will be heard or seen by others. An example from either side:

It was an act of extreme insensitivity on the part of the seven Jews to force their way into the Carmelite convent by scaling the walls. It is utterly foreign to Catholic tradition, indeed it would be a mark of extreme irreverence, for men to enter a cloistered convent of women religious. Catholics are entitled to be as outraged by this action as Jews would be if a group of Christians stormed the Holy of Holies, or entered a synagogue and gave the impression that they were going to desecrate the scrolls of the Torah. Particularly in controversial and highly charged situations, members of one religious tradition have a high obligation to reflect on how their particular actions will be interpreted by members of another religious tradition, and refrain from demeaning what is holy to the other. No one, knowing about the Catholic tradition of cloistered nuns, set apart from the world for a life of intercessory prayer, has a right to force his or her way into the inner sanctuary of private devotion. In the present case, such an action showed insensitivity, if not contempt, for the highly developed exercise of Catholic spirituality.

But the principle must work both ways. And here Christians must try to put themselves in the mind-set of Jews who come to Auschwitz, perhaps to mourn the loss of entire families in the furnaces of death. Although many people have commented on the proximity of the convent to the soil of Auschwitz, few have reflected on the mark of that proximity—a cross more than twenty feet high—or on the meanings associated with that particular symbolism in that particular place.[2]

To Christians, *at their best*, the cross is the pre-eminent symbol of the love of God for all humankind. It is a visible reminder that when God shared our human lot in Jesus of Nazareth, dwelling in our midst as one of us, this act of love and identification was very costly; the same Jesus who came in love was killed by the Roman authorities, who could not tolerate his challenges to their political and economic system.

But Christians are not usually "at their best." Very early in its history, the Christian church, in the name of the one who died on the cross, took the cross and made it a symbol not of love but of terror—a symbol in the name of which Christians felt entitled to force "conversions" from Jews, subject them to ghettoization, bloody pogroms, and outright murder. And so to Jews the cross has almost always been a symbol not of divine love but of the very human hatred it was meant to overthrow.

With that past record, Christians should not be surprised when the presence of a cross suggests to others, and particularly to Jews, a deity who is at least in complicity with human evil, if not the direct inspirer of it. When Christians visit Auschwitz and see a large cross at the edge of its precincts, they see it, at their best, as a reminder of the presence of Jesus, a Jew of Nazareth, suffering in the very midst of the place where so many other Jews likewise suffered—a statement that God is in the midst of the suffering of God's children, whoever they are, bearing it along with them.

But Christians have a responsibility to take seriously the message their symbol communicates to others, and to realize that to Jews who visit Auschwitz the cross gives an entirely different message. The presence of that large cross is a stark and painful reminder to them that if the killers at Auschwitz gave allegiance to any god, it was to the one symbolized by the cross, and that millions of church members and "believers" were acquiescent in, or active agents of, the death of 6 million Jews. Particularly in Poland, where antisemitism has had a long and bitter reign, the juxtaposition of extermination camp and cross only reinforces in the minds of Jews that the leaders of the camp believed they were carrying out the wishes of the one impaled upon the cross.

No Christian, with sensitivity to how the central Christian symbol is interpreted by Jews, will want to insist that at *that* place the cross should be displayed.

4. We can remove the issue of "conversion" from our agendas.

Even the faintest suggestion that the Carmelites were praying for "the conversion of the Jews" was enough to charge the ecumenical atmosphere. According to some Catholics, however, this should not bother Jews at all. William Buckley (as is frequently the case when he ventures into the theological realm) got it all wrong: "On the matter of praying for the conversion of the Jews, ecumenism has really gone too far. The subtlest form of anti-Semitism is to act as though it were not worth it to pray for the conversion of Jews to Christianity."[3] I think it is safe to say that there has never been a Jew, living or dead, who has felt discriminated against, and a victim of antisemitism, because some Christian here or there was *not* praying for his or her conversion to Christianity. If that is "the subtlest form of anti-Semitism," Jews must surely react: Let us have more of it. The authentic Jewish reaction on this matter is the passionate comment of Rabbi Abraham Joshua Heschel: "I had rather enter the gates of Auschwitz than be a candidate for conversion." So let us lay Mr. Buckley's most recent ecumenical excursion to rest. We need not take him seriously.

Obviously, no one can dictate to another what he or she may or may not pray for, especially if the two belong to different faiths. But the matter of prayer for the conversion of another is serious business with a long history, and it deserves a fresh look after all the centuries in which it has been taken for granted as appropriate.

Some lessons can be learned from the ecumenical events that immediately preceded the more recent Christian-Jewish discussions, namely, the earlier Catholic-Protestant dialogue that began in the late 1950s. As a Protestant participant in many of these events, I can well remember the early days of the era, when my Protestant friends were warning me that I was "soft on Catholicism" (which, in the 1950s was as heinous as being "soft on communism") and that I had better be aware that the recent interest in dialogue from the Catholic side was only a trick to soften Protestant sensibilities and pave the way for the ultimate conversion of Protestants to Catholicism.

Initially, to be sure, there may have been reason for the fears. My wife and I had good Catholic friends who said very honestly that they did not want us to convert just yet, since that would give a wrong signal to others, but that they would pray for deathbed conversions so that we could all enjoy eternity together. Again, early versions of the Christian Unity Octave—eight days of prayer in the Catholic liturgical year—for Christian unity, were quite explicit in praying for the conversion to Catholicism of various groups of Protestant "schismatics and heretics" (I think our day was Thursday). But when the climate began to change, as we got to know one another better, it became clear that making "unity" equal "capitulation" was not going to foster good feeling and trust, let alone lead to the creation of a more inclusive Christian family. As a result, a whole new approach was developed, and somewhat to our initial amazement, Protestants and Catholics began to find ourselves praying *together* in that January liturgical week, not for the triumph of one faith over the other, but for more openness to whatever leadings of the Spirit might help both move into greater possession of the gifts God wished to bestow—whatever that might mean for the status of our present structural and denominational arrangements. Catholic-Protestant ecumenism began to move into high gear only when we Protestants realized that Catholics were really not out to make us Catholics, but to search with us for whatever could make all of us better Christians.

I believe Jews today are in somewhat the same position as Protestants yesterday. There is an analogous Jewish suspicion that the end of the road of dialogue, as far as Christians are concerned, is that Jews convert. But for Jews the situation is even more serious, for whereas for Protestants conversion would initially have meant capitulation, for Jews conversion would mean annihilation as well—for if the "Christian mission," according to this reading, is not complete until the whole world has been "won for Christ," this is simply another way of describing a world in which there will be no more Jews.

So long as conversion is the hidden (or open) Christian agenda, Jews are entitled to be wary and even noncooperative. So it must be a high item on both Christian and Jewish agendas to deal *forthrightly* with the appropriateness, or lack thereof, of a Christian mission to the Jews.

Few things, it must be acknowledged, do more to upset conservative Protestants and traditional Catholics than the suggestion that they are not supposed to convert any and all human beings—Jews, Muslims, secular humanists, or whoever—to their own particular brand of faith. There is not space here for a full-blown discussion of the matter, but I think there are at least two things that militate persuasively against Christians trying to convert Jews: (1) *Sociologically*, it is intolerable to expect Jews to respond favorably to joining an institution that has had such an abysmally consistent track record of Jewish persecution almost from the time of its founding; and (2) *theologically*, Christians and Jews are already inheritors, Jews by birth and Christians by adoption, of the same promises by the same God. Christians come, through faith in Jesus Christ, to know the God of the Jews—the God of Abraham, Isaac, and Jacob (and Sarah, Leah, and Rachel) with whom the Jews are *already* in covenant relationship. Put another way, Jesus is the missionary arm of Judaism, reaching out to make it possible for the rest of us, non-Jews, to enter into covenant with a God the Jews already know.

Whatever one thinks of the above highly compressed argument, it is surely arguable that Christians and Jews need to work out ways of living side by side without conversion being part of the *modus vivendi*.

5. We can rethink our theology from the perspective these events furnish.

We have already initiated a process of theological reflection and rethinking in relation to the issue of "conversion." A creative result of the distressing events surrounding the Carmelite convent would be that we extend our theological thinking in other directions as well. I will briefly indicate three further ways in which the discussion could move.

First, the overwhelming theological question in relation to the Holocaust is always, of course, *Where was God when all this was going on?* Shattered forever are traditional views of an omnipotent God who is directly in control of all that happens in the universe. Did such a God exist? That God would be directly responsible for the slaughter of 6 million Jews and at least 5 million other victims of Hitler's war machine, and it would be an obligation of faith to repudiate any deity so conceived. What alternative is there?

From his prison cell in Germany, Dietrich Bonhoeffer, a Lutheran pastor who helped Jews escape to Switzerland and was hanged for his part in the July 20, 1944, plot against Hitler's life, wrote in the final months before his execution that "Only the suffering God can help."[4] By this he meant that in the insoluble mystery of the relation of God to evil, we must at least locate God in the midst of the *victims* rather than among the executioners. Otherwise God is aloof and noncaring—and malevolent.

Jews have many ways of making the claim about a caring and vulnerable and involved God out of the Hebrew Scriptures and the subsequent tradition, and I continually learn from them. Christians who struggle with the question can begin by asking where Jesus would have been found in the death camps. Would he have been at the side of the exterminators, many of whom were members of Christian churches dedicated to worshipping him as God's supreme revelation? Or would he have been found with the exterminated—Jews like himself—dying as a member of a persecuted minority? One can only locate him with the latter group and reflect on the irony that it would have been Christians, "only obeying orders," who would have destroyed him.

Those are not the only things that can be said about God's presence or absence at Auschwitz, but they are surely starting points for further reflection about God and the past.

Second, what, then, do we do with our own past? Both Judaism and Christianity are historical faiths, asserting that God is not found exclusively or even primarily in an ethereal realm, but in the midst of human life. This means that our second question is not *Where is God?* but, at least as poignantly, *Where were we?* Where were the members of the human family when these events were coming to pass? If it is difficult to relate God to the Holocaust, it is at least as difficult to relate humanity to it, and the conclusions when we do are equally devastating. Many people, looking at the brutality and naked human evil in the camps, have concluded that there is no reminder of creative human possibilities for the future, and that the only realism is to live cynically within a fatalistic construct devoid of light and hope and encompassed by darkness and despair.

I believe no one has measured the evil of the Holocaust who has not been deeply attracted to such a conclusion. And yet (those saving words that Elie Wiesel has engrained upon our hearts): there were tiny rays of light piercing even the darkness of Auschwitz: a guard who was kind to the inmates and was killed by his superiors for not displaying the appropriate ''Aryan virtues''; a starving parent who gave his or her full day's ration to a starving child; a believer who repeated the *Sh'ma Yisrael* on the way to the gas chamber, as an ultimate act of refusal to become like the enemy; a woman who saw her own child killed by a Nazi bayonet and then mothered an orphaned child whose parents had been similarly dispatched.

There were torrents of evil. But there were also droplets of good.

What do we do with such a past? There can be only one answer: we pick and choose. We remember all that is good in human experience even at its most desolate, searching for those tiny moments that reveal an indubitable spirit. And we embrace them no matter how few they are, so that in our own lives we can emulate them. But—and equally—we remember the very moments of horror and ugliness that we would like with every fiber of our being to excise from the collective human memory but dare not—for fear that, being forgotten, they will someday be repeated. So we remember good *and* evil, memory offended *and* memory redeemed, and are called upon to make the amazing and scarcely to be validated choice that, after the manner of Joshua, we will choose to affirm life, over death, blessing over curse, so that we and our descendants may live.[5]

Third, *can there be forgiveness?* Dietrich Bonhoeffer, to whom reference has already been made, wrote an essay in 1937 on ''Costly Grace'' that is, among other things, a polemic against what he calls ''cheap grace.''[6] Cheap grace is not only a temptation for Lutherans but for all human beings who (from whatever theological perspective) presume on the benevolence of God, or the order of things, to exonerate them of wrongdoing and wipe the moral slate clean at little or no cost to themselves. ''God will forgive,'' Heine wrote, in a perfect example of cheap grace, ''that's what He's here for.''

So much we can easily dispense with as theological trivia. But there is a deep claim, in the Hebrew prophets, in Jesus, and in Paul, that it is the nature of the divine love to offer ever fresh chances to human beings who genuinely repent of their wrongdoing, and to make that offer not out of indulgence but out of love. Sins can be confessed, forgiven, and the book closed on them forever.

New possibilities are always offered. The mercies of God, Scripture says definitively, are fresh every morning.

In various ways, the great religions all affirm that the relation between God and humanity is not based on a human claim to deserve God's love, but on a divine claim to offer love precisely to the undeserving. This is not only a message of consolation but of challenge. Paraphrasing Luther: If I, undeserving, have nevertheless been forgiven, even so, surely, must I reach out to those who appear to me to be undeserving, and offer them forgiveness as well. It is a glorious conviction when it is not abused.

But does all of that venerable tradition "work" with Auschwitz? Are there not some sins that are beyond the pale of forgiveness? Can there possibly be a message of forgiveness to the perpetrators of the most heinous crimes in human history, such as the burning of babies in front of their parents? Would not the promise of forgiveness to such persons make God sentimentally indulgent, and tear apart the moral fabric of a universe in which we must be held responsible for the consequences of what we do? If people can asphyxiate and burn other people with impunity, have not love and justice and decency been destroyed as universal values?

For such reasons as these, many people have come to feel—post-Holocaust if not before—that forgiveness is a weak virtue, a retreat from moral toughness, and an invitation, as Paul put it on numerous occasions, "to sin bravely that grace may abound." If forgiveness is only the capital on which people feel they can draw in advance to cover forthcoming sins, then it is surely an invitation to moral license. "I like committing crimes. God likes forgiving them. Really the world is admirably arranged," is the way a character in Auden's *For the Time Being* puts it.[7]

For many, therefore, the message of the Holocaust has by contrast been crystallized in the formula "Never forget, never forgive," and while it would be hard to quarrel with the first two words, it is with extreme reluctance that some people affirm the last two. So we need to rethink the possibility that forgiveness could be a strong virtue, offering an ultimate mercy that does not assure people ahead of time that they will not be held accountable. It is difficult, if not impossible, to conceive of a torturer in a death camp being given a fresh start in which all past transgressions have been put aside and cancelled from the moral ledger. And yet, if our ultimate destiny is to be predicated only on the extent of our worthiness, who could ever hope to pass such a test?

This is, to be sure, an ancient theological dilemma, with which all great religions have to wrestle, and for which there is no satisfactory resolution, but the instance of the Holocaust assures at least that we will not adopt views of grace and forgiveness that are indulgent or "cheap." But also, as a result of the Holocaust, we have to ask whether, if vindictiveness was the last word in running the death camps, we want to construct a post-Holocaust world defined by the same criterion. Perhaps this would be "Hitler's posthumous victory" about which Emil Fackenheim writes so powerfully.[8]

Forgiveness, it should be said finally, is not ours to bestow or withhold. It can finally be offered only by those who have been wronged, or by a God who has also, in some analogical sense, been "wronged" as well.[9]

This is a discussion that will not soon be terminated.

I conclude this exercise of hope for the power of memory redeemed, by recounting a further Auschwitz memory, one of my own, because it reminds me every time I recall it of the ease with which we embrace those twin evils, forgetfulness and accommodation.[10]

It was on a Sunday morning in January 1988, close to the noon hour, that a group of us concluded our visit to Auschwitz by entering one of the crematoria and standing silently in front of the furnaces, with their still glistening tracks positioned for the more "efficient" disposal of the corpses. A rabbi led some prayers. A Polish priest read Scripture, the *De profundis* ("Out of the depths") from Psalm 130. The Jews present began to recite the Kaddish, the prayer for the dead.

And then it happened. . . . Interrupting the Kaddish and continuing in clamorous competition with its high solemnity as though wishing to shut it out, the church bells from just outside the camp began to peal, celebrating the consecration of the host at the Mass in the parish church.

My mind involuntarily and instantaneously took a leap back forty-five years. I reflected that at that time real guards would have been in the room in which we are now standing, thrusting real corpses into real ovens heated to temperatures extreme enough to dispose of the corpses quickly, and that the same guards who were burning those same bodies would have gone out of that same camp, walked the few hundred yards to that same church, been absolved of their sins, received communion, and returned that afternoon or the next morning to continue the same grisly occupation—quite unaware of any contradiction between receiving the body and blood of the Jew Jesus, and destroying the body and blood of millions of other Jews.

Memory offended? Yes.

Memory redeemed? Only if we use such memories as occasions for repentance and new beginnings.

NOTES

1. See *Origins* 19 (15 October 1989): 294. This document is also reprinted in the appendix of this book.

2. The following four paragraphs are adapted from my article, "A Symbol Is a Symbol Is a Symbol," *Christianity and Crisis*, 23 October 1989.

3. See *Sunday Times* (Scranton, Pennsylvania), 3 September 1989.

4. Dietrich Bonhoeffer, *Letters and Papers from Prison*, enlarged edition (New York: Macmillan, 1972), 361.

5. Cf. Deuteronomy 30:19.

6. Dietrich Bonhoeffer, *The Cost of Discipleship* (New York: Macmillan, 1959), 35–47.

7. W. H. Auden, *The Collected Poetry of W. H. Auden* (New York: Random House, 1945), 459.

8. Emil Fackenheim, *God's Presence in History* (New York: New York University Press, 1970). See especially chapter 3, "The Commanding Voice of Auschwitz," 67–104.

9. A variety of views on the issue of forgiveness is contained in Simon Wiesenthal, *The Sunflower* (New York: Schocken Books, 1976).

10. The following three paragraphs are adapted from my article "Nobelists, Auschwitz and Survival," *Christianity and Crisis*, 7 March 1988.

Afterword: No Armistice from the Inhuman

Carol Rittner and John K. Roth

> Given all the problems facing humankind, where on the list of priorities do you place the controversy over the Auschwitz Carmelite convent?
> —Carol Rittner to Elie Wiesel

As this book went to press in February 1991, the Carmelite nuns were still in the convent at Auschwitz. War scourged the Persian Gulf. Israelis, many still bearing Auschwitz scars, were on alert against gas attacks that threatened Jews again. The problems facing humankind have not diminished since Carol Rittner asked Elie Wiesel about the Auschwitz Carmelite convent controversy on August 29, 1989. The list of priorities has grown.

A broken world so badly needs mending because humankind's inhumanity offers no armistice. Its destructiveness will rage unless vigilance checks it. Thus, the Auschwitz convent controversy still deserves attention because that unfinished episode could show, as Robert McAfee Brown suggests, that memory offended can become memory redeemed and redeeming.

In late January 1991, the *National Catholic Register* noted that Rabbi Avraham Weiss intends to visit Poland to check reports about "a new Carmelite convent" at Birkenau.[1] Apparently Weiss is suspicious that the Vatican plans a network of convents at Nazi concentration and death camp sites. Church sources deny the existence of a convent at Birkenau, although a few nuns work and live at a parish church that has existed there since the early 1980s. This church, according to the *National Catholic Register*, is "located in a former Nazi building just outside the camp's barbed-wire perimeter." As of this writing, it is unclear how controversial the Birkenau situation may become. It is clear, however, that since the end of September 1989, when the Vatican issued a statement supporting the nun's relocation from the Old Theater at Auschwitz I, there have been many positive changes. If they get good care, and are not compromised by new difficulties at Birkenau or elsewhere, there will be improved understanding and deepened solidarity among Christians and Jews. Here are some of those promising developments.

Signed by Jewish and Catholic leaders, the February 1987 Geneva agreement stipulated "no permanent Catholic place of worship on the site of the Auschwitz and Birkenau camps." This aim is being implemented by the relocation of the Auschwitz convent. On February 19, 1990, ground was broken for "a center of information, education, meeting and prayer." The new center will be inside Oswiecim but outside the Auschwitz-Birkenau camps.[2] There, as the Geneva agreement put it, "the Carmelites' initiative of prayer" will "find its place, confirmation and true meaning."

According to Wladyslaw T. Bartoszewski, secretary of the Institute for Polish-Jewish studies at Oxford and a scholar who has closely followed the controversy, by the end of 1991, the Carmelite Convent will have been moved from the old theater in Auschwitz."[3] Meanwhile, although constructive dialogue between the world Jewish community and the Vatican broke down at times during the heat of the convent controversy, productive talks have resumed. In September 1990, for example, the International Catholic-Jewish Liaison Committee, representing the Vatican and several international Jewish organizations, met in Prague, Czechoslovakia. The delegates discussed the centuries-old roots of religious and secular antisemitism—including its relationship to the *Shoah*. Archbishop Edward Cassidy, president of the Vatican's commission, publicly stated: "That anti-Semitism has found a place in Christian thought and practice calls for an act of *Teshuvah* (repentance) and of reconciliation on our part. . . . "[4]

Signs of such repentance could be found at Czestochowa in late November 1990, when Poland's 244 cardinals, archbishops, and bishops, including Cardinal Jozef Glemp, met in a plenary conference. To mark "The 25th Anniversary of the Proclamation of the Conciliar Declaration *Nostra Aetate*," they prepared a pastoral letter. Read in every Catholic church in Poland on Sunday, January 20, 1991, it addressed controversies that have divided Polish Catholics and Jews for much of the twentieth century: the role of Poles during the Holocaust, for instance, and antisemitism during Poland's Communist period.

In their letter the Polish bishops expressed "sincere regret for all the incidents of anti-Semitism which were committed at any time or by anyone on Polish soil." They also asked "forgiveness of our Jewish brothers and sisters" for any Polish Catholic who could have helped Jews during the Holocaust but failed to do so. In addition, they affirmed that the "most important way to overcome the difficulties that still exist today is the establishment of a dialogue which would lead to the elimination of distrust, prejudices and stereotypes."[5] These statements—indeed the entire pastoral letter—make a strong, albeit indirect, response to the Auschwitz convent controversy and in spirit affirm the new center under way at Oswiecim.

In a December 6, 1990, meeting at the Vatican with an international delegation from several Jewish organizations, Pope John Paul II endorsed the statement drawn up during the previously mentioned September 1990 meeting in Prague. In doing so he acknowledged further that some aspects of Catholic teaching and practice have fostered antisemitism. Significantly, the Prague statement endorsed by the pope also outlines plans for combating the re-emergence of antisemitism in Eastern Europe. Just before the December session with the pope began, Archbishop Cassidy announced to the assembled delegates that money—pledged by the Vatican in September 1989 to assist with the relocation of the Auschwitz convent—had recently been sent to Poland. In his remarks during the meeting, John Paul II added, "no dialogue between Christians and Jews can overlook the painful and terrible experience of the *Shoah*."[6]

The convent controversy gripped not only Jews and Catholics but also the new, non-Communist government of Poland. In the autumn of 1989, Prime Minister Tadeusz Mazowiecki established a commission to consider the future of the State Museum at Auschwitz.[7] The commission has met several times to discuss the organizational and educational aspects of the Auschwitz-Birkenau camp sites, the enrichment of exhibits and correction of information about them, and the relation of the museum to other institutions in Oswiecim, including the center for information, education, meeting and prayer.[8]

The Auschwitz convent controversy involved many dimensions of memory offended—Polish Catholic–Jewish relations, the experiences of two peoples during World War II and the Holocaust, a clash of world views, and the "symbolic ownership" of Auschwitz, to recall only a few. Disagreement was rife in the tangle. But at least one injunction—*Remember*—was as widely shared as it was stressed and stressful. Elie Wiesel's words—"If we stop remembering, we stop being"—might have been spoken by, to, and for everyone who has felt deeply about the Auschwitz convent. And by remembering together—perhaps haltingly, confrontationally, and with difficulty at first but then more honestly, openly, and painfully, too—caring women and men did check the inhuman inclinations that lurked in the controversy.

That there can be human healing is as important to remember as the fact that there is no armistice from the inhuman. Without reading too much into the prospects, if the Auschwitz convent controversy leads to genuine reconciliation, and there are good chances it might, that outcome can provide much needed hope as "live" television coverage of the world at war warns us that humankind's inhumanity may not yet have done its worst.

The American Protestant theologian, Reinhold Niebuhr, often suggested that the best moral and religious ideals "can be victorious only by snatching victory out of defeat."[9] Victory may be too optimistic a word to use, but Niebuhr was right to remind us that healing, reconciliation, and mending of the world remain possible. Realizing those possibilities requires coming to terms with the reasons for memory offended and learning to use memory, as Elie Wiesel has said, for the sake of the future.

NOTES

1. See "WorldNotes," *National Catholic Register*, 27 January 1991.

2. Press Release, Polish Cultural Institute, London, October 1990.

3. Wladyslaw T. Bartoszewski, *The Convent at Auschwitz* (London: Bowerdean Press, 1990), 160. This timely and informative book by a significant Polish scholar provides worthwhile background and analysis about the Auschwitz convent controversy. Bartoszewski's father, himself an Auschwitz prisoner, was a liaison between the Polish underground and the Jewish leadership in the Warsaw ghetto. At great personal risk, the elder Bartoszewski helped to rescue Jews from the Nazis.

4. *Catholic New York*, 18 October 1990, 13.

5. The pastoral letter is reprinted in this book's Appendix K. For an analysis of the letter, see A. James Rudin, "An Analysis of the Polish Bishops' Pastoral Letter," American Jewish Committee, 8 January 1991.

6. Peter Steinfels, "Pope Endorses Statement on Anti-Semitism," *New York Times*, 7 December 1990.

7. See Bartoszewski, *The Convent at Auschwitz*, 158–59.

8. *Christian Jewish Relations*, 22 (Autumn/Winter 1989): 139–40. See also this book's Appendix B.

9. Reinhold Niebuhr, *Leaves from the Notebook of a Tamed Cynic* (San Francisco: Harper & Row, 1980), 39.

Key Documents about the Auschwitz Convent Controversy

PREFATORY NOTE

The controversy surrounding the presence of a small group of Discalced Carmelite nuns living at Auschwitz is well documented. Many declarations, statements, and counterstatements have been made by both Jews and Christians, individuals and organizations, in an effort to resolve the situation.

Originally, the most important documents appeared in diverse sources. Here we reprint the ones that seem particularly crucial for the discussion this book provides on the questions and issues raised by the Auschwitz convent controversy and its impact on Jewish-Christian relations.

We are especially grateful to *Christian Jewish Relations* for permission to reprint the entire documentation section that appeared in its Autumn/Winter 1989 issue. Its contents include documents from February 1987 to December 1989.

Our documentation begins with the July 22, 1986, "Declaration Concerning the Carmelite Convent at Auschwitz by an Official Delegation of Catholics and Jews, Geneva," an important precursor for the key statement of February 22, 1987, that defined so many of the controversy's issues. The former document is not included in the pages we have reprinted from *Christian Jewish Relations*. Following the 1986 document, however, the material from *Christian Jewish Relations* appears chronologically in its entirety. Subsequently, we include some additional items. A few of these provide more complete versions of statements edited by *Christian Jewish Relations*, but most of these supplementary entries are not duplicates at all.

Further documentation on the convent controversy can be found in *Christian Jewish Relations* 20 (Summer 1987): 52–60 and in *Christian Jewish Relations* 22 (Spring 1989): 39–52. The latter focuses in detail on the period January to May 1989.

Declaration Concerning the Carmelite Convent at Auschwitz by an Official Delegation of Catholics and Jews, Geneva, July 22, 1986

I July 22, 1986

To the women and men of our time, to those in time to come:

Zakhor — Remember!

The lonely sites of Auschwitz and Birkenau are recognized today as symbols of the Final Solution, under which title the Nazis carried out the extermination (known as the *Shoah*) of six million Jews, one and a half million of whom were children, simply because they were Jews.

They died abandoned by an indifferent world.

Let us bow our heads and, in the silence of our hearts, remember the Shoah.

May our silent prayer help us today and tomorrow to better respect the rights of others, of all others, to life, liberty and dignity.

Let us remember that all of those murdered at Auschwitz and Birkenau — Jews, Poles, Gypsies, Russian prisoners of war — could cry out each day in the words of the prophet Zephaniah (1:15):

A day of wrath is that day,

a day of distress and anguish,

a day of ruin and devastation,

a day of darkness and gloom,

a day of clouds and thick darkness.

Signatories:

Maître Théo Klein, President of the "Conseil Représentatif des Institutions Juives", France; President of the European Jewish Congress

Cardinal Albert Decourtray, Archbishop of Lyons

Chief Rabbi René-Samuel Sirat, Chief Rabbi of France

Prof. Ady Steg, President of the "Alliance Israëlite Universelle"   .

M. Markus Pardès, President of the "Comité des Organisations Juives" of Belgium

Prof. Tullia Zevi, President of the "Unione delle Comunità Israelitiche" of Italy

Cardinal Franciszek Macharski, Archbishop of Cracow

Cardinal Godfried Danneels, Archbishop of Mechelen-Brussels

Cardinal Jean-Marie Lustiger, Archbishop of Paris

P. Stanislaw Musial, S.J., M. Jerzy Turowicz, members of the Polish Episcopal Commission for Relations with Judaism

Source: Reprinted by permission from *SIDIC* 19 (1987): 28–29.

The Carmelite Convent at Auschwitz: Statements February 1987 to December 1989

In CHRISTIAN JEWISH RELATIONS, vol. 22, no. 1, spring 1989, from page 39 on-wards we published documents on the Convent controversy for the period January-May 1989, together with a list of previous articles in CHRISTIAN JEWISH RELATIONS on the theme. Here we complete the 1989 documentation. For readers' convenience we have reproduced the text of the 1987 agreement, but all other documents appear in our pages for the first time.

We have checked texts against documents in the original languages wherever possible, and frequently discovered that inaccurate versions have been widely disseminated. One instance of this is the 6 September statement of the Polish Bishops' Commission for Dialogue with Judaism; even Reuters originally put out a version which omitted some key paragraphs.

The selection of texts was not easy. Some, for instance, may feel that we have given too much prominence to those relating to Cardinal Glemp; we felt, however, that so much confusion had been generated with regard to his statements and opinions that it was necessary for us to give our readers the fullest opportunity to judge for themselves. Even so, it has to be said that there are allegations that, at Czestochowa, he departed somewhat from the 'official' text we have used.

The Institute of Jewish Affairs, London, has published two Research Reports *on the Carmelite controversy; no. 8, 1987, by Alan Montague and no. 7, 1989, by Karen Adler. Amongst the collections of documents published elsewhere are (in French)* Carmel d'Auschwitz *(Bayard Presses, Paris 1989) and those in various issues of* SIDIC (Service International de Documentation Judéo-Chretienne) *published in English (as well as other languages) by the Sisters of Sion in Rome.*

Declaration adopted at the meeting of dignitaries of the Catholic Church and Jewish leaders in Geneva on 22 February 1987

Having recalled the terms of the declaration of 22 July 1986 recognizing that Auschwitz remains eternally the symbolic place of the Shoah which arose from the Nazi aim of destroying the Jewish people in a unique, unthinkable and unspeakable enterprise.

In the common desire to ensure respect for the memory of the dead in the places where Nazi crimes were perpetrated and, in particular, where the extermination of the vast majority of the Jewish communities of Europe was carried out.

Source: The documents in part B are from *Christian Jewish Relations* 22 (Autumn/Winter 1989): 112–40. Reprinted by permission of the Institute of Jewish Affairs Ltd, London.

Recalling this dramatic period which also demands profound respect for and devout meditation upon the sufferings of the Polish nation at this time and in this place.

The undersigned are in solemn agreement on what follows:

1   The Catholic delegation declares that, taking a stronger sense of its responsibilities towards future generations, it undertakes to embark upon a project, to be carried out by the European Churches, which will create a centre of information, education, meeting and prayer. This centre will established outside the area of Auschwitz-Birkenau camps. To this effect steps have already been taken to involve the Catholic Churches in Europe and all other Churches likely to support this project. It aims will be:

   a)   to encourage exchanges between the European Churches on the subject of the Shoah and also on the martyrdom of the Polish people and other peoples in Europe during the totalitarian horror throughout the war of 1939-1945;

   b)   to combat disinformation and trivialization of the Shoah, and to combat revisionism;

   c)   to receive groups of visitors to the camps to complete their information;

   d)   to encourage colloquia between Jews and Christians.

2   The establishment of this centre is the continuation and the consequence of engagements undertaken at the meeting of 22 July 1986 in Geneva. It implies that the Carmelites' initiative of prayer will find its place, confirmation and true meaning in this new context, and also that due account has been taken of the legitimate sentiments expressed by the Jewish delegation. There will, therefore, be no permanent Catholic place of worship on the site of the Auschwitz and Birkenau camps. Everyone will be able to pray there according to the dictates of his own heart, religion and faith.

3   The Catholic delegation specifies that Cardinal Macharski is to oversee the implementation of this project, while the bishops of other countries undertake to raise the means for its realization within the period of twenty-four months. Cardinal Macharski will keep President Théo Klein informed about progress in the realization of this project.

4   The Jewish delegation takes note of the foregoing undertakings made by the Catholic delegation.

5   Both delegations are conscious of having conducted their dialogue in a common desire to emphasize the uniqueness of the Shoah within the tragedy of the Hitler era, which has so cruelly affected the peoples of Europe and in particular the Polish people, and to ensure respect for the identity and the faith of every man and woman, both in their lifetime and at the place of their death.

Signed by all participants in the meeting:

The Catholic Delegation

CARDINAL GODFRIED DANNEELS, Malines-Bruxelles

CARDINAL ALBERT DECOURTRAY, Lyon

CARDINAL JEAN-MARIE LUSTIGER, Paris

CARDINAL FRANCISZEK MACHARSKI, Cracow

MSGR KAZIMIERZ JAN GORNY , Auxiliary Bishop of Cracow

FATHER BERNARD DUPUY, Paris, Secretary of the French Bishops' Commission for Relations with Judaism

FATHER JEAN DUJARDIN, Paris, Member of the French Bishops' Commission for Relations with Judaism

FATHER STANISLAW MUSIAL, Cracow, Member of the Polish Bishops' Commission for Relations with Judaism

MR JERZY TUROWICZ, Cracow, Member of the Polish Bishops' Commission for Relations with Judaism

The Jewish Delegation

LE GRAN RABBIN RENE SAMUEL SIRAT, Chief Rabbi of France

MAITRE THEO KLEIN, President of the European Jewish Congress and of CRIF

DR E.L. EHRLICH, European Representative of B'nai B'rith International

MR SAM HOFFENBERG, Delegate of B'nai B'rith at UNESCO

MAITRE MARKUS PARDES, President, Comité de Coordination des Organisations Juives de Belgique

DR GERHARD M. RIEGNER, Co-Chairman, Governing Board of the World Jewish Congress, Delegate of the International Jewish Committee on Inter-religious Consultations

PROFESSOR GEORGE SCHNECK, President, Consistoire Israelite de Belgique

PROFESSOR ADY STEG, President, Alliance Israelite Universelle

MRS TULLIA ZEVI, President, Union of the Italian Jewish Communities

The Pope's speech at Vienna, 24 June 1989

Extract, in which the plan for the Centre is endorsed, though transfer of the convent is not specified

From among the various initiatives being taken today in the spirit of the Council in support of dialogue I wish to point to the Centre for Information, Education, Meetings and Prayer being established in Poland. The Centre is to serve research into the Shoah and the martyrology of the Polish and other European nations during the period of national socialism and the spiritual confrontation with these problems. It is to be desired that it should yield abundant fruit and that it should constitute an example for other nations to follow.

Polish Bishops' Conference, Resolution 233, 9 March 1989

Extract, in which the plan for the Centre is endorsed, and transfer of the convent is specified

Auschwitz, which was the place of martyrdom of the sons and daughters of many nations, has an exceptional significance in the history and conscience of the Polish nation. The Polish bishops acknowledge the great importance of the Centre for Information, Education, Meetings and Prayer, which is being put into effect by the Archbishop of Cracow, Cardinal Franciszek Macharski, and is to embrace the new convent as well.

Communiqué from the meeting of the Polish Bishops' Commission for Dialogue with Judaism, 23 April 1989

*From the Polish Bishops' Press Office (*Tygodnik Powszechny, *21 May 1989)*

On 23 April this year, under the chairmanship of Mgr Henryk Muszynski, the Bishop of Wloclawek, a meeting took place in the Secretariat of the Episcopate at Warsaw of the Committee for Dialogue with Judaism in its new, enlarged form. The Commission appointed a new vice-president in the person of Mgr André Suski, Auxiliary Bishop of Plock, and a secretary in the person of Fr. Stanislaw Musial, SJ, of Cracow.

The Commission considered all aspects of the complex and difficult question of the centre at Auschwitz. In doing so it based itself on Resolution 233 of the Plenary Conference of Polish Bishops, which took place this year between 7 and 9 March. The Conference had discussed at length and emphasized the importance of the future creation of a Centre for Education, Meetings and Prayer, which would also include the new Carmelite convent.

The idea of opening the Centre — formulated by Cardinal Macharski, Archbishop of Cracow — is to bring about a lofty ambition — rapprochement between Jews, Christians and other nations. For that reason it greatly transcends Poland and Polish-Jewish relations. The Centre will serve to eliminate preconceived ideas and ignorance and to develop dialogue and the education of future generations in a spirit of tolerance and mutual understanding. As this place will become a centre for prayer, it cannot be understood without a religious dimension and an orientation of this kind.

The annihilation, on Polish soil, of the Jewish people (the Shoah) by the German Nazis, as well as the martyrdrom of the Polish people and other nations — the symbol of which is Auschwitz — constitutes a tragic end of the many centuries of common Jewish and Polish history in this land. Despite the many centuries of history, and the common drama of annihilation, Jews and Christians relate to Auschwitz in different fashions. The enormity of the crime and the unlimited immensity of suffering of those sacrificed to Nazi ideology force Jews and Christians not only to respect their differences but also to transcend the limits of their own perspectives, and to work so that this

tragedy may become the basis for rapprochement and for positive development in the world. It was with this in mind that the document on relations
between Jews and Christians was drawn up by the Commission. Equally, all
the Church texts dealing with this question—Judaism and Jews—have been
translated into Polish.

For this reason, perceiving and feeling the importance of this problem,
the Commission addresses a fervent appeal to all to conduct an open
dialogue. This means defending one's own point of view at the same time as
making the necessary effort to understand that of the partner, to
acknowledge his point of view and not shut oneself off from his sensitivities.
It is in the hope of mutual rapprochement that the Commission takes on the
task of clarifying the problem in the most objective fashion possible, granted
its great complexity, and with due regard to the religious problem on both
sides.

Christians, Poles, sons and daughters of the Church, do not forget that
everywhere and always the witness of love guides all things!

A meeting with the Organization of Jewish Communities, 24 May 1989

*The following is a slightly shortened version of the press release issued in East
Berlin by the Federation of Protestant Churches in the German Democratic
Republic on 25 May 1989.*

At the invitation of the Federation of Protestant Churches (Bund der
Evangelischen Kirchen in der DDR) in the GDR, the first official meeting of
representatives of the Union of Jewish Communities in the GDR (Verband
der Jüdischen Gemeinden) with members of the Federation of Protestant
Churches, representatives of the Working Party on Church and Judaism,
took place on 24 May, at the premises of the Berlin Secretariat.

In his speech of welcome Bishop Werner Leich recalled the fiftieth anniversary of the Pogromnacht of 9 November 1938, which gave the Protestant Church a duty to address itself intensively to the renewal of relationships
with Judaism, so that 9 November 1988 should not have been a one-off day
of remembrance but should have significant consequences for the future
relationship. He recalled the agreement of the Protestant Church on this anniversary that not only the burden of the past but also the common tradition
should be addressed. For the future relationship it was particularly important to speak to one another and to listen to one another. Consideration of
guilt and the burden of the past placed a special duty on the Protestant
Church to see that its own communities were better informed on Jewry and
Jewish beliefs. For this the help and guidance of the Union of Jewish Communities was necessary. This meeting could be regarded as a follow-up to the
successful meeting of the International Council of Christians and Jews at
Buckow in August 1987. The Association of Protestant Churches should

continue to be open to exchanges, educational trips and a deepened reciprocal relationship.

The president of the Organization of Jewish Communities, Siegmund Rotstein, gave thanks on behalf of the representatives of the Jewish community for the invitation to attend this meeting. He said that the fiftieth anniversary had contributed to making later developments better known. Particularly for the younger generation, it was necessary to know the whole truth, and to know the role of the Jews in Germany, not only under persecution. The memory of the 6 million martyrs would oblige them constantly to renew the oath 'Never again'. Only a tiny remnant of the Jewish population remained, and they were not always in the places where questions were being asked and research was being done. There would have to be a joint undertaking to give information not only about the past but also about the life and culture of Judaism.

During the three-hour meeting, there was an intensive exchange of views on the importance of and possibility of transmitting the experiences of the older generation. The danger was recognized that recollection of the pogrom might give too negative a picture of Judaism, as well as of Christianity, and that the identity of Judaism should not be reduced to that of victim and persecuted. Moreover, in a comprehensive historical analysis, antisemitism should not be reduced merely to its theological roots.

Dr Peter Kirchner, chairman of the Berlin Jewish community, informed the gathering about the progress of the work and the future events of the Jewish Centre in the Oranienburger Strasse in Berlin.

It was decided to hold annual meetings within the same framework.

Letter from Maître Théo Klein, ex-President of CRIF, to Cardinal Decourtray, 20 July 1989

I learned with regret on reading your letter dated 15 June 1989 that if at long last some progress is being made concerning the plot of land, this progress could and would have been made more than a year ago had not Cardinal Macharski, as we have just found out, yielded to the temptation of a plot of land opposite the Old Theatre.

However, your letter offers no definitive schedule and we find ourselves back in the situation in which, according to your letter of 14 February 1989, you were to request the temporary relocation of the Sisters.

We would like to have confirmation that this step is to be taken, as was envisaged by the Superior General of the Carmelites, amongst others, in this serious situation.

Such is now the situation that we have learned that the mere removal of the cross — installed despite previous undertakings — would create insoluble problems.

Both you and ourselves have made repeated efforts to calm the emotions and to conduct this sad affair in an open spirit.

So far as we are concerned — and in any case as far as concerns me — it seems impossible to continue the Jewish-Catholic dialogue at the level we would wish for, since the concrete facts by which we are confronted are at this point in time in contradiction with the words.

Catholicism, spurred on by the faith of its adherents, has constructed cathedrals and spread Stations of the Cross, while we Jews have been content with the study of the Book; that is to say, you attach importance to a material presence on the ground, and you must therefore feel a commanding obligation to demonstrate by concrete acts, even if belatedly, your will to ensure respect to the word you have given.

This is what we expect henceforth, in the hope of being able to resume a dialogue to which in all conscience we believe we have made a generous and sincere contribution.

Monsieur Cardinal, I beg you in the name of our common efforts, that cruel silence of which the Church speaks and sometimes wishes to repent — should it in truth be prolonged today by the fear of causing offence to those who still refuse to confront the insurmountable truth of the Shoah?

Communiqué from Cardinal Albert Decourtray, Archbishop of Lyon, 22 July 1989

22 July 1989 marks the third anniversary of the declaration 'Zakhor-Remember!', which recognizes the unspeakable pain of the Jewish people symbolised by the concentration camp at Auschwitz-Birkenau.

For this anniversary we had hoped to be able to give a concrete sign which would demonstrate to all that the fulfilment of the agreement signed in Geneva on 22 February 1987 concerning the Carmelite convent at Auschwitz was on schedule.

Administrative delays and psychological obstacles due to a lack of understanding have not permitted this sign to be given on the date envisaged. This saddens us greatly. The new delay is hurtful to our personal desire that there should be some tangible sign indicating the Church's respect in the presence of the Shoah. We beg our Jewish dialogue partners to forgive this delay, which is due to real obstacles, the seriousness of which was not recognized by any of the signatories to the agreement.

It would cause dismay if demonstrations of impatience on one side or acts of intolerance on the other were to interfere with the deepening of relations between Jews and Catholics or were to destroy the effort at mutual recognition of the drama of the Shoah perpetrated by the Nazi followers of Hitler as well as of the martyrdom of the Polish people and other nations.

The concentration camp at Auschwitz is on Polish territory at Oswiecim. We are aware of the numerous difficulties which beset Poland at the present time. Knowing these, the Polish Bishops have confirmed several times in their communiqués that the agreement will be implemented in full, however long the delays in implementation may be. On 15 June, in the name of the Catholic delegation, I sent to M. Théo Klein, President of the Jewish Delegation, an assurance given even more recently by Cardinal Macharski that the Carmelites would leave the theatre building as soon as the new convent was constructed. Together with him, as with Cardinals Danneels and Lustiger, we are determined to make every effort within our power to see that the transfer is effected with the least possible delay. Tangible proof of the good faith of those responsible for the construction of the new convent has been given. These are not just promises in words, as some fear; nor are they those which were expected.

The feeling of injustice due to the failure to honour the schedule fixed at Geneva, and suspicion with regard to the intentions of those who signed the agreement, should not be allowed to lead to acts which would damage that which men of peace have patiently constructed: dialogue between Jews and Catholics in respect for the truth.

Cardinal Macharski calls for suspension of project, 8 August 1989

. . . violent campaign of accusations and insinuations on the part of some Jewish circles in the West . . . insulting aggression expressed not only in words. Attitudes and actions of this kind make it impossible to continue the construction of the Centre. In this atmosphere of aggressive demands and unrest, one cannot work together to give attention to the construction of a place of mutual respect without abdicating one's own religious and national convictions.

Cardinal Decourtray insists convent must move, 11 August 1989

Extract of a declaration by Cardinal Albert Decourtray, Archbishop of Lyon, a signatory of the Geneva Agreements

The Geneva decisions cannot be called into question. An agreement is obligatory on those who sign it. Cardinals Danneels, Lustiger and myself have been informed of Cardinal Macharski's declaration that the implementation of the agreement is suspended owing to the present climate. Neither the demonstrations nor the regrettable reactions can be permitted to impede the fulfilment of the agreement. . . .

Pax Christi International Seminar on the Christian-Jewish Dialogue, 18 August 1989
CARDINAL FRANZ KÖNIG

Closing speech by Cardinal Franz König, International President of Pax Christi and former Archbishop of Austria

This seminar has been an important event for Pax Christi International. It has helped us greatly to gain a better understanding of the many things that unite believers of the Christian and of the Jewish faiths: their common origin in the Bible, their belief in one God, their shared concern for peace and justice in this world. At the same time this seminar has made us realize that if we are to make progress in the Jewish-Christian dialogue, we have to be aware of the different sensitivities that may exist within different communities.

Some of the participants in this seminar have just returned from a visit to Poland, organized by Pax Christi International. To begin with the participants visited the former concentration camp of Auschwitz, where millions of Jews and Poles perished at the hands of the Nazis. It is very painful to us all that this place of common sorrow has now turned into an area of controversy, centered around the presence of a Carmelite convent on the grounds of the camp.

We understand the feelings of our many Jewish friends, for whom Auschwitz is a place of silent mourning, a place of recollection before the unspeakable terror of the Shoah or Holocaust. At the same time we understand the feelings of our many Polish Catholic friends. For them as well, Auschwitz is a symbolic place, a symbol of the terrible suffering of the Polish people under the tyranny of the Nazi regime, the place where the Polish people commemorate Maximilian Kolbe, who accepted martyrdom out of love for his fellow human beings.

We are striving for understanding, but at the same time we must ask ourselves whether it is not shameful that victims should be having such discussions a few weeks before the anniversary of the outbreak of the Second World War, with its campaign of extermination launched by a diabolical regime against God and humanity. What we need now are wisdom and restraint on the part of all those concerned. What we need are words that do not hurt, words that build bridges.

I appeal to our Jewish friends not to doubt the sincerity of the motives of the Church, especially the Polish Church. The Carmelite nuns' intention is not the 'Christianization' of Auschwitz, the symbol of the Holocaust; it is not a Christian imposition. The nuns want to repent for the terrible things done to all the victims, and they want to do so within sight of this place of horror, where millions of men, women and children suffered, Jews and non-Jews, Polish and non-Polish alike. They do so on the basis of a tradition which may be alien to the Jews, who do not build houses of worship at a place of death, but which is important to Christians.

The Church, which too often remained silent during the time of the Holocaust, has to address itself to the Shoah today with great sorrow and restraint: It is in this spirit that the Carmelite nuns want their prayer, their life of repentance, to be understood as the expression of sorrowful reflection.

On the other hand, I ask our Polish Catholic friends to be more sensitive to the feelings of the Jewish people. If prayer at a particular place is offensive to a whole community, why not say this prayer a few hundred metres further away? Prayers can be said anywhere. Would a prayer be less pleasing to God if it was for some time said in a provisional building?

The Geneva Agreement of February 1987 has to be carried out. The impression should not be given that Catholics do not keep their word. This agreement applies not only to those who signed it on both sides. With them, the whole Catholic Church and the whole Jewish community have committed themselves to treat one another with great respect and to be sensitive to the feelings and emotions connected to certain places and certain symbols, as is customary among close relatives.

We should not put at risk the breakthrough which Vatican Council II brought about in relations between Jews and Christians with its declaration *Nostra Aetate*. In this document, the Church not only stressed the close bond linking God's people of the New Covenant with God's people of the Ancient Covenant; it also confessed its guilt in a way that should prevent Catholics at any time from giving in to anti-Jewish feelings, even in the mildest possible way: 'Mindful of her common patrimony with the Jews, and motivated by the Gospel's spiritual love and by no political considerations, the Church deplores the hatred, persecutions and displays of antisemitism directed against the Jews at any time and from any source.'

I would like to state it once again. We do not want to pass a judgement today, but on the occasion of the fiftieth anniversary of the beginning of the Second World War, we have to admit that too many Catholics behaved badly towards the Jews. Therefore, the Church as a community carries a special responsibility. Acknowledging this does not deny the fact that Catholics were also victims of the Nazi regime. This acknowledgement calls upon us, however, to bring a special measure of understanding towards our 'elder brothers', the Jews, and to undertake the actions that spring forth from this understanding.

We trust in the capital of wisdom
CARDINAL JOZEF GLEMP

Homily pronounced during the celebrations to mark the feast of the Most Holy Mary, Madonna of Czestochowa, Jasna Gora, 'On the Summit', 26 August 1989

Let Jesus be praised!
Eminent Cardinals, Archbishops, Bishops, Prime Minister, Ministers, Clergymen, Lay Sisters, Pilgrims, Dear Sisters and Brothers!

1 Wisdom, the foundation of order
'I was set up from everlasting, from the beginning, or ever the earth was' (Proverbs 8, 23). These words from the Bible tell us of the masterpiece of God that is Wisdom. In order to better our understanding of this attribute of God, the author of Proverbs compares Divine Wisdom to a person who exists

before all creation and who accompanied God when God created the world. God is not only all-knowing; He gives every work of creation meaning, He knows its development and its harmonious place among 'things seen and unseen'. Thanks to all-encompassing Wisdom, God tamed a world of waters and gave vent to gushing springs, formed rocky mountains, hillocks and fields, adorned the sky with clouds and laid down the foundations of the earth, and all of this without effort, with great pleasure, as if in play. In the text of the first lesson we sense the great harmony of creation. God loves all his handiwork, which is a delight for him, and yet this joy has its particular expression 'with the sons of men' (Proverbs 8, 31). Thus the appeal to mankind: ' . . . Now therefore hearken unto me. . . . Hear instruction, and be wise, and refuse it not' (32-3).

The liturgy applies the words about Wisdom to the Most Holy Mother. This is completely understandable because She, a Virgin from Nazareth, received the Wisdom of God and expressed it in obedience, in total faith in God. For Divine Wisdom, it is a joy to be with such children as Mary and Her followers. For mankind to participate, through obedience, in Divine Wisdom is to enter into an understanding of reality, into the harmony between God and Creation — that means to be in possession of peace.

2 'The Lord loveth the gates of Zion' (Psalms 87, 2)

We can say: He loves the gates of Jasna Gora, behind which is the Mother of God, present in the painting donated as 'a most wonderful help and defence' (prayer of the day), the Queen of Poland. We come here on the feast day of the Lady of Jasna Gora with our troubles. Through our obedience to Jesus Christ we want to acquire the wisdom necessary to achieve peace and development in our Fatherland. The blessed Capuchin, Father Honorat, son of St. Francis, aids us in our entreaties. It was he who, during the period of servitude and coming changes, which found their loudest expression in 1905,[1] undertook efforts to reinstate the holy day of the Mother of God of Czestochowa. The holy day was celebrated for the first time in 1906 and in the same year Father Honorat organized a national pilgrimage to Jasna Gora. It is he, whose beatification was announced last year, who, together with us, asks Mary for peace for our country.

The question of peace comes to the fore today not only because we are on the eve of solemn ecumenical prayers for the gift of Divine Peace for the world on the fiftieth anniversary of the outbreak of the Second World War, but also because of the necessity of clearing up the ravages of war, which, like a spiritual splinter, have been passed on to the post-war generation and cripple the world of moral values. What I am referring to is the difficulty of extricating the Poles from a reality bristling with mistakes, as well as to the establishing of friendly relations with those nations towards whom resentment has remained because of the war. What I particularly have in mind are Polish attitudes towards Germans and Jews. Peace, as the Church teaches us, is a gift from God, and should therefore be asked for and skilfully nursed. In its social meaning, peace is an agreement between people, based above all on justice. We would like to add, at once, that it is also to be based on liberty, truth and love. The path to this peace is dialogue, patient and wise, which can overcome the barriers along the way to correct relations between nations. Let us stop to consider this problem, limiting ourselves to areas where the Church plays a role.

3 Dialogue with the Germans

The starting-point for successful dialogue is for partners to treat each other equally, with mutual respect, even when one is strong and wealthy and the other weak and poor. The Church in Poland undertook this kind of dialogue when it held out its hand in a gesture of mutual forgiveness to the German Episcopate on the occasion of celebrating 1,000 years of Christianity in Poland. It could have made such a gesture only by basing itself on the Gospel, which goes beyond the passions which stirred up both nations after the experience of the war, and reminds one to 'love one another, love your enemies'. That act of 1965, which came out of faith, was received earnestly and with good will by German Christians and bore good fruit, not only on the ecclesiastical level but also on the social level. It also laid the foundations for further dialogue and explanation between the churches of those matters which can be complicated on the political level. As we recall in prayers the fiftieth anniversary of the Nazi invasion of Poland, we are conscious of the existence of these paths established by the Church. By continuing to follow them we can further the cause of peace in both nations. The proof that these paths exist is the presence today of Cardinal Hengsback, Bishop Homeyer and groups of lay Catholics from Germany as well as our Prime Minister, Mr Mazowiecki. Only recently Catholics from both nations, almost all of them lay members, published a declaration on the anniversary of the outbreak of war, which we noted with great respect and satisfaction.

We very much wish for our relations with Western neighbours to become increasingly broader and friendlier. With gratitude we observe works of charity. What remains to be done is to form, together, integral respect.

The celebrations of 1,000 years of Christianity in Russia have thrown a shaft of light on our Eastern neighbours and have removed much prejudice. The path to peace is open. We want to embark on it with Christian sensitivity.

4 Dialogue with the Jews

Despite all, life does not conform to established patterns and does not define relations between nations in friend-enemy terms. For us this is particularly true of the Jewish nation, which was never a neighbour but a member of our household and whose otherness both enriched us and caused problems. For many Jews, Poland was their Fatherland not only because of citizenship but also because of the authentic love they felt for it. We read in *Pan Tadeusz*[2] about Jankiel (the Jewish character in the poem):

. . . Speaking, he continued to sob,
The kind-hearted Jew loved the Fatherland like a Pole.

Along with the Jewish innkeeper who got the peasants drunk and those
Jews who propagated communism, there were also people among the
Israelites who gave their talents and their lives to Poland. We were not indifferent to one another, which is why phenomena like antipolonism and antisemitism came into being. In order to understand the complexity and the in-
terpenetration of the Polish-Jewish problem, let us ask ourselves the following questions. Were there in Poland aversion to and quarrels with the Jews?
There were. Were there in Poland Jewish businessmen who were disrespect-
ful and scornful towards Poles? There were. Were there, during the occupation, Jews who collaborated and did not live up to the example set by the
heroes of the ghetto? There were. Were there times in Poland when the suffering and victimization of the Jews were concealed? There were. Were there
Poles who sacrificed their lives to save Jews? There were. The remembrance
of the fiftieth anniversary of the outbreak of the Second World War puts us
on the same side of the barricade, on the side of destruction and death. Jews,
Gypsies, Poles—these peoples were condemned to annihilation in the Nazi
strategy, but according to different plans and on different scales. For Poles,
for example, it was the intelligentsia that was destroyed first. A common fate
joined the persecuted. At the Polish cemetery of soldiers killed in action at
Monte Casino, next to the crosses on Catholic graves are erected 'stella' with
the Star of David—also Polish soldiers. Among the mass graves of murdered
Polish officers in Katyn there are surely also Jewish graves. The brotherhood
of shared martyrdom and the community of ashes have a particular eloquence. Antoni Slominski, the Polish poet who did not hide his Jewish
origins, brought out the truth about the nameless heroes of Warsaw when he
wrote:

> For you my song and my tears,
> Ordinary, simple, not great,
> Hundreds more of you fell in battle,
> But who will remember your names?
> Porters, cobblers, artisans,
> Doctors, tailors and servants,
> Wives and sisters, who for months,
> Hidden among the rubble in cellars,
> Because of this, the madness of blood and glory
> In agony, in grief were dying,
> For you my tears, my hot tears.
> (From 'Mogila nieznanego mieszkanca Warszawy',
>   'The grave of an unknown Warsaw resident')

Many Jews sunk into Polish culture and Christianity, but the cross
which is visible on their grave did not take away from them the love they had
for their nation.

So why did the problem of Auschwitz and the Carmelite convent come
about? Why did it blow up suddenly, forty years after the extinguishing of

the crematorium ovens? These questions torment many when we speak of peace, which is supposed to heal the ravages of war. I would like, in humility and in the desire of reconciliation, to talk about this. Given that so many issues have been distorted, dialogue is necessary, a dialogue which systematically clarifies difficult matters, not putting forward demands. We have committed our faults against the Jews, but one would like to say: 'Dear Jews, don't talk with us from the position of a nation above all others and don't lay down conditions which are impossible to fulfil.'

The Carmelite sisters living next to the camp in Auschwitz wanted, and continue to want, to be a sign of that human solidarity which embraces the dead and the living. Do you not, respected Jews, see that in your actions against them you injure the feelings of all Poles, and our sovereignty obtained with such difficulty? Your power is the mass media, which are, in many countries, at your disposal. Do not let them act to kindle antipolonism. Not long ago a squad of seven Jews from New York committed an assault on the convent in Auschwitz. It's true that it didn't come to the murder of the sisters, nor to the destruction of the convent, because they were stopped, but don't call these assailants heroes. Let us maintain the standards of the civilization in which we live. Let us make sure that we are able to distinguish between certain simplified and certain confused matters. Let us differentiate between Oswiecim-Auschwitz, where mostly Poles and other nations perished, and Brzezinka-Birkenau, the camp a few kilometres away, where mostly Jews perished. Let us then distinguish the secular from the theological plane. Let the new doctrine on the question of the presence or absence of God in the place of sacrifice be justified and understandable to all people believing in God, but let it not be a political instrument in the hand of a group of people, especially non-believers.

We who pay homage to Mary of Nazareth and have in common with you, Jews, many holy places of worship, let us undertake dialogue in sincerity and truth. If there is no antipolonism, there will be no antisemitism in us. Our wish for you is that in the Holy Land of Palestine no one will pelt you with stones, that the noises of shooting die away, that no one will die from a bullet and that peace-*shalom* will be wherever you are.

5 Towards peace

Dearest pilgrims!

Divine Wisdom is the constant companion of the creatures of God, and the joy of Wisdom is to be 'with the sons of man'. Today let us ask Mary, the Capital of Wisdom, to bring us closer to Divine Wisdom. The words of Vatican II read: 'Our era, more than previous ones, needs that wisdom which would make new, great matters more human' (KDK 15). We are the witnesses of the achievement of new and important changes in our Fatherland. We must be equal to the challenge of history; we must not look on passively, cynically or with enmity at the efforts of people who want to lead Poland on to the path of development and economic efficiency — that is, on the path of peace. What is needed, therefore, is wisdom, which sees the possibilities and the impossibilities, which knows how to fall into line in order to overcome together the difficult moments, which does not threaten with fists and doesn't stamp feet, which doesn't stop a wheel in full motion at a factory but gives good cheer to those who are faltering.

The matters of our Fatherland — of the Church and of the Nation — we put into the hands of the Queen of Poland at Jasna Gora. Full of faith and confidence, once again, as always, we trust in the Capital of Wisdom that is Our Lady of Jasna Gora. Amen.

Notes

1 After the 'Bloody Sunday' massacre in St. Petersburg a series of strikes swept across Poland, then divided between Russia, Prussia and Austria.
2 By Adam Mickiewicz, Poland's foremost romantic poet of the nineteenth century.

Extract from Pope John Paul II's Encyclical of 27 August 1989 on the fiftieth anniversary of the outbreak of the Second World War

5 But of all the anti-human measures one remains for ever as a disgrace to humanity: the calculated barbarity let loose against the Jewish people.

The Jews, objects of a 'final solution' dreamed up by a perverse ideology, were subjected to deprivations and almost indescribable sufferings. At first persecuted through harsh and discriminatory laws, ultimately millions of them ended in the extermination camps.

The Jews of Poland more than others lived this Calvary; the images of the siege of the Warsaw ghetto as well as what has been learned of the camps of Auschwitz, Maidanek and Treblinka exceed in their horror the limits of human imagination.

One must remember also that this murderous lunacy was directed towards many other groups which committed the error of being 'different' or of rebelling against the tyranny of the occupation.

On the occasion of this sad anniversary, I again call upon all men to overcome their prejudices and to fight all forms of racism, as they learn to recognize the fundamental dignity and good that are in every man and to be mindful always of belonging to a unique human family wanted and brought together by God.

I wish to repeat here emphatically that hostility or hatred towards Judaism is in complete contradiction to the Christian view of the dignity of man. . . .

Cardinal Glemp's Italian interview, 2 September 1989

On 2 September the Italian journal La Repubblica *published an interview with Cardinal Glemp in which the following exchange occurred.*

Interviewer: Was not this agreement to remove the convent signed two years ago in Geneva by eminent Church dignitaries?

Glemp:	No, by Cardinal Macharski and a group of people lacking competence.
Interviewer:	Indeed? Were not Cardinals Lustiger of Paris, Decourtray of Lyon and Danneels of Brussels also present?
Glemp:	I would like the agreement to be renegotiated. This should be done by competent persons, not by some Cardinal who does not understand matters.
Interviewer:	So Macharski does not understand?
Glemp:	Macharski did not understand the situation of the people.
Interviewer:	So what should be done now?
Glemp:	The whole thing should be renegotiated, calmly, in dialogue, as I propose. It must be looked at again, but by competent people. And Poles should not be excluded.
Interviewer:	But isn't Macharski, who negotiated it, Polish?
Glemp:	Macharski alone? How can that be? He represents only the Cracow Church. The problem is larger than that.
Interviewer:	So you don't approve of what Macharski did?
Glemp:	I can only think Macharski signed because things were done rather too hurriedly.

Communiqué from Cardinals Albert Decourtray, Jean-Marie Lustiger and Gottfried Danneels, 3 September 1989

According to the text of an interview which appeared in the Italian journal La Repubblica *on 2 September 1989, Cardinal Glemp said that the Geneva Agreement should be renegotiated and that this should be done by competent persons and not by 'some Cardinal or other who did not understand things'.*

If the Jewish delegation to the Geneva meetings led by Maître Théo Klein, then President of the European Jewish Congress, is not competent — who is?

And if four Cardinals, including the Archbishop of Cracow, are not qualified to represent the Catholic side, then who possibly could be?

The Auschwitz camp is in the Diocese of Cracow. According to the law of the Church, its Archbishop is the first to have full authority there. The Cardinals who joined with him belong to those nations which, in the West, were the principal victims of Hitler's barbarity.

The agreements were patiently and loyally negotiated over two years. The Catholic signatories undertook not to impose any financial obligation on the Diocese of Cracow and still less on Poland.

Cardinal Glemp could have expressed no more than a personal opinion in speaking of renegotiation of the Geneva Agreements. Moreover, until then he always made it known that Cardinal Macharski alone was responsible and that the Conference of Polish Bishops on 9 March 1989 had committed itself to uphold the implementation of the Agreement.

The undertakings which were signed must therefore be fulfilled: they recognize the legitimacy of the Carmelite convent at Auschwitz outside the perimeter of the concentration camp which UNESCO, in recognition of its 'exceptional universal value', included on its list of World Cultural Heritages in October 1979 at the request of the then government of Poland.

Declaration of the Polish Bishops' Commission for Dialogue with Judaism, 6 September 1989

Several inaccurate versions of this document have appeared in the international press. We have retranslated the Polish original—Editor

In connection with difficulties that have arisen recently around the construction of a Centre for Information, Education, Meetings and Prayer, together with a new Carmelite convent in Auschwitz, the Polish Bishops' Commission for Dialogue with Judaism, being aware of the gravity of the problem, states the following.

The Centre for Information, Education, Meetings and Prayer, including the nuns' prayer at Auschwitz, was to serve the dialogue between Christians and Jews, a dialogue that envisages mutual respect for one's own identity, fuller knowledge of each other, and the will to co-operate. Obstacles, however, started to become apparent during the implementation of this important project, and the polemical discussions, arguments and violent protests that ensued have become a serious threat to the very idea of the Centre.

In these circumstances Cardinal Franciszek Macharski, the Archbishop of Cracow, felt obliged to issue a statement, part of which reads as follows: 'Such attitudes and actions make it impossible to further implement the construction of the Centre', as it is not possible to 'attend to the building of a place of mutual respect without shaking off one's own religious and national beliefs'.

The Commission expresses the conviction that Cardinal Macharski's declaration did not contradict the position formulated in communiqué 233 of the Bishops' Conference, dated 9 March, and confirms the explanations given by the secretary of the commission, Father Stanislaw Musial, SJ, in the article he published in circular no. 22/89/1110, 29 May 1989, of the Press Bureau of the Polish Bishops.

The conflict over the Carmelite convent in Auschwitz almost completely ruptured Christian-Jewish dialogue in the world. The renewal of dialogue seems impossible without a solution to the conflict, and this confirms the urgent need to build the Centre. However, we state with regret that the idea of the Centre has not met with appropriate interest and understanding from the Jewish side. Jewish public opinion has followed only one thread of the Geneva declarations—that is, the moving of the convent.

The exceptional importance of Auschwitz as a place commemorating the death of millions of innocent victims calls for a special commitment to use all means possible to remove existing tensions and misunderstandings. The Commission welcomes with satisfaction the statement of Jewish organizations in Poland on their readiness to participate in work aimed at overcoming present difficulties. The Commission for its part announces the readiness to co-operate with all people of good will in Poland and abroad.

The fiftieth anniversary of the outbreak of the war with which the criminal plans of Hitler's Germany for the total suppression of the Jews and the destruction of the Polish People were linked carries with it a special obligation to undertake this collaboration. 'Of all the anti-human measures, one remains as an eternal shame to humanity, the calculated barbarity unleashed against the Jewish people' (Pope John Paul II, apostolic letter on the occasion of the fiftieth anniversary of the outbreak of the Second World War).

In his message to the Polish Bishops' Conference, Pope John Paul II indicated: 'The Church with the people of our times, the people of Europe and the world, seeks to find a path towards the future.'

In response to his words, the Commission issues this call. Let us not allow difficult and sad, but transitory, problems to blind us to the right aim, the importance of which cannot be exaggerated, or allow our emotions to run away with wisdom. Let us not be blind to the true ordering of values. If, as believers in two religions involved in the eternal plan for salvation of the one and only God, we were to break contact, we would no longer be, in the eyes of the world, worthy witnesses of faith, and all of us would be held responsible by Him.

The resumption of talks in the spirit of the Geneva meetings, with no additional conditions, will, we trust, make it possible to find realistic opportunities for constructing the centre in which 'the initiative of the prayer of Carmelite nuns will find its place, its confirmation and its true sense in this new context' (the Geneva declaration).

Let us end the dispute

CARDINAL GLEMP interviewed by PROFESSOR JACEK WOZNIAKOWSKI

The interview was conducted in Wroclaw at the Archbishop's residence on 9 September 1989 and published in Tygodnik Powszechny, *17 September 1989.*

A week ago a Day of Prayer for Peace was held in Warsaw at Your Eminence's initiative. May I ask Your Eminence to share your thoughts on this subject with the readers of *Tygodnik Powszechny?*

Just as on such days in the past, beginning in Assisi and most recently in Warsaw — and I would say that in Warsaw the occasion took on a particular significance because we were praying on the fiftieth anniversary of the outbreak of the Second World War—we were rediscovering together certain very simple and very profound truths. First, we rediscovered how very precious is the praying together of people who follow different roads to God. Second, how rich and how little known to each other are the new spiritual trends in Christianity, Buddhism or Islam. For example, I was struck by the way in which the Moslems from North Africa with whom we met were genuinely interested in the theology of the Virgin Mary, and also by their desire to gain a better and more consistent insight into the love commandment. Third, we saw how friendship between the representatives of different faiths and different nations develops from this shared prayer. What could be of greater value to us than the strengthening of such friendship with the Germans, the Russians and the Jews? I consider ties with the latter particularly important because, as I have said on a recent occasion, the Jews were members of our household rather than neighbours.

> In this light the controversy surrounding the convent of the Carmelite sisters in Auschwitz has grown out of all proportion. It seems so sad and so unnecessary.

A multitude of misunderstandings has come to light with regard to this matter. It is a pity that the Jews did not state their case earlier. As you know, the first critical voice regarding the location of the convent was heard in the Belgian press over a year after the sisters settled at the wall of Auschwitz I. From the legal point of view, their presence on that site is entirely proper and nobody can question this aspect of the matter. As far as other aspects are concerned, such as the meaning and perceived significance of their expiatory prayers, one comes across a variety of reactions, which must be respected and taken into consideration, even if one does not entirely share them. However, one must also respect the basic human rights of the Carmelite sisters. Friendly relations should not be founded on transgressions of form. Generally, the sisters must not be treated as objects; they must take part in the making of decisions which concern them.

> This last point seems self-evident. I do not doubt that the nuns, who settled at the wall of the concentration camp in order to bring peace and reconciliation to the very site where horrendous crimes were perpetrated, will recognize themselves that since their convent became, through no fault of their own, the object of dispute, it would be much better if it were moved half a kilometre away, in accordance with the Geneva Agreements. The removal of the convent would not represent a great inconvenience and surely the Lord will hear their prayers in the new location too.

Of course, but I am a lawyer, and, moreover, I must take into account a variety of opinions. Polish Catholics were not sufficiently familiar with Jewish views and with the wounds still open after the Shoah. We should have done more, and still can do more, while the new negotiations take place, to raise awareness among our faithful, and the Jews should help us sensibly in this endeavour. The contacts between the two sides have been too haphazard. It was unfortunate that there was no representative of Polish Jewry in Geneva. Fortunately, for the last few weeks we have had in Poland Chief Rabbi Joskowicz, who came to see me on 5 July. We had a very amicable and worthwhile conversation. The Nissenbaum Foundation is also active in Poland.

> Does your mention of the renegotiation of the Geneva Agreements mean that Your Eminence is thinking of including these persons in future discussions?

Yes, these and other experts. I believe that if Cardinal Macharski had relied on a wider circle of experts, the conclusions that came out of the Geneva Agreements would have carried greater weight in the eyes of both Polish and foreign public opinion.

> In that case, if I understand you correctly, Your Eminence does not exclude the possibility that the renegotiated conclusions will be very similar to those signed in Geneva?

Not in the least. On the contrary, having familiarized myself with the statement of the Polish Episcopate's Commission for Dialogue with Judaism and with the statements of Cardinals Decourtray, Danneels and Lustiger, I think that would be best. Renegotiation does not necessarily imply that agreements already reached are invalidated; it can mean that their form is further improved. In this respect the Geneva negotiations had some flaws — among others that the two sides were ill-balanced. As I understand it, the Jewish side was represented by a highly structured ethnic group, while the Catholic side was represented by, to use a sociological term, an informal religious group. I do not mean by this remark that I fail to appreciate the great efforts made and the importance of the positions taken on this difficult issue by the three cardinals mentioned earlier.

> In Your Eminence's opinion, is it therefore worth delaying the instructions to implement? The refinement of legal and formal elements is not the most important thing in this matter. How much more essential are the other aspects Your Eminence mentioned earlier, especially the intention of all those concerned to come to an agreement even if — especially if — our understanding of each other is not complete.

Let us hope for such a general intention. But the matter is greatly hindered by the clamour surrounding the convent and the violent demonstrations of the kind held by the New York Jews within its grounds. This form of pressure provokes only negative public opinion.

> I accept that the clamour makes it difficult for the Church authorities to take further steps, but I hope nobody believes that it exempts us from the intentions we expressed and the promises we made in Geneva. Please

forgive me, Your Eminence, but the Jews could rightly think, especially after Geneva, that it is we who hinder the issue — in the first place by delaying matters, and then through various statements which are not always clear and which are on occasion frankly inconceivable. These have offended not only Jews but also many of us.

Indeed, certain reactions in the press made me realize that some of my phrases had not been interpreted in accordance with my intentions. I relied on the fact that my entire message about the need for friendly dialogue between Catholics and Jews was sufficiently clear to leave no room for doubt and offence. However, some words, especially those in which I tried to show what absurd consequences can result from the behaviour of demonstrators, gave rise to just this sort of doubts and offence. I wanted to make it understood that actions contravening generally accepted forms of behaviour should not be condoned or praised. I would like to use this occasion to make an appeal for texts to be read in their entirety and their intentions to be understood as a whole, without singling out particular sentences which, in the emotive atmosphere surrounding the convent, can sound improper, distorting the meaning of the whole message.

I am very grateful to your Eminence for this elucidation. May I point out, however, that these emotions exist and, as a result, our reputation, not only among Jews but also among Christians of the whole world, gets worse every day? Reading the foreign press I can see very clearly that time is of the essence if our dialogue with the Jews and our reputation in the eyes of the world, which is not always well disposed towards us, are not to be seriously damaged. I am anticipating here the decisions of the Church authorities, but I am also taking advantage of the rights and duties of the laity as defined by the last Vatican Council. Together with my friends at the *Tygodnik Powszechny*, I believe that the Commission for the construction of the Centre, as well as the reporting committee — two bodies which ought to be created immediately — should undertake their work without delay, beginning with the setting of realistic deadlines and the making of decisions about financial priorities. Meanwhile, the process of informing public opinion and discussions with the sisters could be taking place in peace, a peace which we have the right to expect and demand. Does Your Eminence agree that construction work, to be paid for by the European Churches, should begin at once, with accurate information given about it?

This seems to be the right suggestion, especially in the light of the statement issued by the Polish Episcopate's Commission for Dialogue with Judaism. I am confident that together with Cardinal Macharski and many people of good will, we shall be able to further the cause of friendly dialogue begun some years ago by the present Pope, John Paul II.

I am grateful for the opportunity to communicate this clarification to people at large through *Tygodnik Powszechny*. However, the case of the

Carmelite convent has made us aware of other, more serious problems which it is impossible to go into fully here. I shall mention briefly two points, but please consider what I am going to say only as seeds for future discussion.

The first problem is obvious and yet very sensitive. When we talk about conflicts on a social scale, we usually mean conflicts of interests. Much less palpable, but also more serious, are conflicts of feelings. The second problem is extremely difficult. It is the problem of the Shoah, especially from the theological point of view. I personally am very absorbed by it, and I think that similar questions are asked by our partners in the Polish-Jewish dialogue. Two questions come to the fore: first, the horror of the Shoah has caused many often remarkable people to lose their faith and yet, how is it possible for an agnostic to participate fully in the life of Israel? It must be a great dilemma; I would like to understand it better. The second question is how to reconcile the uniqueness of the terrible tragedy of the Shoah with the ordinary existence of Israel within the human family? It is my impresson that Israel is still anxiously seeking such an ordinary place. I would be very grateful to God if our Polish-Jewish controversy were in some measure to help this distinguished nation regain its proper place in the family of nations.

Resolution on the Carmelite convent adopted by the European Jewish Congress at its Annual General Assembly, London, 10-11 September 1989

Representatives of the Jewish Communities in Austria, Belgium, Czechoslovakia, Denmark, Federal Republic of Germany, Finland, France, Greece, Holland, Italy, Poland, Romania, Spain, Sweden, Switzerland, United Kingdom, Yugoslavia, who are members of the European Jewish Congress, meeting in London on 10-11 September 1989, for their Annual General Assembly:

Deplore the failure to comply within the specified time with the Agreement signed in Geneva on 22 February 1987, between a Catholic and a Jewish delegation, on the relocation of the Carmelite convent from the Auschwitz-Birkenau extermination camp, where human beings of all creeds were martyred and which is the tragic symbol of the Shoah, when millions of Jews were put to death because they were Jews;

Request that on the basis of this Agreement, the Convent promptly be relocated outside the camp;

Appreciate the voices being raised in the Catholic world, demanding that the Geneva Agreement be honoured;

Express their approval of and confidence in the Jewish delegation dealing with the matter and encourage them to carry on their task;

Hope that the hitherto fruitful Jewish-Catholic dialogue, strongly affected by the situation resulting from the non-relocation of the Carmelite convent, will not suffer lasting damage.

The Church living in the richness of cultures
CARDINAL JOZEF GLEMP

This address was delivered by Jozef, Cardinal Glemp, the Polish Primate, to the Sixth Congress of Polish Theologians, held at the Catholic University of Lublin on 12 September 1989.

(Part 3) The Church and the building of the human family in peace

I would like to refer to the international prayer for peace recently held in Warsaw. This prayer was initiated by the Holy Father in 1986 at Assisi and continued by the St. Isidore Fraternity, which meets at the Santa Maria Basilica in Trastevere. By God's will, I happen to be the titular cardinal of that church, and my ties with the Fraternity enabled me to initiate, at first with some timidity and uncertainty, the great international and interdenominational prayer for peace on the fiftieth anniversary of the outbreak of the Second World War in Warsaw—that is, in the very city where destruction and contempt for human rights and human dignity began. Fifty years later, in that very place, we were able to speak aloud, together with all the world's believers represented there, and make an urgent plea to God and to the people, to society. All this gives us a place within the human family—that is to say, the community of feelings and interests, the common good towards which we are striving and to which we wish to make our own contribution.

However, we are not always successful in our endeavours to build the human family with due respect for national identities. We are not always able to solve difficult problems in a mature and serene fashion. I am referring here to the great culture and tradition of the Jewish people, with whom our contacts have become very inflamed, very vociferous—not so much here at home, but largely abroad, which is doing us great injustice. Let us reflect for a while on the great cultural world that is Judaism. It seems to me that the Shoah is one of the most complicated problems for the theologians of today. I would like us to acquire a deep understanding of the way Jews see the Shoah from a theological point of view. It is, undoubtedly, a deeply theological problem, arising out of the theological premises and methods formulated by believing Jews. We would like to familiarize ourselves with it and I am therefore appealing to one of our institutions of higher learning, perhaps the Catholic University of Lublin, to make this issue, in its wider religious and theological dimensions, more accessible to us and our society. But the case of the Shoah is not only theological; it is also ideological. And ideology is always the instrument of political processes which has to be known and understood. In any case, I wish to stress very clearly and categorically that in building the human family we have no desire to solve anything by violence, shouting or anger. Everyone's rights must be protected, with due respect for each individual. We wish to respect all religions, but we too wish to defend our position, because we too have the right to demand that our position and feelings be respected. The anger which has broken out in the world concerns, it would at first appear, a rather insignificant matter—the Carmelite convent in Auschwitz. Of course, this is the point at which these great ideological roads cross. A considerable problem, a problem of the conflict of feelings on the international scene.

Until now the world has worked out ways of diffusing conflicts of interests. However, as far as feelings and perceptions are concerned, in a situation of opposing emotional positions, we do not have any international frameworks to enable us to solve such conflicts methodically. Again, we are dealing here with anger, and arguments dictated by anger are the weakest, the most one-sided and circumstantial; they do not bring the truth any closer. The case of the Carmelite convent in Auschwitz points to a conflict of feelings. We want to understand Jewish feelings so that our own feelings can be understood too. The conflict over the Carmelite convent presents an ethical as well as a legal problem and we cannot impose an unethical solution, no matter how great the pressure. As far as ethics are concerned, two important points have to be considered. The first is the accusation of promises or undertakings not kept. Let us examine this carefully. The document arising out of the Geneva meetings is not an agreement; it is a declaration of intent. Undertakings can be made only through proper agreements in which both sides undertake to do things that are possible. An agreement is not proper if it is flawed, if only one side is burdened with its implementation. It must be possible to carry out these undertakings. Considering the issue from the ethical point of view, we do not go back on anything that will truly advance a solution of this conflict of feelings. But it must be carried out in a dignified fashion which will guarantee respect for the law and respect for accepted forms of behaviour. The second point concerns the ethics behind the removal of the Carmelite nuns. We cannot simply say, 'You are being removed from the site', for the nuns have their own legally acquired rights, which were not contested in the first few years of their presence there. The Church cannot remove them and take upon itself the responsibility for violating the rights and human dignity of these women, who are entitled to live there. Our wish is to consider these difficult matters with honesty and composure, but it cannot be done amidst the shouting and clamour of unjust accusations. The truth is that in spite of these pressures, there is no anti-semitism in Poland. It really does not exist here.

I return now to the thought which encapsulates the theme of this Congress. Its aim is to show the mutual enrichment which different cultures derive from one another as they embrace elements of the spiritual heritage and achievements of others. Perhaps what is happening today will bring about a creative ferment. Because truth must prevail and we want to build our society in the truth which grows out of a spirit of deep understanding of other cultures, in the common enrichment which our Christian heritage brings. We want to contribute our own heritage to the human family and work for its cohesion. God bless!

Letter

Andrzej Friedman   Stanislaw Krajewski
Al. Ujazdowskie 16 m 21   Walicow 20 m 515
00-478 Warsaw   00-851 Warsaw
Poland   Poland

Warsaw, 15 September 1989

His Excellency
Yitzhak Shamir
Prime Minister of the State of Israel

Your Excellency,

We are writing to you as Polish Jews who are active members of the Polish-Israeli Friendship Society.

With pain we witness the recent deterioration of Polish-Jewish and Christian-Jewish relations. It is very sad that your remark about Polish antisemitism has made the situation even worse.

In Poland antisemitism was very widespread. It is present also now. However, now it is usually not considered a respectable attitude, and — even more important — it is much less common among younger Poles. And it is not rare, especially among intelligentsia, to find sympathy for Jews and Judaism, fascination with the former Jewish presence in Poland, and support for the State of Israel. A number of persons with such pro-Jewish views are members of our Society.

The identification of Poles with antisemitism is a false generalization. It is harmful and insulting to our Catholic friends from the Polish-Israeli Friendship Society, and to all Poles of good will, including ourselves. It is especially insulting to the memory of those Poles who lost their lives trying to help Jews during the Second World War.

Your remark, suggesting the incurability of antisemitism in Poland, can only strengthen the antisemitic tendencies in our country. We think that anti-Polish generalizations are as morally unacceptable as antisemitic ones. We know, however, that the roots of antisemitism are deeper, and we are aware of the fact that real harm caused by anti-Polishness is incomparable to that caused by antisemitism. These distinctions are apparently not understood by the Primate of Poland. It is very sad that Primate Glemp, in his declaration in Czestochowa, was not only tactless but also seemed to suggest that antisemitism could be a legitimate defence. We would like to add that we condemn the arrogant form of Rabbi Weiss's protests at Auschwitz. It is wrong to require respect for one's feelings without showing respect to others. Yet we were shocked that the Primate implied that those Jews wanted to murder the nuns. We believe, however, that one unfair statement cannot justify another.

We believe that we Jews, who have been for centuries victims of stereotyping, should not perceive others in terms of schematic stereotypes.

Your additional remark about the Poles who are free of antisemitism shows that we may find common ground. We hope that the amelioration of Polish-Jewish relations is as important for you as it is for us.

Sincerely yours,
Andrzej Friedman and Stanislaw Krajewski

Vatican Commission's statement, 19 September 1989

The Vatican's Commission for Religious Relations with the Jews issued the following statement on 19 September. The statement was signed by the President of the Commission, Cardinal Johannes Willebrands.

The Holy See's Commission for Religious Relations with the Jews has noted with satisfaction the communiqué published on 6 September 1989 by Bishop Henryk Muszynski, President of the Polish Bishops' Commission for Dialogue with Judaism.

The intention expressed of establishing a Centre for Information, Education, Meetings and Prayer, as the Geneva declaration of February 1987 provides, is welcomed positively since the Holy See is convinced that such a Centre would contribute significantly to the development of good relations between Christians and Jews.

Indeed, the Holy Father, in his address to the Jewish community of Vienna on 24 June 1988, expressed the hope that 'this Centre may produce fruitful results and serve as a model for other nations'.

The prayer and dedicated life of the Carmelites, whose monastery (convent) will be in some way at the heart of this Centre, will contribute decisively to its success.

In order to support the implementation of this important but costly project, the Holy See is prepared to make its own financial contribution.

Letter
Prymas Polski
Kardynal Jozef Glemp

London, 20 September 1989

Dear Sir Sigmund,

With reference to your Telex message, you have no doubt seen that I have stated that the best solution to the dispute involving the Carmelite convent at Auschwitz would be for work to start as soon as possible. It is my intention that the Geneva Declaration of 1987 should be implemented and I am therefore keen to work on a friendly dialogue between Christians and Jews.

I have seen the Prime Minister's letter sent to you, in which he refers to the 'untold suffering of the Jewish people whose each and every member stands unequalled among all martyrised nations. The tragedy and sacrifice of Shoah defies any comparison. It will remain a warning for all until the end of this world.'

I am also aware of the Holy Father's reference to the immense 'suffering of the Jews in Poland'. Until you sent your messages I was unaware of the moderating voices, therefore I was glad that some of the shrill voices do not reflect the feelings of world Jewry and aggression is not part of Jewish philosophy.

There has been a great deal of ill feeling and misunderstanding which we would like to clear up. We are a people of our word and we understand that the implementation of the Declaration can only take place in a tranquil atmosphere. It is essential not only to move the convent outside the perimeter of the site, but also to set up the new cultural centre. This will help us to continue the dialogue which is so dear to us.

I understand from the Ambassador that you have accepted the Prime Minister's, Mr Tadeusz Mazowiecki, invitation to visit Poland. I shall be pleased to meet you and discuss with you the speedy implementation of the Geneva Declaration.

Auschwitz should never be a place of controversy.

Yours respectfully
Jozef, Cardinal Glemp

Sir Sigmund Sternberg
Star House
Grafton Road
London NW5

Barefoot Carmelites' statement, 23 September 1989

The following statement was issued on 23 September by Fr. Anthony Morello, the Barefoot Carmelites' English-speaking general councillor in Rome.

During his visit to Rome, Sir Sigmund Sternberg, chairman of the International Council of Christians and Jews, accompanied by Bishop Gerald Mahon, vice-chairman of the British Council of Christians and Jews, met with Fr. Anthony Morello, OCD, the English-speaking general councillor, at the generalate of the Barefoot Carmelite order. Sir Sigmund handed Fr. Anthony copies of two letters addressed to himself: one from Tadeusz Mazowiecki, chairman of the Council of Ministers of the Polish People's Republic, dated 8 September 1989, and one from Cardinal Jozef Glemp, dated 20 September 1989, pledging the implementation of the Geneva declaration of 1987.

Fr. Anthony expressed great satisfaction at the content of the letters and affirmed that all along the position of the general of the order, Fr. Philip Sainz de Baranda, OCD, has been that agreements must be honoured.

A good rapport was established between Sir Sigmund Sternberg and the generalate. Sir Sigmund is a knight commander of the Equestrian Pontifical Order of St Gregory the Great and a leading figure in several organizations connected with interfaith dialogue.

A letter from the Superior General of the Carmelite Order, Fr. Philip Sainz de Baranda, to M. Théo Klein, appeared in CHRISTIAN JEWISH RELATIONS, vol. 22, no. 1, 1989, 41.

Communiqué

On 1-2 December 1989 there took place in Auschwitz a meeting of the committee concerned with the future of the State Museum of Auschwitz. The meeting was chaired by the Minister Krystyna Marszalek-Mlynczyk, Under-Secretary of State at the Ministry of Culture and Art. The meeting was also attended by Dr Jonathan Webber, Fellow of the Oxford Centre for Hebrew Studies.

The committee undertook a survey of the individual exhibitions and their structure, and it also acquainted itself with the problems and requirements of the museum. The committee discussed questions concerning the organizational and educational aspects of visiting. The committee paid attention to the relationship between the museum and the town of Oswiecim, as well as the responsibilities of other institutions with similar interests, such as the Miedzynarodowy Dom Spotkan Mlodziczy (International Youth Meeting Centre) and the future Osrodek Informacji, Wychowania, Dialogu i Modlitwy (Centre for Information, Education, Meetings and Prayer). The committee also underlined the significance of a conservation belt round the museum.

The committee put forward various suggestions and proposals, as follows:

1 The broadening of the exhibitions to include elements illustrating the place of the Jews in Auschwitz and the uniqueness of the Shoah;
2 The enrichment of the exhibitions with information and documentation illustrating the resistance against the attempts at degredation and the specific type of dehumanization of the camp inmates, and illustrating their struggle for dignity and solidarity, for faith and hope;
3 The creation of an exhibition illustrating the life and fate of the Romanies (Gypsies) during the years of the Second World War;
4 The replacement of the present film about the liberation of the camp by others which would better serve the purpose of preparing the visitor for a tour of the museum;
5 The suggestion of different itineraries for visitors which would answer the wishes and needs of different social groups, particularly those of young visitors;
6 The preparation of differentiated guide-books and information-

sheets corresponding to the varying interests of Polish and foreign
social groups, together with those of young visitors;

7 The conducting of further sociological research on the visitors to
enable a better orientation of the interests and needs of the present-
day young generation;

8 The organization of a workshop for foreign journalists to give them a
better understanding of the role and problems of the museum;

9 The organization, in 1990 — corresponding to the fiftieth anniversary
of the incarceration of the first prisoners to the camp and also the
forty-fifth anniversary of its liberation — of an international conference devoted to the problems connected with Auschwitz.

The committee greeted with satisfaction the information concerning
proposed changes to exhibitions in the national pavilions.

The committee expressed its appreciation to the museum's employees
and its thanks to all the institutions and social groups collaborating with it,
particularly the youth organizations.

Statement by Gerhart M. Riegner

This statement by Dr. Riegner, Co-Chairman of the World Jewish Congress Governing Board and member of the International Jewish Committee on Interreligious Consultations, was published in Regards, 12–25 March 1987.

I am very happy that we have reached an agreement with the representatives of the Catholic Church on the transfer of the Carmelite convent in Auschwitz. I have always believed that such an agreement was possible and that our legitimate sensitivity was understood by a growing number of Christians. The transfer of the Carmelite convent is not the only cause for satisfaction. It is also extremely important that this agreement has the support of the cardinals in a number of Western countries acting in the name of all European churches. Thus, for the first time, the Catholic episcopate will actively help to establish a Catholic center for reflection, study, and interfaith encounters in commemoration of the *Shoah* and other victims of Nazi monstrosity. It remains to be hoped that the Polish authorities, who should never have given their consent to the establishment of the convent without consulting us, will do their utmost to facilitate and accelerate the creation of the new center and the transfer of the convent as stipulated in the Geneva agreement.

Source: Reprinted by permission from Israel Singer, Secretary General, World Jewish Congress.

D

Extract from the Address of Pope John Paul II to the Leaders of the Jewish Community in Vienna, June 24, 1988

" . . . You and we are still burdened by the mercy of the *Shoah*, the murder of millions of Jews in the concentration camps. . . . Here is revealed the dreadful face of a world without and even against God, whose intentions to kill were clearly directed against the Jewish people, but also against the faith of those who revere in the Jew Jesus of Nazareth the Redeemer of the world. . . . The process of complete reconciliation between the Jews and Christians has to be carried on in full force on all levels of relationships between our communities. Collaboration and common studies should help to explore in a deeper way the significance of the *Shoah*. . . . Among the manifold modern initiatives which have arisen in the spirit of the Council for the Jewish-Christian Dialogue, I would like to point to the Center for Information, Education, Meeting and Prayer which will be established in Poland. Its purpose is to explore the *Shoah* as well as the martyrdom of the Polish people and that of the other European nations during the time of National Socialism and also to enter into discussions about them. We hope that it will bear rich fruit and also enrich the civil life of all social groups, animating them to care in mutual respect for the weak, the needy, and marginalized, to overcome hostilities and prejudices, as well as to defend human rights, especially the right to religious freedom for each individual and community. . . . "

Source: Reprinted by permission from Dr. Eugene Fisher, Executive Secretary, Secretariat for Catholic-Jewish Relations, National Conference of Catholic Bishops, Washington, D.C.

Pope John Paul II's Remarks in English at His Weekly General Audience, August 2, 1989

Dear brothers and sisters,

Today we consider the coming of the Holy Spirit at Pentecost as the fulfillment of the new and everlasting covenant between God and humanity. Jesus sealed this new covenant with his own blood, as he indicated at the Last Supper when he said: "This cup is the new covenant in my blood."

The new and everlasting covenant sealed in the blood of Jesus and completed when the Spirit came at Pentecost was prepared and foretold in the Old Testament. In the covenant with Noah, God showed his intention to establish a covenant not only with humanity but also with the created world. By choosing Abraham and his descendants as sharers in a covenant with himself, God revealed his plan to choose a specific people, Israel, from which the promised Messiah would be born.

In the covenant which he established with Moses on Mount Sinai, God gave the law, the Ten Commandments. God would continue to regard Israel as his special people, as "a kingdom of priests and a holy nation," on condition that they remained faithful to his law. But the history of the Old Testament shows many instances of Israel's infidelity to God. Hence God sent the prophets as his messengers to call the people to conversion, to warn them of their hardness of heart and to foretell a new covenant still to come.

The new covenant foretold by the prophets was established through Christ's redemptive sacrifice and through the power of the Holy Spirit. In the wonderful event of Pentecost God offers the Holy Spirit as a gift to all men and women of every age. This "perfect gift from above" descends to fill the hearts of all people and to gather them into the church, constituting them the people of God of the new and everlasting covenant.

I wish to welcome the group of Salesian Sisters of St. John Bosco who have come from the United States. My greetings go also to the members of the Nigerian Armed Forces Pilgrimage. I likewise welcome the international group of young people who have been involved in work camps near Rome during the month of July. May this experience of cooperation bear fruit in strengthening the bonds of trust between peoples of different

cultural and religious backgrounds. And upon all the English-speaking visitors and pilgrims here today I invoke God's blessings of peace and joy.

Source: The text is from the wire service of the Catholic News Service. Copyright 1989 by Catholic
News Service. Reprinted by permission.

Statement by Cardinal Franciszek Macharski, Archbishop of Cracow, August 8, 1989

I had hoped that this serious problem, raised by Jewish feeling in the West, would be solved by setting up a "center for information, education and prayer" at Auschwitz, in that this center would act as a common meeting point for people of all nations and religions in a spirit of mutual respect. This would be a place where they could strive for understanding and harmony, to warn people about, and protect them from, war, terror and all those forms of violence and hatred which once thrived there.

It proved impossible to get the center ready in the time proposed and this delay fostered a violent campaign of accusations and defamation in some Western Jewish communities. This offensive attack, which was not solely verbal, has had repercussions in Auschwitz.

The human and Christian dignity of the sisters has not been respected, thus disrupting the peace to which they have every right. Christianity and the symbols of its faith and worship have not been respected. Our wishes and our intentions have been constantly misinterpreted and misrepresented in bad faith.

With regard to the intrusion within the convent itself and the subsequent attempt to take control of it, I have only heard one voice raised in an appeal for calm, and it belonged to the Jewish organizations of Poland.

This sort of attitude and behavior make it impossible for me to create the center as I had planned. In this climate of aggressive demands and uncertainty which has sprung up between us, it is not possible for us to work side by side in the creation of a place dedicated to mutual respect, without violating our personal religious and national convictions. Any plan for peace has to be founded on a genuine desire for peace. I want peace, and I will not disturb it, and I would remind my community that if necessary we must keep our dignity and moderate our words and our actions. I deplore the fact that this has not been appreciated by the leaders of some Jewish organizations.

Our position corresponds to the attitude on the Jewish faith taken by the church at the Second Vatican Council and which has been consolidated by subsequent decisions taken by the Holy See. This relates to all previous questions as well as to all forms of anti-Semitism which the church—prompted by evangelical love—deplores. As the anniversary of the outbreak of World War II approaches, we pray to God with ever increasing fervor for peace, which flows from him. And we implore all humankind to seek out the ways of peace in a mutual attempt to communicate, however difficult that may prove to be.

Source: Reprinted by permission from *Origins*, 14 September 1989, 250. The translation is by the Catholic News Service.

Pope John Paul II's Remarks in English at His Weekly General Audience, August 9, 1989

Dear brothers and sisters,

The descent of the Holy Spirit at Pentacost was the definitive fulfillment of Christ's paschal mystery. As such, it was also the fulfillment of the entire Old Testament. God had established his covenant with Israel by giving the chosen people his law. But because of Israel's infidelity, he had promised, through the prophets, that he would establish a new covenant with his people. In this new covenant, God's law would no longer be written on tablets of stone. Instead, it would be written by the Spirit upon man's very heart.

We have received this new law, this new covenant, in Jesus Christ. Through the outpouring of the Holy Spirit, we have been transformed and have been enabled to fulfill Christ's commandments to love God and our neighbor. Deep within our hearts, the Holy Spirit guides us to imitate the teachings and example of Jesus. This new "law of the Spirit" in no way restricts our human freedom. Rather, it restores and perfects that freedom, so that we may live and act fully in accordance with God's plan, sharing in the life which he has offered us in Christ. The law of the Spirit is a law that sets us free.

The book of the Acts of the Apostles reveals how the gift of the Holy Spirit enabled the early Christians to fulfill Christ's law of love. Through the enduring power of the Spirit, we have received the possibility of living according to a new morality that is not merely a code of laws, but the life of the new and eternal covenant, the life of the Spirit. Through the Spirit who dwells in our hearts, we receive the power to love God and our neighbor with all our heart, as Christ has taught us.

I wish to greet the various groups of pilgrims, especially those from Hong Kong, Taiwan and the United States. I am pleased to welcome my brothers and sisters from the Church of Sweden, who have come to Rome from Jonkoping. And I extend a particular greeting to all those who are here from South Korea, assuring you of my prayers as I prepare to visit Korea in October, for the conclusion of the International Eucharistic Congress. To all the English-speaking visitors present at today's audience I cordially impart my apostolic blessing.

Source: The text is from the wire service of the Catholic News Service. Copyright 1989 by Catholic News Service. Reprinted by permission.

Yehuda Bauer, "Auschwitz: The Dangers of Distortion," September 30, 1989

THE FUROR around the Carmelite convent in Auschwitz is not only a matter of Catholic-Jewish or Polish-Jewish relations. The background to it is a misunderstanding on all sides—including the Jewish one—of what Auschwitz actually was and what really happened there. The danger lies in the fact that this misunderstanding has created a myth that is endangering the accurate memory of the Holocaust.

Israel TV has followed the BBC, the curator of the Auschwitz museum, Kazimierz Smolen, and now also Netanel Lorch (*Jerusalem Post* daily, September 3) in falling into the trap of claiming that four million people died in Auschwitz. Indeed, that is the figure engraved in stone in Auschwitz itself, and our Israeli pundits accept it without bothering to check.

Official Polish propagandists then claim that out of these four million victims, two-and-a-half million were Jews, implying that as the Auschwitz concentration camp was predominantly Polish, most if not all of the other 1.5 million victims were Poles.

If those who make these statements didn't know any better, one might understand this as a grievous but unintentional error. But this is not so. Historians have shown each one of these statements to be patently untrue, and while one can understand Israel TV's Haim Yavin or Netanel Lorch unwittingly repeating this kind of error, one cannot understand how Polish curators and English investigators can fall into the same trap.

There were never four million victims in Auschwitz. According to a painstakingly researched paper by the doyen of French Jewish Holocaust historians, Georges Wellers ("Essai de Determination du nombre de Morts au Camp d'Auschwitz," *Le Monde Juif*, Fall 1983), which is now accepted as a basis for understanding the horror statistics of Auschwitz, the total number of people who died there, both by gassing in the extermination camp at Birkenau and by starvation, torture, execution or disease in the concentration camp and its satellite camps, was in the neighborhood of 1.6 million.

A total of 215,409 Poles were brought to Auschwitz. Of these, 3,665 were gassed in the gas chambers; 79,345 died or were murdered in the camp; a total of 83,010 Polish victims. The number of Gypsies who were gassed is 6,430; 13,825 died in the camp. A total of 11,685 Russians were also gassed.

The figure for Jews murdered by gassing is 1,323,000, with 29,980 dying in the camp: a total of about 1,350,000. (Obviously, these figures, despite their apparent detail, cannot be taken as totally accurate, but they give a general indication.) The basis for these figures is the clandestine registration carried out by a group of very courageous men and women who worked as clerks in the camp administration and had a fairly clear picture of what was going on.

One of the reasons for the misinformation disseminated about Auschwitz lies in the fact, demonstrated by a number of authoritative historical research projects, mainly by my colleague Yisrael Gutman, that from the end of 1942 on, Auschwitz ceased to be a predominantly Polish camp.

At that time, Himmler decided to transfer the Jews from all the other camps to Auschwitz; parallel to that, Poles were gradually shipped out of there to other camps. Himmler's order was not completely carried out, and many Jews remained in the camps they were in at the end of 1942, or to which they were brought later.

The partial execution of the order, however, meant that the three main Auschwitz camps and their satellites received large transports of Jews, most of whom were not gassed on arrival; and from 1943, Auschwitz became a predominantly Jewish camp. Many of the 200,000 Poles brought to Auschwitz died not there but in other camps— but, of course, a majority survived.

Mr. Lorch's suggestion, that we say to Cardinal Glemp: "Fine, you give us Birkenau to establish our memorial there, and you have yours at Auschwitz, which was a Polish camp," may be brilliant politics, but it has nothing at all to do with the grim realities of 1943–1945. False history establishes false consciousness and creates false myths. Are we really interested in doing this?

Why then, one must ask, do some Poles disseminate the wrong figures? In my view, the answer is simple. In order to create a national myth, there has to be at least a well-understood hint that the Holocaust included Poles as well as Jews. Once that is accepted, the Poles' concept of themselves as the crucified nation, the real sufferers of Europe, can be accepted too, with the obvious practical consequences.

This is Cardinal Glemp's real line. Rather than have the Auschwitz complex remain a universal, international monument to suffering, one which Jews can accept because they are then free to relate it to the overwhelming disaster brought upon the Jewish people, and upon them primarily, he appropriates Auschwitz for the Polish nation, by self-definition a Catholic nation.

Hence the nuns in the Auschwitz convent, in their prayers, then appropriate the Jewish dead and, in fact, all the other dead as well, within a nationalist Polish self-concept. Glemp then proceeds to emulate a predecessor of his, Cardinal Augustus Hlond, who, in the wake of the 1946 pogrom at Kielce—in which the Catholic hierarchy played a less than distinguished role—also said a few things about Jewish-controlled media. So deep does this kind of anti-Semitism go, that I do not even believe it is conscious.

One hastens to add that a good part of the Polish intelligentsia, including liberal Catholics, rejects this interpretation completely in favour of saying that what the Nazis intended for the Poles was slavery and national extinction, but not total murder, as was the case with the Jews. They were and are among those who resist the propaganda about the four million victims at Auschwitz.

Our own Zevulun Hammer then returns from Warsaw, having discussed the matter with the appropriate dignitaries there, and suggests that we adopt the low-key, conciliatory approach of a slow, diplomatic effort. The odour of political considerations that have little to do with the memory of the Holocaust can be discerned in these statements. The point is that historical falsifications are ultimately counterproductive.

Yes, of course, discussion should be encouraged, because this kind of disagreement provides a posthumous victory for Hitler. But the convent has to go, and the site has to revert to being the universal memorial it was slowly becoming. The shame of a closed "Jewish" barrack, which is opened only when Jewish visitors arrange for it, has to be erased. The fact that Auschwitz lies in Poland makes the Poles the custodians of it, nothing more. Nobody "owns" the dead.

By definition, a myth is an untruthful interpretation of reality. The fact that Israeli politicians and the media accept the four million figure with all its disastrous ramifications can perhaps be explained by the conscious or unconscious effort made in this country to create a Holocaust myth that is totally different from the reality it supposedly relates to. If two-and-a-half million Jews were gassed at Auschwitz, that is "better" for propaganda than the truth, as though the truth were not horrible enough.

It is added to the other myths that are being created: that Jabotinsky or Uri-Zvi Greenberg foresaw the Holocaust, that *all* the European nations stood by while the Jews were being murdered, and lately, that the fact of Jewish resistance, in which left-wingers were predominant, was itself a myth.

Poles and Jews alike are supplying the denyers of the Holocaust with the best possible arguments. It is very easy to prove that four million people could never have been murdered at Auschwitz. On the basis of prisoner statistics, it is equally easy to disprove Polish claims about Polish victims. We are simply doing all the Nazis' and neo-Nazis' work for them.

In the ceaseless battle against the misuse of the Holocaust, against the distortions and lies and their unwitting dissemination, this is another battle that has to be fought. Catholics and Jews, Poles and Israelis alike should have a common, if extremely painful and agonizing, interest in fighting it.

Source: Reprinted by permission from the *Jerusalem Post* (International Edition), 30 September 1989. Yehuda Bauer is the Jona M. Machover Professor of Holocaust Studies at the Institute of Contemporary Jewry of the Hebrew University.

Rabbi Avraham Weiss, "Let the Nuns Pray Elsewhere," October 15, 1989

When we flew to Poland to peacefully protest against the Carmelite convent located at the Auschwitz death camp where 3 million Jews had been annihilated, we never imagined we would challenge so many institutions. We did not expect to be attacked by Polish workers or castigated by the Communist press. Neither did we anticipate that Poland's Jozef Cardinal Glemp would spew forth anti-Semitic canards in denouncing us. Nor did we believe we would be shaking the foundation of Catholic-Jewish dialogue. And we certainly never expected to be described by some Western newspapers as "militants" who "stormed the convent."

As the leader of the group that generated this furor, an account of what occurred is in order.

The target of our demonstration, the Carmelite convent, is located in the building that had been used to store the canisters of Zyklon B gas used by the Nazis to carry out their program of mass killings. The convent was established in 1984 when a group of nuns took over the building at the camp entrance.

Faced with mounting protest against the location of the convent at a site so bitterly emblematic of the greatest calamity ever to befall the Jewish people, Catholic representatives, including four cardinals, met in 1987 with Jewish leaders in Geneva and signed an accord providing for the removal of the convent no later than Feb. 22, 1989.

By July 1989, the convent had not been relocated. Instead, it was expanded and refurbished; a 24-foot cross was erected in an adjacent area; the nuns, claiming to be praying for "the 4 million victims of Auschwitz, most of whom were Jewish," were more entrenched than ever. Aid to the Church in Distress, an organization that helped finance establishment of the convent, had declared the nuns would pray for "the conversion of strayed brothers." The Jewish community is highly sensitive and, indeed, offended by any hint of prayer for the conversion of Jews.

PEACEFUL VOICES

Moreover, the nuns occupied the building in violation of the 1972 UN Convention for the Protection of the World Cultural and National Heritage, an agreement designed to preserve intact sites of cultural and national interest. Auschwitz, including the building the nuns occupy, is on the World Heritage List at Poland's request.

We came to Auschwitz in July 1989, five months after the deadline for removal of the convent had passed, to peacefully raise a voice of moral conscience.

After approaching the fence surrounding the convent, we rang the bell, declaring that we had come in peace. When our attempts at opening a dialogue about the convent's removal were ignored, we climbed the fence, wrapped ourselves in our prayer shawls and sang and studied Torah on the convent porch.

By climbing the fence after being denied entry, we did not regard ourselves as trespassers. In the most tragic and unwanted way, Auschwitz had become Jewish—ours. It is a Jewish cemetery; the bones and ashes of Jews are strewn across its ground to this very day.

It is not we who violated the convent, but the convent that is violating the peace of the dead. We were no more "invading" the convent than the Rev. Martin Luther King Jr. was "invading" lunch counters and buses.

Soon after we began our demonstration, workers from inside the convent threw buckets of water mixed with urine and paint over our heads. Several hours later, the workers attacked us again, this time kicking and punching and dragging us from the area. Their leader yelled, "Heil Hitler."

Nuns peered through the convent windows as we were beaten. A Polish priest cried, "Rip off their skullcaps! Drag them out!" Uniformed and plainclothes police watched without intervening. As we were hauled away, dogs were set loose to patrol the area. A Reuters reporter observing all of this wept openly.

Outrage at what was done to us has been expressed in many quarters. The State Department, the Israeli Foreign Ministry, Jewish organizations, and many in the Western press have all joined in condemning the attack.

Jacek Kuron, a Solidarity leader, now Poland's minister of labor, told us: "I feel very much ashamed as a Pole for what happened to you." His statement was published on the front page of the Solidarity newspaper *Gazeta Wyborcza*.

Even the Polish press agency, PAP, which originally reported that we had "come to attack the nuns," reversed its position and apologized. At a meeting with Janusz Solecki, director general of PAP, he admitted that no reporter had been present at Auschwitz the day we were beaten. In a subsequent story, PAP stated: "The director general of PAP apologized to the participants of the meeting for the unfortunate terms used in the PAP story about the incident at Auschwitz."

Indeed, a few days after we were attacked, Polish Deputy Foreign Minister, Jan Majewski said to Mordechai Palzur, Israel's representative in Poland: "Because of the latest incidents at the Carmelite convent at Auschwitz, the government has decided to intervene to insure its removal."

Only after months of silence did the Vatican concede that the nuns should move into an interfaith prayer center to be built in accordance with the 1987 Geneva agreement. But no timetable has been given. One Vatican official said it may take years. Every day the nuns remain is a violation of the agreement.

Marcus Pardes, a Jewish signatory to the Geneva agreement, said: "When our brothers and sisters met their deaths in Auschwitz, they were surrounded by a total silence on the part of the world, and a very significant silence on the part of the church. We cannot tolerate that prayers should take place, even in the best intentions, in this place from those who could have at the right time raised their voices for our brothers and sisters and who did not do so."

Furthermore, the Vatican has failed to censure Glemp for his egregious anti-Semitic comments of Aug. 26. Unless Glemp recants, we, for our part, intend to travel to Poland to pursue our defamation suit against him for alleging that we had come to kill the nuns and for his slander against the Jewish people.

Even if the nuns move, the convent at Auschwitz is perceived by many to be part of the Vatican's larger attempt to Christianize the Holocaust. Churches now exist at the death camps of Sobibor (where 99% of those murdered were Jews) and Dachau (where the majority of the victims were Jewish). Many Jews fear that soon the world will begin to believe that the Holocaust was a Nazi attempt to murder Christians rather than Jews. Unless the State of Israel administers the death camps, no one will know that Jews were murdered there. One high Vatican official was reported to have said that the church's mistake was building the convent 20 years too soon.

The image of Jews being beaten at Auschwitz in the very place in which, not so long ago, millions of Jews were beaten, tortured and gassed, evokes in Jews today flashbacks of memory so painful as to cause them to rub their eyes in disbelief.

Didn't the world learn something from Auschwitz, especially the Poles? Especially the church? And most especially, the nuns who came to Auschwitz to, of all things, pray?

We did not come to Auschwitz to be beaten. We came to demand that the convent be removed, the nuns leave and the cross, erected on ground that tragically has become sacred to us, be removed.

Let the nuns who say they are praying for those who died in Auschwitz pray elsewhere. Let them cease praying for the Jews who were murdered there. Those who died as Jews should be left to rest in peace as Jews.

Source: Reprinted from the *New York Daily News*, 15 October 1989, by permission from Rabbi Avraham Weiss. Rabbi Weiss heads the Hebrew Institute of Riverdale, New York, and is assistant professor of Judaic studies at Stern College, Yeshiva University. He is chairman of the Coalition of Concern.

Francis A. Winiarz, "We're Not Moving a Single Inch," November 1, 1989, and Sidebar

On September 29, 1989, this writer had an opportunity to visit and chat with Sister Teresa, the Mother Superior of the Carmelite Sisters' Cloistered Convent, in Oswiecim, Poland, which was recently invaded by a group of seven American Jews, led by Rabbi Avraham Weiss from New York City.

We spent some three-and-one-half hours discussing this incident, the Jewish question in general, and her plans for now and in the future.

To be in the presence of Sister Teresa, and to hear her recite the history of Poland as it relates to the Jewish question, and the current onslaught on her convent, is to gain a clear insight into my own Polishness.

As most Poles, she is friendly, affable, and quite a scrapper. A short, very attractive young lady, she is determined to stand her ground and not budge an inch to the pressure that she move her convent elsewhere. And here is why.

The cross and the convent building objected to by the Jews do not stand on the grounds of the Auschwitz concentration camp. The cross was erected on the very spot where some 22,000 Polish people, mostly the Polish intelligentsia, were murdered by the Nazis in 1940, some two years prior to the arrival of any Jewish inmates.

The first shipment of Jews to Auschwitz took place in the spring of 1942. Therefore, the cross was erected in memory of the Polish souls, on the very spot where they died. And that is where she is determined to keep it.

At this point, she reviewed how good the Poles have been to the Jews for centuries. They were expelled from England in 1290, from France in 1306 and again in 1394, and from Spain in 1492.

In Poland they began to appear in the 13th century, granted refuge by numerous Polish princes, together with the right to conduct their own affairs with their own laws.

It was not until King Kazimierz Wielki (1310–1370) that their privileges were extended over the entire land. They became a state within a state. They had their own boroughs, their own courts of law, etc. They enjoyed rights in Poland denied to them by Western Europe.

According to Sister Teresa, most of the Jews perished not in Auschwitz, but rather in Birkenau, Belzec, Majdanek, Sobibor, and Treblinka camps which were erected by the German Nazis in occupied Poland. Those were the main crematoria built for the specific decimation of the Jews.

Of course, some did perish in the Auschwitz concentration camp proper. Of the 4.5 million people who perished there, there were 28 different nationalities represented. The Jews comprised approximately 30 percent of that number.

The sisters have no objections if the Jews wish to build a synagogue next door to them, or across the street from them, or in the very center of the Auschwitz complex. In fact, the Jews are the only group that already has a synagogue in the center of the Auschwitz camp. One of the former inmate-barracks was given to them as a pro-tem synagogue. They conduct their prayers and services there, as well as other social functions.

We then touched on the subject of Zygmund Nissenbaum, a Jewish millionaire, now residing in West Germany, and a former inmate of Auschwitz concentration camp, who offered to donate a million dollars to the nuns so that they could build their convent elsewhere.

Her reply was a vehement "We don't want a single penny from him. His offer has a string attached to it. He wants to introduce a new brand of liquor to Poland, and that million is to be realized from that source by giving us 15 percent of his liquor profits. Frankly, Poland has already more vodka than this country needs."

Then, the point of the Geneva Conference was raised, where a commitment was made to have the convent moved. Question? Did either Cardinal Macharski or Cardinal Glemp consult with you prior to that meeting in Geneva?

"Definitely not," was her quick and very emotional response. "We had no consultation with either of them."

Representing the nuns in Geneva from Poland were Cardinal Franciszek Macharski, Bishop Kazimierz Gorny, Father Stanislaw Musial, and the Editor-in-Chief of the Catholic Weekly, the "Tygodnik Powszechny," Jerzy Turowicz. It is very interesting to note that the Editor-in-Chief, a Jew and a member of the Jewish Council in Poland, represented the Catholics at this meeting.

Also present at the conference in Geneva and representing the Catholic side were two French clergymen, namely Cardinal Decourtray and Bishop Lustiger, both of whom are Jewish converts. Naturally, the outcome of that Geneva Conference was one-sided in favor of the World Jewry.

The Geneva Conference agreed to the following four points:

One, Cardinal Macharski was to oversee the building of this new center for information, meetings, and prayer.

Two, the center was to be constructed within 24 months. The cost was to be assumed by the Polish bishops and the Polish bishops from other countries. The Jews did not commit themselves to any part of the cost of such a center. The entire burden was to fall on Poland and the World-Polonia.

Three, Cardinal Macharski was instructed to report on the progress of such a center to a Jewish lawyer, Theo Klein, who was the chairman of this conference.

Four, the Jewish delegation made it abundantly clear that they are not obligating themselves financially to anything undertaken by the Catholic delegation.

The questions here arise, she said: "Why do the Jews want special laws and treatment in Auschwitz only for themselves? Why don't they realize that the best arrangement for everyone would be if each religion built its own temple of prayer? Do they still consider themselves the chosen people?''

Sister Teresa stated, ''There is no good or bad God. God is one. Let the Jews understand that the prayers of the Carmelite nuns are also offered for the souls of those victims who were also of the Jewish persuasion.''

In a very perplexed manner, she asked, ''Why are the Jews, in this particular point in time, when Poland has so many serious problems and is attempting to build a new political system, creating such a disturbance for us?

''Jews are accusing the Poles of anti-Semitism. If they know their history, they would know that in this country they had their biggest economical and political privileges. And besides that, didn't the Poles suffer thousands of deaths for attempting to help the Jews during World War II?

''Israel,'' she continued, ''receives three billion dollars from the United States only because it is building a democratic country; however, the daily press reports in detail how they are mistreating the Arabs. Greater anti-Semites are hard to find.''

Poland now wishes to build a democratic form of government. It needs financial help from the United States and the World Bank. They don't want a dole-out. They want a good credit rating. Being an industrious and a greatly responsible nation, it would soon put its economic system on target. The Poles are an honorable breed.

According to Mother Teresa, following World War II, the fate of the Polish economy was in the hands of Henry Minc, a Jew. Military Affairs Minister was Jacob Bermann, another Jew. The entire Polish Government consisted of 75 percent Polish Communist Jews, appointed by Joseph Stalin, with the specific instructions to introduce atheism into Poland.

Schools and churches were closed by the Jews in power. Because the Poles wished to be Catholic, many of them were imprisoned. Churches were devastated. The results of that political period are well known and recorded in the annals of the Polish history.

It is worthy to note that the Jews are continually accusing the Poles of anti-Semitism. However, it must be noted that following World War II, the Minister of Defense was Marian Spyhalski, a Jew. He held this position from 1956 to 1968. In 1963, he received the title of ''Marshall'' in spite of the fact that he never served a day in the military.

Another Jew was the president of Poland prior to Wojciech Jaruzelski. His name? Heinrik Grunbaum, changed to Henry Jablonski. He served from 1972 to 1982.

There were many ministers, judges, and members of important committees, etc. of Jewish persuasion. When one compares this with the very small percentage of Jews in Poland prior to World War II (10 percent out of 35 million people), one can easily deduce that there was very little anti-Semitism in Poland to speak of. The Jews were an insignificant minority group in Poland with a majority of privileges.

Finally, Sister Teresa concluded, that Auschwitz is a place of many people's tragedy.

''We must honor that. We must bow our heads over this land, and pray in many languages, and according to many beliefs. We cannot say that only one nation was chosen, and that the nation has the right to dictate to others what it should do. That was the exact attitude of Hitler and his henchmen.''

Her final goodbye to me was, ''You can tell the Americans that we are not moving a single inch. And like the Pauline monks who bravely withstood the Swedish siege of their monastery at Czestochowa in 1655, we are here to stay!''

My report to that was a ''thumbs-up'' sign, and a ''Nazi Gora'' remark.

She smiled broadly and replied, "Nawzajem!"

Accompanying this article in the *Polish Daily News* was a sidebar. Headed by the words "Poland Is Beautiful," it went on to say:

Nine times since his retirement 15 years ago as an aviation and clinical psychologist with the United States Air Force, Col. Francis A. Winiarz has led groups of people on visits to Poland.

"I've been all over the world and always thought Italy was the most beautiful country in the world. But nothing can beat Poland. All of it, from top to bottom, is beautiful."

Born in Buffalo, N.Y., 74 years ago, Winiarz, who now lives in Eggertsville, N.Y., shares a memorable moment from his most recent journey to Poland, a visit with the nuns at the Carmelite convent outside the gate of the Auschwitz concentration camp in Oswiecim, Poland.

"One thing I didn't put in my article," Winiarz said, "is that Sister Teresa told me that if she and her sister nuns (there are 14 in the convent) were forced to move out, they would leave Poland and resettle elsewhere.

"But she didn't think that the situation would come to that."

Winiarz's brother, Fr. Cellistus, a Franciscan priest, was a former pastor of St. Hedwig Parish on Detroit's west side.

Source: Reprinted by permission from the *Polish Daily News*, 1 November 1989.

K

Polish Pastoral Letter, November 30, 1990, "Pastoral on Jewish-Catholic Relations"

"We express our sincere regret for all the incidents of anti-Semitism which were committed at any time or by anyone on Polish soil," the Polish bishops state in a pastoral letter read in all Polish parishes Jan. 20. The bishops also write that even if there were only one Christian who could have helped but "did not stretch out a helping hand to a Jew during the time of danger or caused his death, we must ask for forgiveness of our Jewish brothers and sisters." The pastoral, dated Nov. 30, 1990, was released in observance of the 25th anniversary of Vatican Council II's Declaration on Non-Christian Religions, "Nostra Aetate." The bishops continue, "in expressing our sorrow for all the injustices and harm done to Jews, we cannot forget that we consider untrue and deeply harmful the use by many of the concept of what is called 'Polish anti-Semitism,' " which frequently connects "the concentration camps not with those who were actually involved with them but with Poles in a Poland occupied by Germans." The following text is based on a translation of the pastoral by Thomas Bird of Queens College in New York, prepared for the Interreligious Affairs Department of the American Jewish Committee.

We address you today about the very important issue of our relationship to the Jewish people and to the Mosaic religion, with which we Christians are uniquely linked. We do this on the occasion of the 25th anniversary of the proclamation of the conciliar declaration *Nostra Aetate*, in which the church defined more precisely its relations to non-Christian religions, among them the Jewish religion.

This declaration, adopted on Oct. 27, 1965, has lost none of its importance or contemporary value today. Our Holy Father John Paul II has repeated this on numerous occasions, saying "I would like to confirm with the deepest conviction that the teaching of the church, given during the Second Vatican Council in the declaration *Nostra Aetate*

...always remains for us, for the Catholic Church, for the episcopate...and for the pope, a teaching to which one must adhere, a teaching which one must accept not only as something relevant but even more, as an expression of faith, as an inspiration of the Holy Spirit, as a word of divine wisdom'' (Speech to the Jewish community in Venezuela, Jan. 15, 1985).

The conciliar declaration points out first and foremost the multiplicity and diversity of ties that exist between the church, the Jewish religion and the Jewish people. There is no other religion with which the church has such close relations nor is there any other people with which it is so closely linked. ''The church of Christ,'' write the fathers of the council, ''acknowledges that in God's plan of salvation the beginning of her faith and election is to be found in the patriarchs, Moses and the prophets'' (*Nostra Aetate*, 4). Therefore, John Paul II, who after St. Peter, was the first of his successors to visit a synagogue, having visited the synagogue in Rome on April 13, 1986, could address the Jews as ''our elder brothers'' in the faith.

The church is rooted in the Jewish people and in the faith of the Jews most of all because of the fact that Jesus Christ, according to the flesh, came from that people. This central event in the history of salvation was from its very inception intended by God in his original plan of salvation. To that people God disclosed his name and made a covenant with them. This election was not only an exclusive privilege, but also a great commitment to the faith and fidelity to the one God, including the testimony of suffering and, quite often, of death as well. To this people God entrusted the special mission of uniting everyone in the true faith in one God and awaiting the Messiah, the Savior. When the time was fulfilled, the eternally true word of God, the only begotten Son of the Father, took flesh from the Virgin Mary, a daughter of the Jewish people. Announced by the prophets and awaited by his own people, Jesus Christ was born in Bethlehem as ''a son of David, a son of Abraham'' (Mt.1:1). From the Jewish people came also ''the apostles, the pillars on which the church stands,'' as well as ''many of those early disciples who proclaimed the Gospel of Christ to the world'' (*Nostra Aetate*, 4).

The church, as God's people of the new election and covenant, did not disinherit God's people of the first election and covenant of the gifts received from God. As St. Paul teaches, the Israelites, because of their forefathers, are the subject of love (Rom. 11:28), and therefore the gift of grace and the calling of God are irrevocable (Rom. 11:29). To them belong also ''the sonship, the glory, the covenants, the giving of the law, the worship and the promises'' (Rom. 9:4). God thus has not revoked his selection of the Jewish people as the chosen people, but continues to bestow his love. He and only he, the almighty and merciful God, knows the day ''when all people will call on God with one voice and serve him shoulder to shoulder (*Nostra Aetate*, 4).

The fathers of the council, in the declaration, deny in a clear and decisive manner the main accusation that all Jews bear responsibility for the death of Christ. The declaration states, ''Even though the Jewish authorities and those who followed their lead pressed for the death of Christ, neither all Jews indiscriminately at that time nor Jews today can be charged with crimes committed during his passion'' (ibid). Some people, however, quoting the words of St. Matthew's Gospel, ''Let his blood be upon us and upon our children,'' (Mt. 27:25) accuse the Jews of the death of Christ. In reality, these words mean: We accept the full responsibility for that death. But it was not the entire Jewish people who said this, only the unruly crowd gathered in front of Pilate's palace. One should not forget that for these people, as for all of us, Jesus prayed on the cross: ''Father, forgive them, for they know not what they do'' (Lk. 23:34).

The catechism of the Council of Trent treats the question of the responsibility for the death of Christ as follows: "Christian sinners are more responsible for the death of Christ in comparison with certain Jews who participated in it. The latter really 'did not know what they did, whereas we know only too well' " (Part 1, Chap. 5, Quest. 9). The declaration *Nostra Aetate* reminds us of the traditional teaching of the church that "Christ . . . freely underwent suffering and death because of the sins of all" (No. 4).

The teaching of the church in that declaration was developed in later documents of the Apostolic See. Especially important is a document of 1985 titled "Notes on the Correct Way to Present Jews and Judaism in Preaching and Catechesis in the Roman Catholic Church." This deserves the widest possible dissemination, especially among pastors and catechists.

We Poles have particular ties with the Jewish people from as early as the first centuries of our history. Poland became for many Jews a second fatherland. The majority of Jews living in the world today are by origin from the territories of the previous and current Polish commonwealth. Unfortunately, in our century this particular land became the grave for several million Jews. Not by our wish, and not by our hands. Here is what our Holy Father said recently, on Sept. 26 of this year, about our common history:

"There is still one other nation, one particular people: the people of the patriarchs, of Moses and the prophets, the inheritors of the faith of Abraham. . . . This people lived side by side with us for generations on the same land, which became, as it were, a new fatherland of their diaspora. This people underwent the terrible death of millions of their sons and daughters. At first they were stigmatized in a particular way. Later, they were pushed into the ghetto in separate neighborhoods. Then they were taken to the gas chambers, they underwent death—only because they were children of this people. Murderers did this on our land—perhaps in order to dishonor it. One cannot dishonor a land by the death of innocent victims. Through such death a land becomes a sacred relic" (Speech to Poles during a Wednesday audience, Sept. 26, 1990).

During his historic meeting in 1987 with the few Jews living in Poland, in Warsaw, the Holy Father said, "Be assured, dear brothers, that the Poles, this Polish church is in a spirit of profound solidarity with you when she looks closely at the terrible reality of the extermination—the unconditional extermination—of your nation, an extermination carried out with premeditation. The threat against you was also a threat against us; this latter was not realized to the same extent because it did not have time to be realized to the same extent. It was you who suffered this terrible sacrifice of extermination: One might say that you suffered it also on behalf of those who were likewise to have been exterminated" (L'Osservatore Romano, June 1987).

Many Poles saved Jews during the last war. Hundreds, if not thousands, paid for this with their own lives and the lives of their loved ones. For each of the Jews saved there was a whole chain of hearts of people of good will and helping hands. The express testimony of that help to Jews in the years of the Hitler occupation are the many trees dedicated to Poles in Yad Vashem, the place of national memory in Jerusalem, with the honored title, "The Just Among the Nations" given to many Poles. In spite of so many heroic examples of help on the part of Polish Christians, there were also people who remained indifferent to this incomprehensible tragedy. We are especially disheartened by those among Catholics who in some way were the cause of the death of Jews. They will forever gnaw at our conscience on the social plane. If only one Christian could have helped and did not stretch out a helping hand to a Jew during the time of danger or caused his death, we must ask for forgiveness of our Jewish brothers and sisters. We are aware that many of our compatriots still remember the injustices and injuries committed by the postwar communist authorities, in which people of Jewish origin also took part. We must acknowledge, however, that the source of inspiration of their activity was clearly neither their origin nor religion, but the communist ideology, from which the Jews themselves, in fact, suffered many injustices.

We express our sincere regret for all the incidents of anti-Semitism which were committed at any time or by anyone on Polish soil. We do this with the deep conviction that all incidents of anti-Semitism are contrary to the spirit of the Gospel and—as Pope John Paul II recently emphasized—"remain opposed to the Christian vision of human dignity" (John Paul II on the 50th anniversary of the outbreak of World War II).

In expressing our sorrow for all the injustices and harm done to Jews, we cannot forget that we consider untrue and deeply harmful the use by many of the concept of what is called "Polish anti-Semitism" as an especially threatening form of that anti-Semitism; and in addition, frequently connecting the concentration camps not with those who were actually involved with them, but with Poles in a Poland occupied by the Germans. Speaking of the unprecedented extermination of Jews, one cannot forget and even less pass over in silence the fact that the Poles as a nation were one of the first victims of the same criminal racist ideology of Hitler's Nazism.

The same land, which for centuries was the common fatherland of Poles and Jews, of blood spilled together, the sea of horrific suffering and of injuries shared—should not divide us but unites us. For this commonality cries out to us—especially the places of execution and, in many cases, common graves. We Christians and Jews are also united in our belief in one God, the Creator and Lord of the entire universe, who created man in his image and likeness. We are united by the commonly accepted ethical principles included in the Ten Commandments, crowned by the love of God and neighbor. We are united in our respect for the biblical books of the Old Testament as the word of God and by common traditions of prayer. Last, we are united in the common hope of the final coming of the kingdom of God. Together we await the Messiah, the Savior, although we, believing that he is Jesus Christ of Nazareth—await not his first, but his final coming, no more in the poverty of the manger in Bethlehem, but in power and glory.

The most important way to overcome the difficulties that still exist today is the establishment of a dialogue which would lead to the elimination of distrust, prejudices and stereotypes, and to mutual acquaintance and understanding based on respect for our separate religious traditions as well as opening the way to cooperation in many fields. It is important, moreover, that while doing this we learn to experience and appreciate the proper religious contexts of Jews and Christians as they are lived by Jews and Christians themselves.

We conclude our pastoral homily, dear brothers and sisters, recalling the recent statement of the Holy Father about our common temporal and final destinies: "The (Jewish) people who lived with us for many generations remained with us after the terrible death of many millions of their sons and daughters. Together we wait for the day of judgment and resurrection" (Speech to Poles during the Wednesday audience, Sept. 26, 1990.)

Commending to the merciful God all the victims of force and hatred, we bless you from our hearts, praying that "the God of peace may be always with you" (Phil. 4:9).

Source: English language text translated from the pastoral by Thomas E. Byrd of Queen's College, City University of New York, prepared for the Interreligious Affairs Department of the American Jewish Committee.

Selected Political Cartoons

Benson

Source: From the *Arizona Republic* [Phoenix, Arizona], 31 August 1989. Reprinted by permission: Tribune Media Services.

"Let us pray for that antisemite, Cardinal Glemp."

Source: From the *Los Angeles Times*, 1 September 1989. Copyright, 1989, Los Angeles Times. Reprinted by permission.

Source: From the *Chicago Tribune*, 8 September 1989. Reprinted by permission: Tribune Media
Services.

Source: From *Present Tense*, November-December 1989. Reprinted by permission from Jack Tom. This cartoon accompanied an article by Arthur Hertzberg, "Doing Unto Others," which focused on issues about the Auschwitz convent controversy.

Jack Tom

Selected Bibliography

Adler, Karen. "Controversy over the Carmelite Convent at Auschwitz 1988–89." *IJA Research Reports* 7 (1989).

Bailly, Michel. "A Carmelite Convent at Auschwitz." *Christian Jewish Relations* 19 (March 1986): 43–45. This article appeared originally in *Le Soir* (Brussels), 14 October 1985.

Banki, Judith. "The Convent Crisis." *AJC Journal*, Spring 1987.

Bartoszewki, Wladyslaw T. *The Convent at Auschwitz*. London: Bowerdean Press, 1990.

Battiata, Mary. "3 Cardinals Tell Poles to Honor Pact." *Washington Post*, 4 September 1989.

Batzdorff, Susanne M. "Catholics and Jews: Can We Bridge the Abyss?" *America*, 11 March 1989.

———. "A Martyr of Auschwitz." *New York Times Magazine*, 12 April 1987.

Bauer, Yehuda. "Auschwitz: The Dangers of Distortion." *Jerusalem Post* (International Edition), 30 September 1989.

Baum, Geraldine. "Why Nuns' Home Opened Wounds." *Newsday*, 5 September 1989.

Bering-Jensen, Helle. "No Peace for Convent at Auschwitz." *Insight*, 18 September 1989.

Blinken, Antony J. "Postcard Poland: Missing." *The New Republic*, 16 October 1989.

Blonski, Jan. "The Poor Poles Look at the Ghetto." *Christian Jewish Relations* 22 (Autumn/Winter 1989): 5–20.

Bono, Agostino. "Pope Says Murder of Innocent Jews Sanctified Poland." *Catholic News Service*, 26 September 1990.

Breindel, Eric. "The Silence of Pope Pius XII." *New York Post*, 25 August 1989.

Brown, Robert McAfee. "Nobelists, Auschwitz and Survival." *Christianity and Crisis*, 7 March 1988.

———. "A Symbol Is a Symbol Is a Symbol." *Christianity and Crisis*, 23 October 1989.

Brumberg, Abraham. "A Parting for Solidarity and the Church?" *New York Times*, 1 September 1989.

———. "The Problem That Won't Go Away: Anti-Semitism in Poland (Again)." *Tikkun*, January/February 1990.

Buchanan, Patrick J. "Awakening the Sleeping Catholic Giant." *Daily Report* [Ontario, Calif.], 24 September 1989.

———. "Catholics Under Siege." *New York Post*, 24 September 1989.

———. "Hardball Is a Game That Two Can Play." *Washington Times*, 25 September 1989.

———. "In Defense of Pius XII." *New York Times*, 12 September 1989.

———. "Storm Over Auschwitz." *New York Post*, 16 August 1989.

Buckley, William F. "Auschwitz and the Nuns." *National Review*, 13 October 1989.

———. "Elie Wiesel Is Right: The Nuns Should Go and Pray Elsewhere." *Sunday Times* (Scranton, Pa.), 3 September 1989.

Campion, Owen F. "Auschwitz, a Convent, and Hope for Tomorrow." *The Priest*, December 1989.

Cargas, Harry James. "Buchanan, and Others, 'Waldheiming' Auschwitz." *Washington Times*, 6 September 1989.

Catholic-Jewish Scholars Dialogue. "On the Carmelite Convent at Auschwitz." *The New World* (Chicago, Ill.), 25 August 1989.

Chotkowski, Charles. "The Nuns at Auschwitz Are Not Intruders." *Washington Post*, 5 September 1989.

Chrostowski, Waldemar. "Controversy Around the Auschwitz Convent." *Occasional Papers on Religion in Eastern Europe*, June 1990.

———. "Controversy around the Auschwitz Convent." *Christian Jewish Relations* 22 (Autumn/Winter 1989): 21–36.

Cohen, Richard. "Auschwitz: Where Is the Pope?" *Washington Post*, 1 September 1989.

———. "The Site of Auschwitz Was No Accident." *Washington Post*, 18 August 1989.

Curtius, Mary. "Israel's Bittersweet Diplomacy." *Boston Globe*, 24 September 1989.

Davis, Helen. "Poland Begins Seeking Ways to End Bitterness with Jews." *Detroit Jewish News*, 5 January 1990.

Dershowitz, Alan M. "A Pious Anti-Semite." *Jerusalem Post*, 15 November 1989.

Doblin, Alfred. "A Horrible Offense as Political Fodder." *Detroit Jewish News*, 11 August 1989.

Early, Tracy. "ADL Calls a Papal Homily 'Prejudicial.' " *The Jewish Week*, 11 August 1989.

Echikson, William. "Behind the Auschwitz Controversy." *Christian Science Monitor*, 14 September 1989.

———. "Convent at Auschwitz Strains Jewish-Catholic Relations." *Christian Science Monitor*, 31 July 1989.

Estarriol, Ricardo. "Conflict at Auschwitz." *30 Days*, July/August 1989.

———. "The Scandal of the Cross." *30 Days*, July/August 1989.

Firestone, David. "Claims to Auschwitz." *Newsday*, 5 September 1989.

———. "Out of the Synagogue." *Newsday*, 26 July 1989.

Fisher, Dan. "Auschwitz: Jews, Poles Differ on Its Primary Significance." *Los Angeles Times*, 18 September 1989.

Fleischner, Eva. "Contemplation and Controver." *Commonweal*, 30 June 1986.

————. "Learning from History: Resolution by Catholics and Jews." *Commonweal*, 27 March 1987.

Goldman, Ari L. "O'Connor Assails Remarks by Glemp." *New York Times*, 30 August 1989.

Greeley, Andrew. "Cardinal Glemp Outburst Gives Jews Cause to Wonder." *Chicago Sun-Times*, 3 September 1989.

Gudorf, Christine. "Catholics and Auschwitz: Guilt and Beyond." *Christianity and Crisis*, 23 October 1989.

Hausknecht, Murray. "Bensonhurst and Auschwitz." *Dissent* (Winter 1990).

Hebblethwaite, Peter. "Auschwitz Legacy and 'Unholy Mess': Jews and Catholics Vie for Horror Prize." *National Catholic Reporter*, 25 August 1989.

————. "Glemp Stumbles on Rock-strewn Jewish History." *National Catholic Reporter*, 15 September 1989.

————. "An Open Letter to Cardinal Jozef Glemp." *National Catholic Reporter*, 29 September 1989.

Hertzberg, Arthur. "Doing Unto Others." *Present Tense*, November/December 1989.

Hilinski, Joseph T. "Poles, Jews Must Heal Relationship." *Catholic Universe Bulletin*, 15 September 1989.

Husarska, Anna. "Malice or Misunderstanding Over Auschwitz?" *Washington Post*, 17 August 1989.

Hyer, Marjorie. "New Questions Cloud Vatican-Jewish Relations." *Washington Post*, 14 August 1989.

Ibrahim, Youssef M. "3 Cardinals Defend Convent Pact Against Attack by Polish Primate." *New York Times*, 4 September 1989.

Jones, Arthur and Joe Feuerherd. "Convent Flap Spurs Ecumenical Temper Tantrum." *National Catholic Reporter*, 6 October 1989.

Kamin, Ben. " 'What's the Big Deal?': Why Jews Are Disturbed by the Convent at Auschwitz." *Cleveland Plain Dealer*, 6 September 1989.

Kaplan, Allison. "Attack on Jews at Auschwitz Protested." *The Jewish Week*, 21 July 1989.

Kaufman, Michael T. "Poland: The Ghosts of Jews." *Commonweal*, 11 August 1989.

Kempton, Murray. "A Cross for Polish Catholics to Bear." *Los Angeles Times*, 7 September 1989.

Klenicki, Leon. "The Carmelite Convent at Auschwitz, Past and Future." *Anti-Defamation League of B'nai B'rith*, October 1989.

————. "Interreligious Jewish-Catholic Dialogue in Poland: A Prayerful Jewish Reflection." *Studium Papers*, April 1989.

Klenicki, Leon, and Elias Mallon. "Close Enough to Step on Toes." *Commonweal*, 6 October 1989.

Klenicki, Leon, and David Rosen. "ADL Voices Concern on Pope's Remarks." *Detroit Jewish News*, 22 September 1989.

Koenig, Cardinal Franz. "Auschwitz and Catholic-Jewish Dialogue." *Origins*, 5 October 1989.

Krajewski, Stanislaw. "Carmel at Auschwitz: On the Recent Polish Church Document and Its Background." *SIDIC* 22 (1989): 15–19.

————. "The Convent at Auschwitz." *Moment*, December 1986.

Kusielewicz, Eugene. "The Poor Carmelite Nuns at Auschwitz." *Polish-American Journal*, August 1989.

Lerner, Max. " 'Quiet Diplomacy' Happily Prevails." *Washington Times*, 25 September 1989.

Levingston, Judd. "The Legacy of the Convent at Auschwitz." *Sh'ma*, 27 October 1989.

Lewis, Flora. "Flames from Ashes." *New York Times*, 3 September 1989.

Lewis, Kevin. "The Auschwitz Museum and the Clash of Memories." *The Christian Century*, 23 January 1991.

Lewis, Neil A. "Walesa's View of Glemp Irks Jewish Leaders." *New York Times*, 18 November 1989.

Lewis, Paul. "Furor Over the Convent Near Auschwitz." *Christian Jewish Relations* 19 (March 1986): 45–48. This article appeared originally in the *New York Times*, 31 January 1986.

Lipstadt, Deborah E. "Communism Toppled, Prejudice Endures." *Los Angeles Times*, 27 November 1990.

McConnell, Scott. "Dear Pat: Why This Sudden Dark and Medieval Rage?" *New York Post*, 26 September 1989.

MacDonald, Katharine. "Auschwitz Sorrows Behind Tensions." *The Catholic Times*, October 1989.

Malech, Steve. "Students Target Auschwitz Convent—Urge Church and Polish Officials to Act." *Tachlis*, May/June 1989.

Marty, Martin E. "How to Lift a Shadow from Auschwitz." *Newsday*, 11 September 1989.

Matson, Ruth. "Confrontational Rabbi." *Detroit Jewish News*, 3 November 1989.

Metzger, Deena. "Pilgrimage to Auschwitz." *Los Angeles Times*, 19 August 1989.

Montague, Alan. "The Carmelite Convent at Auschwitz: A Documentary Survey." *IJA Research Reports* 8 (October 1987).

Montalbano, William D. "Italian Jews Call on Pope to Act in Auschwitz Dispute." *Los Angeles Times*, 5 September 1989.

Novak, Michael. "To Honor Auschwitz's Catholic Dead—Move the Nuns." *Wall Street Journal*, 12 September 1989.

O'Connor, Cardinal John J. "Auschwitz and Dialogue." *Catholic New York*, 3 August 1989.

Oesterreicher, John M. "Auschwitz . . . Opportunity for Understanding." *The Catholic Advocate* (Camden, N.J.), 27 September 1989.

Paci, Stefano M. "The Convent Again under Fire." *30 Days*, March 1989.

———. " 'We Gave Our Word and Now We Must Keep It.' " *30 Days*, March 1989.

Pallido, Maria et al. "Auschwitz: A Response." *30 Days*, June 1989.

Palmieri-Billig, Lisa. "Focus on Auschwitz." *Jerusalem Post*, 8 September 1989.

———. "Lights and Shadows." *Jerusalem Post*, 27 March 1989.

Parmelee, Jennifer. "Vatican Offers Aid to Move Auschwitz Convent." *Washington Post*, 20 September 1989.

Pawlikowski, John T. "A Sign of Contradiction: Pain to Jews, Shame to Catholics." *Commonweal*, 22 September 1989.

"The Peace of Auschwitz." *The Economist*, 10 March 1990.

Perth-Grabowska, Alina. "The Battle Over Auschwitz." *Studium Papers*, October 1989.

Pfaff, William. "Do Jews or Poles Have the Last Say at Auschwitz?" *Newsday*, 28 August 1989.

Pope John Paul II. "Lessons of World War II." *The Tablet* (London), 2 September 1989.

Pritchard, Bill. "New Tensions Plague Auschwitz Interfaith Project." *Georgia Bulletin*, 17 August 1989.

Reaves, Joseph A. "Solidarity Joins Convent Issue." *Chicago Tribune*, 29 August 1989.

"Replacement for Auschwitz Convent Begun." *World Jewish Congress News & Views*, May/June 1990.

Riding, Alan. "Jewish Group Protests Remarks Made by Pope." *New York Times*, 13 August 1989.

Rittner, Carol. "Interview with Elie Wiesel." *Catholic New Times*, 8 October 1989.

Roth, John K. "The Auschwitz Convent: An Introduction." *Catholic New Times*, 8 October 1989.

———. "When a Faith Exalts Itself Over Others, Hatred Is Born." *Los Angeles Times*, 25 August 1989.

Royko, Mike. "What Is the Point of This Silly Fight?" *Chicago Tribune*, 1 September 1989.

Rudin, A. James. "An Analysis of the Polish Bishops' Pastoral Letter." The American Jewish Committee, New York, N.Y., 8 January 1991.

Schulweis, Harold M. "From the Convent Controversy, Let There Be Light." *Los Angeles Times*, 27 September 1989.

Sgherri, Giuseppe. "The Complexities of Jewish-Christian Relations." *30 Days*, July/August 1989.

Siegman, Henry. "Catholics and Jews, Cool It!" *Washington Post*, 21 August 1989.

Simons, Marlise. "Vatican Declares It Takes No Position on Auschwitz Convent Issue." *New York Times*, 5 September 1989.

———. "Vatican Strongly Urges Removal of Convent at Site of Auschwitz." *New York Times*, 20 September 1989.

Sobel, Henry I. "Let Catholic and Jew Share Where We Hurt and Why." *Los Angeles Times*, 11 September 1989.

Solomon, Norman. "The Carmelite Convent at Auschwitz." *Christian Jewish Relations*, 19 (September 1986): 42–46.

Staszewski, Dorothy. "Stop the Dancing!" *Polish-American Journal*, September 1989.

Steg, Ady. "The Jewish-Christian 'Summit.' " *Christian Jewish Relations* 19 (September 1986): 47–51.

Steinfels, Peter. "Catholics and Jews Exchange Hope and Misunderstanding." *New York Times*, 17 September 1989.

———. "Convent Issue: Divisions Growing within Divisions." *New York Times*, 10 September 1989.

———. "Jewish Reaction to Glemp Comments Is Mixed." *New York Times*, 3 September 1989.

Tagliabue, John. "Cardinal in the Auschwitz Whirlwind." *New York Times*, 5 September 1989.

———. "A Place Where the Past Overwhelms the Present." *New York Times*, 13 September 1989.

———. "Polish Cardinal Terms Agreement on Auschwitz 'Offensive.' " *New York Times*, 3 September 1989.

———. "Polish Prelate Assails Protests by Jews at Auschwitz Convent." *New York Times*, 11 August 1989.

———. "Polish Prelate in Convent Dispute Cancels U.S. Trip." *New York Times*, 19 September 1989.

———. "Polish Primate Criticizes Jews in Dispute on Auschwitz Convent." *New York Times*, 29 August 1989.

———. "Vatican Acts after Persuading Polish Primate to Ease Confrontational Stance." *New York Times*, 20 September 1989.

Tanenbaum, Marc H. "No One Has the Right to Turn Auschwitz into a Christian 'Holy Place.' " *New York Post*, 18 August 1989.

Thavis, John. "No Protests Over Birkenau Church." *National Catholic Reporter*, 22 September 1989.

Tinco, Henri. "À Auschwitz, le carmel de la colère." *Le Monde*, 18 July 1989.

Tanenbaum, Marc H. "Rx for a Malignant Mental Disorder, Anti-Semitism." *The Jewish Week*, 19 October 1990.

Valenti, Connie Ann. "Why Do Nuns Need a Convent in Auschwitz?" *Pittsburgh Catholic*, 15 September 1989.

Wallfish, Asher. "Church 'Annexation' of the Camps." *Jerusalem Post*, 16 August 1989.

Warszawski, Dawid. "The Convent and Solidarity." *Tikkun* 4 (November/December 1989). Dawid Warzawski is the pen name of Konstanty Gebert, a Polish journalist and member of the Solidarity movement.

Watson, Russell et al. "Whose Holocaust? Poland's Nasty Debate Over Auschwitz." *Newsweek*, 11 September 1989.

Webber, Jonathan. "Why the Nuns Should Stay at Auschwitz" [Letter]. *London Jewish Chronicle*, 14 July 1989.

Weiss, Avraham. "Let the Nuns Pray Elsewhere." *New York Daily News*, 5 October 1989.

———. "We Did Not Go to Auschwitz to Be Beaten." *New York Times*, 12 September 1989.

Whitney, Craig R. "Polish Primate Backs Convent Move." *New York Times*, 22 September 1989.

Wiesel, Elie. "God Judges All Nations on Rosh Hashanah." *The Northern California Jewish Bulletin*, 29 September 1989.

———. "A Year of Blood and Ashes." *Baltimore Jewish Times*, September 1989.

Wieseltier, Leon. "At Auschwitz, Decency Dies Again." *New York Times*, 3 September 1989.

Winiarz, Francis A. " 'We're Not Moving a Single Inch.' " *Polish Daily News*, 1 November 1989.

Woodward, Kenneth L. "Detente at a Death Camp: Catholics and Jews Find Some Common Ground." *Newsweek*, 2 October 1989.

———. "Pope John Paul II and the Jews." *Newsweek*, 11 September 1989.

Wyschogrod, Michael. "Was This Fight Necessary?" *Sh'ma*, 27 October 1989.

Zlotowski, Michel. "The Jewish Archbishop [Lustiger] Speaks about the 'Shoah.' " *Jerusalem Post*, 28 April 1989.

Index

About the Editors and Contributors

EDITORS

CAROL RITTNER, R.S.M., Ed.D., formerly Director of The Elie Wiesel Foundation for Humanity, New York, N.Y., is a Sister of Mercy and President of Mercyworks. She is the editor of *Elie Wiesel: Between Memory and Hope*.

JOHN K. ROTH, Ph.D., Pitzer Professor of Philosophy, Claremont McKenna College, Claremont, Calif., is the author of *A Consuming Fire: Encounters with Elie Wiesel and the Holocaust*. He is coeditor, with Michael Berenbaum, of *Holocaust: Religious and Philosophical Implications*.

CONTRIBUTORS

JUDITH HERSHCOPF BANKI, M.A., Associate Director of Interreligious Affairs for the American Jewish Committee, New York, N.Y., has published extensively in the area of Christian-Jewish relations, religious education, and interreligious dialogue.

MICHAEL BERENBAUM, Ph.D., Project Director at the United States Holocaust Memorial Museum, Washington, D.C., is also Professor of Theology at Georgetown University. Dr. Berenbaum is the editor of *A Mosaic of Victims*, a collection of essays about non-Jewish victims of the Nazis, and the author of *After Tragedy and Triumph: Essays in Modern Jewish Thought and the American Experience*.

ROBERT McAFEE BROWN, Ph.D., author of numerous books, including *Elie Wiesel, Messenger to All Humanity*, is Professor Emeritus of Theology and Ethics at Pacific School of Religion in Berkeley, California.

LEO EITINGER, M.D., a survivor of Auschwitz, is a Norwegian scholar and psychiatrist who has given special attention to the problem of refugees and concentration camp survivors. Dr. Eitinger lives in Oslo.

ALBERT H. FRIEDLANDER, Ph.D., Rabbi of Westminster Synagogue and Dean of the Leo Baeck College, London, England, is the editor of *European Judaism: A Journal for the New Europe*. He is the coauthor, with Elie Wiesel, of *The Six Days of Destruction*.

CLAIRE HUCHET-BISHOP, editor in English of Jules Isaac's work, is the past President of the Amitié Judéo-Chrétienne de France and the International Council of Christians and Jews. Madame Huchet-Bishop lives in Paris.

STANISLAW KRAJEWSKI, Ph.D., was born into an assimilated Jewish family in Warsaw. In recent years he has developed actively his Jewish interest and religious identification. Professor Krajewski is a mathematics scholar.

HERMANN LANGBEIN, a survivor of Auschwitz, lives in Vienna, Austria, where he is Secretary of the Comité International des Camps. He has published numerous articles and books about the Holocaust.

MARY JO LEDDY, N.D.S., Ph.D., a member of the Sisters of Our Lady of Sion, is the author of *Memories of War, Promises of Peace*. She is founding editor of *Catholic New Times*, an independent national Catholic newspaper in Canada.

RONALD MODRAS, Ph.D., a Roman Catholic priest and Professor of Theological Studies, St. Louis University, St. Louis, Mo., is an adviser on Polish affairs to the Secretariat for Catholic Jewish Relations of the National Council of Catholic Bishops. During 1989–90, he was a Fellow at the Annenberg Research Institute, Philadelphia, Pa.

GABRIEL MORAN, Ph.D., Director of the Religious Education Program, New York University, is the author of more than a dozen books, including *No Ladder to the Sky: Education and Morality*. He is also the editor of *The Alternative*, a religious education newsletter.

JOHN T. PAWLIKOWSKI, O.S.M., Ph.D., Professor of Social Ethics, Catholic Theological Union, a constituent school of the Chicago Cluster of Theological Schools, has written many essays and books, including *What Are They Saying about Christian-Jewish Relations?* Professor Pawlikowski is a member of the U.S. Holocaust Memorial Council, Washington, D.C.

RICHARD L. RUBENSTEIN, Ph.D., Professor of Religion, Florida State University, and President, Washington Institute for Values in Public Policy, is the author of many books, including *After Auschwitz: Radical Theology and Contemporary Judaism.* He is also coauthor, with John K. Roth, of *Approaches to Auschwitz: The Holocaust and Its Legacy.*

EMANUEL TANAY, M.D., Clinical Professor of Psychiatry, Wayne State University, Detroit, Mich., is a forensic psychiatrist. Dr. Tanay, a survivor of the Holocaust, is working on a book of memoirs.

ELIE WIESEL, winner of the 1986 Nobel Peace Prize, is Andrew Mellon Professor in the Humanities at Boston University. Professor Wiesel is the author of more than thirty books, including *Night,* his memoir of Auschwitz and Buchenwald.